Modern Political Theory

Modern Political Theory

L. J. Macfarlane

Fellow of St. John's College, Oxford

BARNES & NOBLE

BOOKS

10 East 53d St., New York 10022
(a division of Harper & Row Publishers, Inc.)

Published in the U.S.A. 1973 by:
HARPER & ROW PUBLISHERS, INC.
BARNES & NOBLE IMPORT DIVISION

Copyright © L. J. Macfarlane 1970

ISBN 06 494452 2 (cloth)
     06 494453 0 (paper)

Printed in Great Britain by
Fletcher & Son Ltd, Norwich

Contents

TO HELEN, COLIN AND CATHERINE

Preface

In writing this book I have been assisted by my wife's candid comments and by the corrections and suggestions made by my friend and former colleague, Paul Brodetsky of Ruskin College, Oxford. The original conception grew out of the experience gained over a number of years in running classes with Paul Brodetsky in Political and Social Theory for Ruskin students, and out of my dissatisfaction with existing textbooks in the field. It is my belief that the book will help students approaching the study of political theory for the first time, and my hope that my fellow teachers will find it a useful teaching aid. Each of its thirty-six sections is essentially self-contained and designed to lead the student on to the reading of the recommended selected texts. This method of approach has involved a certain amount of repetition of fundamentals, but it makes the book a more valuable tool for the student. Moreover, since the topics are arranged in logical sequence and the thinkers chronologically under each topic, it is possible to read the book either topic by topic or thinker by thinker.[1]

In conclusion, I am pleased to acknowledge my indebtedness to the following publishers who have granted me permission to quote from copyright editions and translations of the works of the political philosophers treated in this volume:

To Allen & Unwin for the quotations from G. W. F. Hegel, *Phenomenology of Mind*, translated with introduction and notes by J. B. Baillie, 1949; and for those from Karl Marx, *Capital*, translated by Eden and Cedar Paul, Everyman's Library edition (J. M. Dent & Sons). To Anchor Books, New York, for the quotations from *Writings of the Young Marx on Philosophy and Society*, edited and translated by Loyd D. Easton and Kurt H. Guddat, 1967. To Cambridge University Press for quotations from Peter Laslett, *John Locke: Two Treatises of Government: a Critical Edition with an Introduction and Apparatus Criticus*, 1960. To J. M.

---

1. Except in the case of Hegel in which students should first read the first section, 'Man and Society', to gain an overall picture of his approach, before tackling any of the more specific sections. (See Introduction p. xiv, below.)

Dent & Sons for quotations from the Everyman's Library editions of
J. J. Rousseau, *Émile or Education*, translated by Barbara Foxley, 1911,
and *The Social Contract and Discourses*, translated and with an introduction by G. D. H. Cole, 1913. To Lawrence & Wishart for quotations
from *Karl Marx: Selected Works in Two Volumes* (Lenin Institute,
Moscow under the editorship of V. Adoratsky), English edition edited
by C. Palme Dutt, 1942; Frederick Engels, *The Origin of the Family,
Private Property and The State*, translated by Alick West and Dona Torr
from the fourth Russian edition, Marxist-Leninist Library, 1942;
Frederick Engels, *Herr Eugen Dühring's Revolution in Science (Anti-
Dühring)*, translated by Emile Burns, Marxist-Leninist Library, 1936;
and Karl Marx and Frederick Engels *Selected Correspondence 1846 to
1895*, translated with commentary and notes by Dona Torr, Marxist-
Leninist Library, 1936. To Thomas Nelson & Sons for the quotations
from Rousseau, *Political Writings*, translated and edited by Frederick
Watkins, 1953. To Oxford University Press for quotations from *Hegel's
Philosophy of Right*, translated with notes by T. M. Knox, 1942; and
Hegel's Political Writings translated by T. M. Knox with introductory
essay by Z. A. Pelczynski, 1964. To Penguin Books for quotations from
Jean-Jacques Rousseau, *The Social Contract*, translated and with introduction by Maurice Cranston, 1968. To C. A. Watts & Co. for quotations from *Karl Marx Selected Writings in Sociology and Social Philosophy*, edited by T. B. Bottomore and Maximilien Rubel, 1956 (Pelican
edition).

Introduction: Ideas in Politics

In common with most other fields of study, politics has in recent years tended to become broken down into a number of separate compartments, each with its own particular approach and concerns and each taught all too often without regard to the rest. The sharp distinction, for example, between the study of political theory and political institutions, which is so marked a feature of university politics teaching, is itself a recent development which finds no parallel in the writings of the 'masters' of politics. Works like Hobbes's *Leviathan* and Hegel's *Philosophy of Right* treat equally of political ideas and political organization. Recently however, the break-up of politics has gone much further. Political sociology has staked a claim to being a separate kind of politics: that of behaviour as distinct from institutions; political history is claimed as a separate discipline from the current problems to which it gives rise or the political structures which it nurtures; political theory is divorced from the searching writings of the political philosophers and reduced to the study of the use of the language of politics. Without doubt this fragmentation has led to considerable gains of knowledge in many areas, but at the expense of coherence and depth of understanding. In consequence attempts have been made in recent years to provide general functional theories of politics which will enable the vast mass of information assembled to be understood and utilized in terms of the principles underlying the working of all political systems. The best known of these is that put forward by David Easton in the United States, but the writings of S. M. Lipset, Gabriel Almond and David Apter have also been very influential. Behind the distinctive approaches of these writers there lies a common conception of the possibility of providing an objective scientific basis for the study of politics. They hold that it is possible to formulate hypotheses, models and conceptual approaches which, by incorporating within themselves the beliefs and ideas which men have as causal elements in the total situation, can overcome the divorce between political facts and political values and provide a total explanation in terms which are valid irrespective of the moral or ideological position of the investigator. There is no place in political science on this view for any theorizing about the validity or justifiability of one set or kind of values as against another, as distinct from investigating the effects which different sets of values have on the participants in the political arena. The former questions are the subject of quite another order of academic discipline existing on a separate and distinct level of inquiry.

This is not the place to deal with this approach in depth[1], but it is pertinent to stress some of the more obvious limitations and dangers of this approach as exemplified particularly in the Eastonian systems analysis. In essence this analysis uses the model of a political decision-making process or system which has to cope with an ever-changing total environmental situation. This total situation provides both the supports on which the political system rests and the demands with which it has to cope. The decisions made themselves react upon the social environment generating new demands and responses. The aim of those concerned with the political decision-making process must be to build up and extend the social supports for the system and to meet or contain the demands made upon it. For this purpose a demand is anything which forces itself upon the public authorities for consideration; whether it be a demand consciously directed at the authorities themselves or at some other body in such a way as to be a matter of public concern, or whether it is simply a vague or general expression of discontent. The supports of a political system are to be found in the social institutions and shared values which uphold it, whether at the level of the total political community, the political régime with its rules and procedures, or the particular groups and individuals in control of the various parts of the decision-making process.[2]

What needs to be stressed about this kind of analysis is that it rests on a number of assumptions and implies a number of values. It assumes that it is possible to subsume all that is political under the function it plays in the formulation and execution of public policy. In particular it assumes that these functions can be treated as part of a controllable process; that politics is concerned with running 'a country' and that

1. A brief and illuminating criticism along the lines indicated above is to be found in Charles Taylor, 'Neutrality in Political Science', *Philosophy, Politics and Society*, Third Series, a collection edited by Peter Laslett and W. G. Runciman, 1969.
2. A simplified account of the Eastonian theory of political systems analysis is to be found in H. V. Wiseman, *Politics in Everyday Life*, Part II, Section 2, 1966.

this is not basically different from, though considerably more complicated than, running a firm or club. The decision-makers have to manage the polity with a view to keeping both themselves and it in business, by meeting as best they can the demands made upon them and the crises which break about them. Managerial politics is a very particular view of politics, a view moreover which is both historically and ideologically conditioned. Where men in general, and those in positions of authority in particular, do not think in these sorts of terms, then the practice of politics is unlikely to fit into the model prescribed. If the role of the king or leader is seen as upholding the traditions and customs of the community, fulfilling the divine purpose, or maintaining the position of the chosen caste or élite, then these concepts will not simply determine how demands are processed but will undermine the very notion of demand processing. The whole approach is then alien to decision-making and the machinery of government is not shaped to that purpose. This applies not only to primitive societies and to the medieval world, but also to a modern community like Maoist China, where any conception of political demands and issues is largely irrelevant, since the whole context of politics is orientated in a completely different direction from that assumed under the systems analysis model. One's duty as a citizen of the Chinese People's Republic is to turn one's back on individualism and factionalism and to strive to realize the truth embodied in the writings and life of Chairman Mao. This involves intense political activity directed, not towards the formulation and expression of sectional demands, but in opposition to those who seek to reduce the Communist state to a mere satisfier of material wants. But even in the Western world of pressure groups and consensus politics, certain demands are not processable, either in the sense that they cannot be catered for within the system or that those who make them do not make them through established channels. It is arguable, for example, that experience shows that the replacement of the existing 'mixed economy' by a Socialist economy is unrealizable within the framework of the Western representative political systems; not in the crude sense that the capitalist class would never allow it, but that the 'demand for Socialism' changes both its form and direction under these conditions. Consequently, if one wants Socialism, as distinct from social reform, one must adopt revolutionary objectives and tactics which, by their nature, are not and cannot be treated as demands made upon the existing system.[1] It is

1. A recent discussion of this point is to be found in R. Miliband, *The State in Capitalist Society*, (1969).

interesting to note that while some political demands appear in the form of claims which could be met within the framework of the system, they may in fact be designed as the first step in the process of undermining it. Thus Marx in 1848 called on the German workers to put forward limited demands which should be stepped up as the struggle proceeded with a view to precipitating a revolutionary dénouement.[1] A similar process can be seen in the demands put forward by the most ideologically committed of the student revolutionaries which appear to moderate students and liberal-minded academics as negotiable, practical proposals, instead of as tactical moves in a struggle which has the paralyzing of the universities as simply the most immediately available of its aims.

The political beliefs and ideas which men hold are not simply a factor to be taken into account in understanding the process of decision-making. These values colour the whole setting of the political and social life of a community, conditioning not simply the way in which particular problems and issues are faced, but, more importantly, conditioning what is seen as an issue and how it is seen. Thus we commonly find different societies approaching the same political problem from such fundamentally different premises that it does not appear to be the same problem. To the vast majority of the newly independent states of black Africa, the forcible overthrow of the South African régime is self-evidently necessary and desirable; while, to the British government, it raises equally fundamental but foreign issues of state sovereignty and non-intervention. Secondly, a change in attitude may over time transform the nature of a problem or even obliterate it. In this way the erosion of the medieval belief that the extirpation of heresy was the moral and social duty of church and state alike changed the whole context of politics in Western Europe. Finally, we may find that the social values of one segment of the population do not coincide with those of another segment. We may contrast the traditional working-class notion of class solidarity with the traditional middle-class defence of individual freedom. This finds expression in the one group despising and molesting strike-breakers and the other demanding police protection for 'black-legs' and the prosecution of strike pickets. Political and social values are important because they move men to act, and they do so precisely because men believe in them. It is necessary therefore in the study of politics to ascertain not simply what men believe, but why they believe. Moreover, as individuals vitally concerned with the basic points at issue in political controversy,

1. See p. 135, below, for a discussion of this point.

we shall ourselves, in the process of testing the force and validity of the arguments adduced in support of the various claims and principles put forward, be shaping and testing our own personal set of values.[1]

The study of the fundamental principles which underlie, or which ought to underlie, the running of civil society is the subject-matter of political theory, and in English universities it has typically been studied through the writings of individual thinkers taken in chronological order. Alongside this approach there has developed the study of the concepts used in political theorizing, concepts which are held to embody some important truth or understanding relevant to the appraisal of man's condition as a social and reflective being. Surprisingly, each of these approaches has normally been carried out quite separately from the other, although it is evident both that individual thinkers were influenced by the nature of the political concepts currently used in theoretical discourse, and that each of the major thinkers themselves made a distinctive contribution to conceptual thinking, whether in terms of undermining old concepts and values or in promoting new ones. The purpose of this book is to provide an introduction to political ideas which will span these two approaches. The particular method used has been to approach the study of some of the main concepts of political theory through the writings of a limited number of major theorists whose works are readily available in English. The choice was confined to a sufficiently small number of writers to permit an adequate treatment of each. By restricting consideration to six theories, it has been possible to get away from the textbook approach and to draw on a wide range of original writing as well as to refer to some of the more important recent scholarly works in each field. It was important to confine the study to writers in the modern Western tradition of political thinking, speaking roughly the same political language, and concerned with the same order of theoretical problem, since only in this way could one significantly

---

1. It is of great interest to note that David Easton himself, in a stimulating Presidential Address 'The New Revolution in Political Science' to the 1969 Annual Meeting of the American Political Studies Association, drew attention to the deep dissatisfaction there is with contemporary politics teaching in America, dominated as it has been by functionalism and behaviourism. He issued a clarion call for reconsideration of the part played by political values and theories in political activity and research, and for the recognition that it is no longer practical or morally tolerable for teachers of politics to stand on the political sidelines and adopt 'neutral' stances. *American Political Science Review* December 1969.

In the same issue of this journal there is a stirring defence of 'Political Theory as a Vocation' by Sheldon S. Wolin.

compare the varied uses to which different writers put the same terms and concepts. Many writers had claims for inclusion, but on the premise set out above the final selection came down to Hobbes, Locke, Rousseau, Bentham and Mill, Hegel, Marx and Engels.

The book opens with an introductory chapter, 'The Individual and Society', with sections giving the broad outlines of the political philosophy of each writer in turn, followed by chapters similarly divided up into sections for each writer, on morality and religion, law and political obligation, liberty and tyranny, equality and property, and the form of the state. In presenting the position taken up by each writer, extensive use has been made of quotations from his original works to show how he developed his case. The fact that each conclusion drawn rests on textual quotation enables the reader to decide for himself whether he accepts the author's interpretation of the thinker concerned. It must be emphasized that the extensive use of quotations is in no way designed to be a substitute for reading the basic writings of the theorists themselves. On the contrary, they are meant to direct the reader to the relevant sections of the original writing, so that he may follow up the author's argument in full at any desired point of special interest. In addition, specific reading from the original sources is given at the end of each section.

A particular problem arises with Hegel's use of language which, from the very nature of what he is discussing, is difficult to follow. While an attempt has been made to elucidate without oversimplifying, the sections on Hegel, and especially the quoted passages from his writings, are not easy to follow. With Hegel the best approach is to push boldly ahead, grasping what one can of the general argument until one reaches the end, then to retread one's steps—recognizing that what Hegel is trying to express is, in terms of his own doctrine, incapable of being fully comprehended in the world as it is. Although this book is primarily an exposition of how selected thinkers dealt with specified concepts, at various points their arguments and conclusions have been critically examined. No attempt has been made to provide a comprehensive detailed criticism of each writer's position; rather those points have been selected in any writer which appeared crucial to his thesis. In some cases, and particularly with Hegel, the thesis itself is so complex and difficult and open to such a range of interpretation, as to require the whole space available to be devoted to exposition. In the case of Marx and Engels the primary need was to correct the narrow simplistic picture popularly presented, by indicating something of the range and depth of their position as displayed in their very extensive writings. In consequence the Marxist exposition is subjected to a considerably less searching review than that of Locke, although the premises of the former are open in many ways to more fundamental dispute than those of the latter. The omission is easily repaired, however, if reference is made to the authors referred to in the suggested reading at the end of the relevant sections.

Experience in teaching political theory over many years convinces me that students can better understand and appraise the writings of a political philosopher after having examined the general context of his thought and the problems he grappled with. There can, of course, be no such thing as an authoritative objective account of the views of such controversial thinkers as Rousseau and Hegel. In a real sense, each reader must construct for himself his own rendering of 'what Marx really meant', but he can be aided in this task by the presentation of the essential ingredients and an indication of the major points on which differences of interpretation arise. What one hopes to arouse in one's readers is not assent to particular views or interpretations, but something of the sense of intellectual excitement which can be found in coming to grips with the ideas of the great political theorists. This is the first of a number of reasons why political theory may be commended as a subject for study. The writings of men like Hobbes and Bentham are of intrinsic interest in themselves. They widen the horizon of our imagination and understanding and direct our concern to new problems and different approaches. Moreover, in the process of coming to understand the often difficult and complex lines of theoretical argument, our intellectual wits are sharpened and extended.

In seeking to understand the writings of any political theorist, it is necessary to appreciate the conditions in which his various works were written and his intentions in writing them. It is important for any understanding of John Locke's *Second Treatise of Government* to know that the greater part of it was probably written, not as the Preface would suggest as a *post hoc* justification of the Glorious Revolution of 1688, but to serve as a theoretical justification for forcing King Charles II to exclude his Catholic brother James, Duke of York, from the succession to the English throne. These moves culminated in the plots of 1681–3 in which not only Locke's patron, Shaftesbury, but Locke himself was deeply implicated.[1] It is even more important in reading Rousseau's

1. See Peter Laslett, 'Locke and the First Earl Shaftesbury', *John Locke Two Treatises of Government*, 1960, pp. 25–37.

Social Contract not to be led astray by his eulogy of civil society in Book I, Chapter 8, and to conclude that Rousseau was a staunch defender of established authority; a mistake which no one would make if acquainted with Rousseau's castigation of the corruptness of contemporary society in the *Discourse on Inequality* and other writings. A political theorist must be judged in the context of the time in which he wrote and his words related to the problems of those times as they were then seen. That is not to say that the political philosopher is not likely to have seen these problems in a less time-tied light than his contemporaries; but only that he wrote primarily for his time and in terms of his time. It might be argued that Professor Macpherson's penetrating study of Hobbes and Locke in *The Political Theory of Possessive Individualism* suffers precisely from this fault[1]. One should also be aware of the danger of imposing coherence on an author by insisting on interpretations which sweep up all his ideas into a neat and balanced pattern. Political theorists are, like other men, inconsistent; they leave loose ends in their works, they grapple with problems they are unable to solve, they change their views in the light of experience or even expediency. On the other hand, while one should beware of obliterating all inconsistency in the cause of doctrinal purity and completeness, one should equally beware of reading fundamental inconsistencies into an author's works. Since the level of intellectual ability and integrity of these thinkers is of a high order, it behoves one to hesitate before proclaiming to the world that Hobbes did not know what Hobbes was talking about. Some other less destructive, if less dramatic, interpretation is not merely possible but likely. It was a predisposition of this sort which led the author to consider critically, and on closer examination of the text, to reject the readings of the Marxist theory of the state provided by Professors Plamenatz and Avineri: viz. that Marx held two conflicting views as to the nature of the state (Plamenatz), and that Marx had a fundamentally different view of the state from Engels – (Avineri).[2]

The importance of understanding something of the political and historical background of the political theorists here studied can be illustrated by reference to the issue of the franchise. Professor Seliger, for example, fails to appreciate that in s. 158 of the *Second Treatise*, Locke is not arguing in modern terms for the right of additional classes of people to be represented in parliament, but in traditional seventeenth-century terms for the right of new areas of adequate size and wealth to

1. Professor Macpherson's views are discussed below, pp. 178–82 and 186–7.
2. See pp. 251–2, below.

secure representation by incorporation as boroughs.[1] More generally, both Mill's support of proportional representation and Marx's conception of the franchise as a revolutionary weapon, must be seen against the background of the Chartist struggles of the 1840s, which led Mill to fear, and Marx to thrill, at the prospect of an enfranchised working-class voting on class lines to alter the existing order of things. At another level it is easy to discern the impact of great social upheavals on the political thinking of contemporaries. The bitter experiences of the English Civil War confirmed Hobbes's gloomiest fears about the social destiny of man; while the threat of a rigid proselytizing Catholic on the throne drove Locke to abandon his earlier assertion that chaos would ensue unless the established authorities had absolute power to determine how men should behave, in favour of the declaration of the right of the people to overthrow a monarch turned tyrant. The impact of the French Revolution of 1789 on political thinking was even more striking than the events of seventeenth-century England had been, as can be seen in the writings of two such contrasting figures as Jeremy Bentham and Friedrich Hegel. In almost all cases our understanding of a political thinker's ideas will be deepened by an appreciation of his life and personality. Rousseau produced the deeply committed and compelling ideas that he did because of the sort of man he was, and we are less likely to be led into distorted interpretations of his ideas if we know something of the man himself as bared to the world in his *Confessions*. In quite a different but no less important way, Marx's life and writings cannot be separated, since he developed his revolutionary ideas in the process of seeking to understand and influence political events. The interaction between theory and practice was the keystone of both Marxist theory and revolutionary practice. His writings cannot be understood except in that context – he sought to understand the workings of capitalist society in order to overthrow it, where understanding itself necessarily involved participation in the struggles of the proletariat.

It is for this reason that Marx's writings are rarely studied for their intrinsic interest but because his ideas are so directly pertinent to the problems of our own day. One does not need to labour the question of relevance with respect to a thinker whose principles are acclaimed as their inspiration by revolutionary movements and states throughout the world. What is self-evident in Marx's case is also true in varying degrees

1. See pp. 191–2 below. Much of the detailed discussion at the time of the 1832 Reform Bill was for and against the representation of particular areas on the basis of their contribution to the life of the community.

of other writers. The ideas which the leading political thinkers have formulated are not simply of academic or historic merit, since the major problems they dealt with were not of passing consequence. We do not turn to Hobbes or Hegel to provide an 'answer' to current political problems (not least perhaps because political problems are not mathematical-style questions to which there is a finite answer),[1] but in the expectation that their particular approaches will highlight the problems from new and revealing angles. Familiarity with the way in which the political philosophers have developed and handled political concepts may suggest how the hidden roots and assumptions lying behind current disputed issues may be exposed and their implications better understood.

Nowhere is this relevance of political thinking to the modern world more apparent than in the realm of political and moral values. The study of political theory is concerned both to bring out the crucial part played by assumed and asserted values at every level of political debate, and to examine critically the validity of the values concerned. This involves going beyond a simple concern with the internal consistency of a set of values to an anlaysis of the reasons adduced or adduceable in its support, and of the consequences which would flow from its adoption. The political concepts which a writer uses are themselves value-laden. He uses the terms he does in the way he does because they enable him to express his purposes and give effect to his ideas. While it might theoretically be possible to accept Marx's conceptual analysis of the nature of class society and yet refuse to identify oneself in any way with the proletariat, in practice this does not happen; just because the analysis has overwhelming moral implications. Capitalism is not, and cannot be, defended in the terms in which Marx portrays it because the moral condemnation of the existing social order is part of the actual analytical approach.

Examples abound of the pertinence to the guilt-torn world of today of the discussion of moral issues by political philosophers. One might commend to Afrikaners Hegel's penetrating analysis of the inherently unstable and indefensible nature of the master–slave relationship; since the degrading forced dependence of the slave can never satisfy his master's need for that recognition of superiority which alone can provide psychological satisfaction and a moral justification for the act of domination. From Hegel, too, comes a heavy assault on the current avowal of purely personal moral judgements. Subjective morality is, he

---

1. This important point is discussed in Bertrand de Jouvenal, *The Pure Theory of Politics*, 1963: Addendum, 'The Myth of the Solution'.

insists, no morality at all, but simply opinion. Men need to identify themselves with and realize themselves in the wider context of a workable moral system; though one may doubt whether complete identification is particularly desirable, especially where the focal point of identification is made to be the state. The discussion in Hegel may be followed up in Rousseau, who draws a much sharper distinction than Hegel does between the state as it is and the state as it might be, if only the common will of all men for the general good were able to triumph over particular wills dedicated to narrow selfish interests. Rousseau's vision of a society in which each will realize his true self in the service of all is the underlying theme of all communalist thinking. In its extreme form it finds expression in a complete rejection not simply of self-assertion at the expense of others, but of the very notion of any self apart from the community. Individualism is viewed as an anti-social disease or even as a political crime in China today. Only by a complete rejection of the notion of self and identification with the person and thoughts of the infallible leader can China build a Communist community of new men. The alternative is to follow the Russian path and to degenerate into a 'Socialist' society dominated by bourgeois acquisitive values. This Maoist vision may be compared with Rousseau's conception of a society in which men have come to subordinate their selfish interests to the common weal.[1] The question of whether this latter conception embraces or involves something like the former is far more than a matter of textual interpretation; it raises the issue of how far holding an ideal of a new society requires for its realization the remoulding of men to some personal conception, and whether such an approach to one's fellow creatures is not both presumptuous and dangerous.

The charge of interference here raised is itself a good example of individualistic thinking and has been recently levelled by Maurice Cowling against John Stuart Mill,[2] often regarded as the high priest of individualism. For Mill does not take up the position of those who applaud all manifestations of personal nonconformity so long as they do not directly injure some non-consenting party. The extreme libertarians of today do not simply defend public copulation on the grounds that those liable to be offended may turn away the blushing cheek, but positively uphold the virtue of unrestrained licence. Mill, however, drew a distinction between the claim which could be made in support of

1. But see pp. 65–6 below, for a discussion of the role of individuality and personal freedom in Rousseau's thinking.
2. Maurice Cowling, *Mill and Liberalism*, 1963.

persons being permitted to do as they think fit, as long as others are not immediately and directly harmed, and the desirability or otherwise of the practices indulged in. While he asserted that, in general terms, it was highly desirable for persons to be encouraged to pursue their own personal pleasures and tastes without being subject to the restrictions of law and opinion, he was far from asserting that all pleasures and tastes should be encouraged. There is no incongruity here. My acceptance of the right of every man to take his own life does not in any way involve my acceptance of the worth of suicide; on the contrary, those who applaud its worth lay themselves open to the charge of inconsistency by their continued existence. The case for permitting licence in any area of activity is different from the case in favour of taking advantage of that licence if granted. Some forms of personal behaviour, like addiction to hard drugs or alcohol, are clearly incapable of defence in terms of individualism, since they undermine the very human quality of purposive conscious existence. A gin-soaked sponge or heroin-controlled husk is no longer a human being but a thing in need of resurrection to the human level. Concern for the capacity of, and opportunity for, each person to be an individual leads one to consider the impact of various forms of behaviour on all parties concerned. A claim to be beyond censure or discussion can only be considered in terms of individualism if others are not harmed, since only absolute self-sufficiency could substantiate a claim to absolute moral sovereignty. If I assert my individuality by making others dependent on my will and whims, I deny the principles of individualism by denying their application to any but myself. Once it is accepted that individualism necessarily involves respect for the personality of all other affected beings, licence has to give way to responsible liberty.

The concept of liberty itself has been the subject of extensive analysis and debate in recent years.[1] What this debate has most clearly revealed is the variety of senses in which the term has been used and the importance of distinguishing between them in political argument. The distinction, for example, between the subjective feeling which a man has of being free and the objective conditions in which he exists, enables us to see that there is nothing inherently contradictory in their being in opposition. A man who feels free in prison is free in his feeling, but because the cell walls do not exist for him as barriers to his will, this does not mean that they are not barriers. As Rousseau argued in the *Discourse on Inequality*, men are often blind to the restraints and fetters

1. See for example, Sir Isaiah Berlin, *Four Essays on Liberty*, 1969.

which encompass them, and the necessary condition of their objective freedom may be to make them conscious of their chains, to make them subjectively unfree. Rousseau draws our attention to the fact that society itself, its values and institutions, may be by far the most important of the forces restraining our free development. Indeed, in one sense this is bound to be so, since the establishment of any social relationship, whether by choice, chance or force, inevitably conditions and restricts our behaviour and limits the range of subsequent choice. As Hobbes points out, I am always free to choose, since there is always some alternative, if it is only death; but once the choice is made this freedom is lost and I am caught up in the consequences of my decision. Nor can it be retained by refusing to choose, since choices do not remain open over time and circumstances change – the freedom not to choose is itself one of the choices open to us. What is important is that I should make the right choice, which in terms of personal freedom means the choice which provides me with the greatest opportunities for self-development and satisfaction. For men, being finite beings, must live within a particular limited context. The whole world cannot be ours, but it does not follow from this that we should be satisfied with the patch offered or available to us. Rousseau saw clearly that bourgeois society curbed men's freedom both by its projection and extolling of acquisitive material values as well as by its commitment of the mass to a sordid animal-like search for the sheer means of livelihood while the rich wallowed in senseless luxury. Alongside his searing moral indictment of social slavery, Rousseau projected his vision of a new world of free equals. What he failed to provide was any clear indication of how the transition might be made or even any compelling reason for believing it was realizable. This omission was filled by Marx, who took over Hegel's conception of history, 'the progress of the consciousness of freedom', and gave it a dialectical twist – freedom remained as the assured goal of human development, but a goal to be secured only by smashing through the distorted image to be seen in contemporary society. The Marxist analysis claimed to show that the existing social order, with its corresponding set of social values, was bound to collapse under the weight of its own inner contradictions and be replaced by a classless society. The future was assured, but its coming to pass might be speeded by the conscious participation of awakened men acting on the side of history and of progress. While no social freedom was possible in class society, a man might shake himself loose of its ideological chains by joining in the struggle for society's overthrow in the sure knowledge that the kingdom of man was at hand. At another level Marx has some penetrating and disturbing remarks to make about the cramping and distorting effect of the bourgeois productive system on those caught up in it. This discussion of the alienation of the worker from both the work process and the product of his labour is highly pertinent to all industrialized societies.

But if social and political systems are attacked in terms of arguments culled from Rousseau and Marx, they are also defended and modified in the light of ideas to be found in writers as varied as Hobbes and Hegel. Hobbes's insistence that the essential basis of any society is the maintenance of law and order and that this requires a willingness to surrender all necessary power to the authorities, where the authorities themselves determine what is necessary and what constitutes law and order, has a very familiar and ominous modern ring about it. It savours of the detention of African nationalists without trial in Rhodesia, before and after U.D.I., and of General Moczar's strong-arm tactics against dissidents in the streets of Warsaw in 1968. Yet Hobbes's own treatment of the theme brings out the essential truth of his avowal that, without the security of law and order, there can be 'no knowledge of the face of the Earth; no account of Time; no Arts; no Letters; no Society; and which is worst of all, continually feare and danger of violent death'. What is at issue here is whose law and order, since permanent revolution against any and every established order is only defensible in abstract nihilistic terms. For Locke the answer is to be found in defending men from the degrading and evil consequences of arbitrary absolute rule. He recognized that the greatest dangers arise not from the absence of political power but from its unreserved concentration in one pair of hands. He argued persuasively that by constitutionalizing power, defining, restricting and balancing its constituent parts, the worst excesses of tyranny might be avoided; while *in extremis* he provided for popular insurrection as a crude and ultimate check against gross misuse of authority by any arm of government. Experience of the horrors of arbitrary rule when it is harnessed to the furtherance of some all-embracing cause or creed, as with Hitlerite Germany and Stalinist Russia, has demonstrated the validity of Locke's analysis. One of the most striking features of both régimes was their spurning of the very conception of legal authority, even though the whole legal apparatus was at their disposal. Omnipotent extra-legal bodies and procedures had to be used if European Jewry was to be exterminated and all Russia paralyzed by fear and terror into acting out the lie of living in the land of Socialist freedom. In these extremities not merely the will to resist but even the conception of resistance itself seems to disappear.

The problem of political resistance and disobedience is in many ways both the most interesting, fundamental and difficult of political concepts to handle, and the most urgent and compelling practical issue which men have to face. American students awaiting draft to Vietnam, Czech communists faced with the reimposition of repression under cover of Soviet military might, Negroes faced with the prospect of permanent ghetto existence as outsiders in the Great Society, Catholics subject to discrimination by the Protestant majority in Ulster – all have to determine on what grounds they might legitimately reject authority.[1] Each of the thinkers discussed in this book deals with the problem in his own distinctive fashion. Hobbes argues that the consequences of disobedience will always be worse than those of conformity to laws held to be wrong. Resistance to authority can only be defended when the individual's life is actually at stake. But while Hobbes sees the propensity to revolt as the main cause of political unrest and reason for repressive measures, Locke argues the reverse. People are very reluctant to take up arms against their rulers and will suffer extreme inefficiency, corruption and repression before doing so. It is not difficult, then, for a ruler to avoid a revolt, but neither is it easy to avoid rulers who make revolt necessary. The solution lies in embodying the notion of constitutional rule, where the ruler is given extensive but defined powers to act on behalf of the community; but where this trust may be withdrawn if he exceeds his powers or undermines the fundamental rights for which the political community exists. This conception receives formal embodiment in the United States Supreme Court; but impressive as the record of that Court has been in recent years in the field of civil and political rights, it has not been able to deal with the root causes of present discontent, which are social and political rather than legal and constitutional. The social basis of disquiet so obviously ignored by Hobbes and Locke was only too obvious to Rousseau; but though he thundered at the misery and injustice of the class-ridden, money-mad society of his time, he was surprisingly reluctant to commend its revolutionary overthrow. There was no guarantee that those who overthrew existing oppressors in the name of freedom might not tie some new and tighter chains round mens' necks when once they came to power. The ills of the modern society stemmed from men identifying themselves with

1. I have discussed this problem at some length in 'Justifying Political Disobedience', *Ethics* (Chicago University Press, October 1968).

false and selfish gods; the way forward lay not in changing the government or amending its laws, but in shifting men's goals from self to community. It was to nationalism rather than revolution that Rousseau looked for deliverance.

Nationalism as an expression of social identification is also a major theme of Hegel's writings, but for Hegel, unlike Rousseau, its focal point is the state, which embodies to a high degree the needs and purposes of its individual members, since all states are in process of realizing themselves as they are destined to be. This process, however, does not rule out, indeed in some sense it involves, a conflict between the form of state as it is and as it ought to be in process of becoming at that particular stage of development. In these circumstances, as in pre-revolutionary France in Hegel's view, the overthrow of the old-established order may be justified for the underlying new order to be enabled to fulfil itself. What is damaging to Hegel's argument is not so much the weakness of his case for accepting constitutional monarchy, Prussian-style, as the appropriate form of state for the Western Europe of his time; but his failure to show how men are to determine when the existing social order is beyond redemption. This deficiency Marx fills with his bold assertion that each phase of class society eventually collapses through its own internal contradictions, which themselves generate class consciousness and resistance among the exploited. The oppressed have no obligation to the political state of their oppressors, but they will not in the mass see their true position, nor be in any position to act, until the society of which they are members ceases to be able to provide for their basic needs. The problem of political obedience is, to Marx, a matter on the one hand of consciousness of one's class position, and on the other of possibilities latent in the objective political situation. It is a tactical rather than a moral problem, to be decided in terms of whether disobedience at a specific time on any particular issue will further a struggle for the overthrow of existing society.

For Bentham, too, practical considerations are paramount; the mischiefs of submission to authority having to be compared with those of resistance. He distinguishes individual resistance – which may be embarked on where an individual is convinced that his own personal act of disobedience will cause less harm than his personal act of submission – from general resistance or revolt. In the latter case, the most important factor to be determined is whether a government is acting contrary to established custom or expectation, and whether therefore it is likely to be obeyed in such actions. It is only when government actions are likely to be challenged or disobeyed on a large scale that resistance can be justified, because only in these circumstances is it likely to succeed.

Bentham's analysis has considerable merits. It suggests that the intellectually honest person, like the conscientious objector in time of war, can always justify personal disobedience in terms of his own conviction that he can demonstrate that more good than evil will stem from refusal to submit.[1] On the other hand, those who would initiate organized revolt or defiance need to demonstrate, not simply that the government act complained of would have specifically evil consequences, but that it would give rise to such public resentment that the organization of resistance would meet with success. Unless the second condition is fulfilled, resistance will probably lead to greater suffering than submission. Political theory is not a subject for academics and students alone, but one for all in which to come to grips with the values which make men act as they do to produce the society that we know.

---

1. He may, of course, argue that the deliberate killing of another person is wrong in itself, irrespective of other consequences.

CHAPTER I

The Individual and Society

1. HOBBES

It was the common lore of writers in the seventeenth century that man was a creature of God endowed with the faculty of reason, but although Thomas Hobbes accepts God as his Maker, he sees reason not as a gift from God but as the reward which comes to those who make the necessary effort. Man makes himself. Children are born with 'the possibility apparent of having the use of Reason in time to come' (p. 21),[1] but this latent possibility may not be realized in adulthood. True reason requires that men should first define their basic terms and then proceed to build up from these terms more complex constructions, consequences and conclusions, as in geometry – 'the onely Science that it hath pleased God hitherto to bestow on mankind' (p. 15). Hobbes's avowed aim was to apply this scientific method to the study of politics.

Richard Peters has described Hobbes as 'the great metaphysician of motion'.[2] Men's motions are, according to Hobbes, of two kinds, voluntary and involuntary, and it is with the latter kind that Hobbes is primarily concerned in *Leviathan*. Voluntary actions proceed from 'foresight of the End, or Consequence of things' (p. 25) and take the form either of movement towards or movement away from the source of stimulus of the senses. Movement towards, Hobbes speaks of as *appetite* or *desire*, and movement away from as *aversion* or *hate*.

> But whatsoever is the object of any mans Appetite or Desire; that is it, which he for his part calleth *Good*: And the object of his Hate and Aversion, *Evill* – There being nothing simply and absolutely so; nor any common Rule of Good and Evill, to be taken from the nature of the objects themselves (p. 24).

1. All quotations of Hobbes are from *Leviathan*, Everyman's Library edition, unless otherwise stated.
2. Richard Peters, *Hobbes*, Penguin Books, 1956, p. 94.

Each man therefore is guided by what satisfies his appetite and nullifies his aversions: these are the springs of his actions. Men are by nature assertive wilful creatures, concerned with self-gratification and self-fulfilment which finds expression in 'a perpetuall and restlesse desire of Power after power, that ceaseth only in Death' (p. 49). Left to his own devices, this restless searching for power makes every man the enemy of every other man.

> In such condition, there is no place for Industry: because the fruit thereof is uncertain: and consequently no Culture of the Earth, no Navigation, nor use of the commodities that may be imported by Sea; no commodious Building; no Instruments of moving, and removing such things as require much force; no Knowledge of the face of the Earth; no account of Time; no Arts; no Letters; no Society; and which is worst of all, continuall feare, and danger of violent death; And the life of man, solitary, poore, nasty, brutish and short (pp. 64–5).

Man, however, is not the complete slave of his own nature. Being possessed of reason, he recognizes that the consequence of directing all his efforts at self-fulfilment at the expense of others is the nullification of these desires. He draws back from a condition which promises insecurity and death rather than self-aggrandisement and easy pleasures. Reason suggests the way out of this predicament, for it enables man to determine what is to his true advantage. Reason supplies man with what Hobbes calls Articles of Peace 'which otherwise are called the Lawes of Nature' (p. 66). These articles differ from the laws of nature so familiar in medieval writings in that, unlike the latter, they are solely directed to the preservation of the individual. They do not restrain or temper individualism, rather they suggest how it can best be realized under conditions where men are in constant contact with one another – 'dictating Peace, for a means of the conservation of men in multitudes' (p. 81). Hobbes wrote,

> These dictates of Reason, men use to call by the name of Lawes; but improperly: for they are but Conclusions, or Theoremes concerning what conduceth to the conservation and defence of themselves; whereas Law, properly is the word of him that by right hath command over others (p. 83).

Though Hobbes lists nineteen laws or theorems it is only the first three which are fundamental to his purpose; for it is from these that the whole framework of his civil society is built and in terms of these that it is justified. The wretchedness of man's natural condition – that is the condition he would find himself in if society did not exist to restrain his wilful nature – stems from the fact that in the natural state every man has a right to everything, for every man is at liberty to use his own power as he thinks most advantageous to himself. There are no unjust claims because the very concept of justice – 'the giving to every man his own' – is meaningless where there is nobody to determine what is a man's own. 'And therefore, as long as this naturall Right of every man to every thing endureth, there can be no security to any man (how strong or wise soever he be) of living out the time, which Nature ordinarily alloweth men to live' (p. 67). The unqualified right to do as one pleases therefore requires substantial modification if men are to have any hope of achieving felicity, i.e. 'continuall prospering' (p. 30). The first law of nature is, 'That every man, ought to endeavour Peace, as farre as he has hope of obtaining it; and when he cannot obtain it, that he may seek, and use, all helps and advantages of Warre' (p. 67). It embraces both the need which all men have to live in peace and the right to defend themselves against those who threaten that peace. This law of self-preservation, which recognizes the need for restraint, is further qualified by the second law which reads, 'That a man be willing, when others are so too, as farre-forth, as for Peace, and defence of himselfe he shall think it necessary to lay down his right to all things; and be contented with so much liberty against other men, as he would allow other men against himselfe' (p. 67). It is important to note that Hobbes does not express this law in the form that men *ought* to divest themselves of their right to all things for the benefit of all, which would make it a moral law. He expresses it as a rule of personal advantage which a rational person will take account of as far as *he* thinks it beneficial to himself and in respect of those claims only which he is prepared to surrender if others surrender the same claims in respect of him. It is clear that Hobbes sees this 'law' essentially as a rule of mutual forebearance by which men will increase their personal felicity by refraining from inter-fering with or hindering one another. Such a rule will, however, only be kept by any man 'when he has the will to keep them, when he can do it safely' (p. 87). It will clearly be to the advantage of any man that others should observe forebearance towards him while he neglects it towards them. Thus, while Hobbes asserts that all men desire peace, he insists that the natural condition of men is not conducive to its realization because men's private appetites and differing judgements give rise to different conceptions of good and evil. The first two laws of nature therefore point the need for the creation of a force capable of producing rules which are sufficiently precise and which are backed by sanctions to ensure that men do not merely desire their realization in general but are required to act in accordance with them.

The need for such a force is clearly seen in Hobbes's third law of nature, 'That men performe their Covenants made' (p. 74), which he derives directly from the first two. His purpose in formulating his own particular laws of nature is now made clear for he now expresses these laws not as theorems of self-interest which every rational man is bound to accept as being for his personal advantage, but as rules 'by which we are obliged to transferre to another, such Rights, as being retained, hinder the peace of Mankind' (p. 74). In place of the recognition by individuals of the mutual need for forebearance in their personal relations, we now have an unqualified demand for the surrender of all rights which stand in the way of peace and security. This mutual renunciation or transference of rights, while it is expressed as a voluntary act undertaken in furtherance of some good to each of the participants, is held to require the existence of 'a common Power set over them both, with right and force sufficient to compel performance' (p. 70), if it is to be a valid covenant. Hobbes distinguishes a covenant from other forms of contract in that it leaves one party to fulfill his obligation after the other has performed his. Thus in calling on men to keep covenants made Hobbes is making his third law of nature a demand for the creation of a civil society which alone can make covenants secure. Reason shows man how wretched his natural state would be were he to live in accordance with the dictates of his passions. The laws of nature are meant to be axioms which reason discloses to be the necessary conditions for the realization of felicity for 'men in multitudes'. They are thus not so much axioms of personal conduct as axioms which lead inexorably to the conclusion that men need to live in an ordered civil society, with power to make laws backed by force. The first of two laws can be seen as rules of rational self-interest which require the institution of civil society for their implementation, while the third is explicable in terms of rational self-interest only for creatures who already exist in civil society.

Hobbes's portrayal of the state of nature as a state of war is a logical prerequisite for the construction, not of civil society generally, but of the Leviathan form of state. This prerequisite was, in Hobbes's view, not only deducible from self-evident propositions about human behaviour, but was confirmed by historical experience; for in many parts of the world savage peoples continued to live in the state of nature, such as he had described. More important, he argued, 'it may be perceived what manner of life there would be, where there was no common Power to feare; by the manner of life, which men that have formerly lived under a peacefull government, use to degenerate into, in a civill Warre' (p. 65). The state of nature is the pit into which men are liable, even likely, to fall, if they do not learn and apply the lessons taught in *Leviathan*. Hobbes purports to show what arrangements are necessary if men are to avoid this evil, not to discuss the actual arrangements which men have made. Thus when Hobbes writes that

> the only way to erect such a Common Power, as may be able to defend them from the invasion of Forraigners, and the injuries of one another – is, to conferre all their power and strength upon one Man or upon one Assembley of men, that may reduce all their Wills, by plurality of voices, into one Will (p. 89),

he is well aware both that most governments were not so instituted and that they did not possess or claim to possess such unqualified power. Hobbes's argument, however, is that anything less than such a conferment will be insufficient to curb the natural passions of men and avoid the danger of degeneration into a state of war.

In Chapter 30 of *Leviathan*, Hobbes discusses the internal diseases which Commonwealths are prone to and which, if unchecked, will lead to their dissolution. All these diseases stem, in his view, from the absence of a single all-powerful directing force in the community. Hobbes's Leviathan is a geometrical construction from elements which he claims to have firmly established. It seeks to show the only way by which man might save himself from the dilemma posed by his own nature. If one accepts Hobbes's view of man then the question which arises is whether his construction is internally self-consistent. One major inconsistency is that a contract to hand over all power to one man or one assembly of men depends for its effectiveness on their future keeping of their promise of unqualified obedience: it is thus in Hobbes's terms a covenant. But covenants cannot be binding, Hobbes has insisted, unless there already exists a common power able to compel compliance. Consequently one cannot covenant to establish a commonwealth if covenants themselves can exist only under commonwealths. Further there seems no necessary reason why the transfer of power under the covenant should be unqualified or made to some person or body not a party to the compact as Hobbes requires. On the question of unqualified transfer it is to be noted that Hobbes himself holds that it is necessary for men on entering civil society to retain some rights 'as right to governe their owne bodies; enjoy aire, water, motion, waies to go from place to place; and all things else without which a man cannot live, or not live well' (p. 80)[1]. This would suggest a limited transfer of rights in those areas which are sources of conflict between men and the creation of a will which would be sovereign in limited fields only. This conclusion, however, conflicts with Hobbes's deep-rooted convictions as to the essential requirements of a well-ordered society; for in his view the reservation of specified rights would open the door to dispute and chaos. Again it is plain that the need to make the sovereign the beneficiary of the covenant but not a party to its making, arises not from the very nature of his formulation of the problem of the human condition but from his own prior conception of what is required for its resolution. He wishes to establish that 'there can happen no breach of Covenant on the part of the Soveraigne, and consequently none of his Subjects, by any pretence or forfeiture, can be freed from his Subjection' (p. 91). For while Hobbes accepts that sovereign power is created for 'the procuration of *the safety of the people*', he holds the sovereign to be responsible not to the people but to God for the fulfilment of that trust.

READING

Hobbes, *Leviathan*, Chs. 4, 5, 14 and 15.

J. Plamenatz, *Man and Society*, Vol. I, Ch. 4, Hobbes section iv, 'The making and keeping of the covenant'.

2. LOCKE

As Peter Laslett has shown, there is strong evidence to suggest that John Locke's *Two Treatises of Government* were, in the main, written in the period 1679–80, when Locke's powerful patron, the Earl of Shaftesbury, was actively considering armed resistance should Charles II refuse to exclude his Catholic brother James from the throne. Locke's

1. See Ch. IV, s.i below for a discussion of the rights and liberties of the subject in the Hobbesian state.

justification of political rebellion was not published until after the 'Glorious Revolution' of 1688, when it appeared prefaced as a work 'to establish the Throne of our Great Restorer, Our present King William; to make good his Title, in the Consent of the People, which being the only one of all lawful Governments, he has more fully and clearly than any Prince in Christendom'. It was precisely, however, because so many people were doubtful about William of Orange's claims, especially after James II reasserted his title rights, that Locke's work had such an impact. Locke was well aware of the dangers to himself which would result from any return of James II and went to great lengths to conceal his authorship.[1]

The two *Treatises* had two different purposes. The *First* (probably written after the more famous *Second Treatise*) was designed to demolish the case for the divine right of kings put forward by Sir Robert Filmer in *Patriarcha* written *c.* 1636–8 and extensively circulated in manuscript before its publication in 1680. Filmer's work quickly established itself as a classic of High Toryism and Royalism. Locke's aim was to show that Sir Robert Filmer's arguments from scripture were not only erroneous, but that their acceptance would undermine all claims to political obedience; placing tyrants and true princes on the same level. In the *Second Treatise* Locke put forward his own views on the nature and limits of political authority in a form which resurrected in a new and essentially secular way the old medieval doctrine of the right of resistance to tyrants, against the new and short-lived 'heresy' of the divine right of kings.

Locke follows the example of Hobbes in seeking to deduce the nature of political society from that of man in his natural state, that is, man abstracted from the political society in which he is normally to be found living.

> To understand Political Power right, and derive it from its Original, we must consider what State all Men are naturally in, and that it is, a *State of perfect Freedom* to order their Actions and dispose of their Possessions, and Persons as they think fit, within the bounds of the Law of Nature, without asking leave, or depending upon the Will of any other Man (II, s. 4).

1. See Peter Laslett, Introduction, section iii, to John Locke's *Two Treatises of Government*, 1960. Laslett's edition has been used throughout this book and references are given to section numbers in I (*First Treatise*) and II (*Second Treatise*).

The hypothetical state of nature was constructed by reference to Locke's conceptions of the nature of man. The most distinctive characteristic of man for Locke was his rationality. In the *Essays on the Law of Nature* written about 1660 Locke talks of reason as 'the discursive faculty of the mind, which advances from things known to things unknown and argues from one point to another in a definite and fixed order of propositions'. He distinguishes this faculty, which works on the perceptions furnished by the senses, from 'right reason', moral principles of conduct 'necessary for the direction of life and the formation of character', which men can discern *through* the faculty of reason.[1] These principles of conduct, which Locke sometimes refers to as the laws of nature, and sometimes as the laws of reason, are binding both because they embody the will of God and because they are part of man's very nature. These two reasons are united through God as the creator of man – 'since man has been made such as he is, equipped with reason and his other faculties and destined for this mode of life, there necessarily result from his inborn constitution some definite duties for him, which cannot be other than they are' (ibid., p. 199). Those who, like idiots, lack the faculty of reason or those in whom it is not yet developed, as with children, are not bound by the laws of nature for 'it is not given to those who are unable to understand it' (ibid., p. 203). On the other hand there are many who through laziness remain ignorant of these laws; while others are 'either carried off by inveterate habit and traditional examples or led aside by their passions, thus yielding to the morality of others; also they follow the herd in the manner of brute beasts, since they do not allow themselves the use of their reason, but give way to appetite' (ibid., p. 203). Men are partial to their own interests and this partiality leads them to refuse to act in accordance with the principles of true reason and to prefer immediate satisfaction to long-term advantage. 'For though the Law of Nature be plain and intelligible to all rational Creatures; yet Men being biassed by their Interest, as well as ignorant for want of study of it, are not apt to allow of it as a Law binding to them in the application of it to their particular Cases' (II, s. 124). These two elements of rationality and partiality are seen as permanent characteristics of men and explain both the human predicament and the measures which must be taken to resolve it.

Locke distinguishes between the state of nature and the state of

1. John Locke, *Essays on the Law of Nature*, edited by W. Von Leyden, 1954, p. 149.

War, conditions which he avers 'some Men' (i.e. the followers of Hobbes) 'have confounded'.

> Men living together according to reason, without a common Superior on Earth, with Authority to judge between them is *properly the State of Nature*. But force, or a declared design of force upon the Person of another, where there is no common Superior on Earth to appeal to for relief, *is the State of War* (II, s. 19).

Locke goes on to make it clear that the state of war can exist within a political society and between political societies as well as outside them. Where no political society exists any man who seeks to force me to do his bidding puts himself in a state of war with me. The same situation may arise in political society where a man seeks to 'take away the *Freedom* belonging to those of that Society or Commonwealth' (II, s. 17). More important, and in sharp contrast to Hobbes, Locke recognizes that those appointed to administer justice may themselves be the authors of injustice;

> where an appeal to the Law, and constituted Judges lies open, but the remedy is deny'd by a manifest perverting of Justice, and a barefaced wresting of the Laws, to protect or indemnifie the violence or injuries of some Men, or Party of Men, *there* it *is* hard to imagine any thing but a *State of War* (II, s. 20).

Since man has according to Locke a Right '*by the Fundamental Law of Nature*' to preserve his own life by destroying those who make war upon him, provided that he is the innocent party, it follows that men who find themselves in a 'state of war' with their ruler have the right to rid themselves of him as they would rid themselves of an armed robber. Whereas outside political society a state of war is likely to result from 'every the least difference' because of the absence of any authority to settle disputes, the state of war in political society will only result on those occasions where the political authority is ineffective or corrupt.

When Locke speaks of the state of nature being 'properly' a condition where men live together 'according to reason without a common Superior on Earth' (II, s. 19), he is using the term in a normative or ideal sense, as the way in which men ought and might live together if they were not led astray by partiality and passion. In this sense the 'state of nature' as a state of peace and social harmony, is contrasted with the 'state of war'. Locke, however, also uses the term 'state of nature' in a less precise sense as simply the condition men find themselves in when they lack a common superior, and here the 'state of nature' includes the possibility of degeneration into a 'state of war'. In this latter sense the 'state of nature' becomes a realistic hypothesis based on men as they are (or rather as Locke sees them as being) not as they might and ought to be. Consequently not only can men be found living in a state of nature, as with the North American Indian, but such a condition is held by Locke to exist in those political societies where all power is concentrated in the ruler's hands.

> For he being suppos'd to have all, both Legislative and Executive Power in himself alone, there is no Judge to be found, no Appeal lies open to any one, who may fairly, and indifferently, (i.e. impartially – my note), and with Authority decide, and from whose decision relief and redress may be expected of any Injury or Inconveniency, that may be suffered from the Prince or by his Order. So that such a Man, however entitled, *Czar*, or *Grand Signior*, or how you please, is as much *in the state of Nature*, with all under his Dominion, as he is with the rest of Mankind (II, s. 91).

This condition is worse than that of 'the ordinary State of Nature' for there each man is at liberty to determine for himself when his rights and interests have been invaded and to take what steps he thinks necessary to protect them. But the 'Slave of an Absolute Prince' –

> whenever his Property is invaded by the Will and Order of his Monarch, he has not only no Appeal, as those in Society ought to have, but as if he were degraded from the common state of Rational Creatures, is denied a liberty to judge of, or to defend his Right, and so is exposed to all the Misery and Inconveniences that a Man can fear from one, who being in the unrestrained state of Nature, is yet corrupted with Flattery and armed with Power (II, s. 91).

Locke seeks to show that his realistic hypothesis of the state of nature (as distinct from his normative ideal state) explains both why men should want to construct a political society and how they are able to do so.

The state of nature for Locke, unlike Hobbes, is a social condition in which men live together in family units with established and recognized property rights.[1] But while life outside political society is possible the dangers of being plunged into a state of war are ever present; for 'the greater part' of men being 'no strict Observers of Equity and Justice, the enjoyment of the property he has in this state

---

1. See Chapter V, section 2, below, for a full discussion of Locke's views on property.

is very unsafe, very unsecure' (II, s. 123). The state of nature lacks firstly 'an establish'd, settled, known *Law*, received and allowed by common consent to be the Standard of Right and Wrong, and the common measure to decide all Controversies between them' (II, s. 124); secondly '*a known and indifferent Judge*, with Authority to determine all differences according to the established Law' (II, s. 125); and thirdly '*Power* to back and support the Sentence when right, and to *give* it due *Execution*' (II, s. 126). 'Thus Mankind, notwithstanding all the Priviledges of the state of Nature, being but an ill condition, while they remain in it, are quickly driven into Society. Hence it comes to pass, that we seldom find any number of Men live any time together in this State' (II, s. 127).

If we construct, as Locke as done, a hypothetical situation of this kind facing men who are by nature 'all free, equal and independent', then it logically follows that 'The only way whereby anyone devests himself of his Natural Liberty, and *puts on the bonds of Civil Society* is by agreeing with other men to joyn and unite into a Community, for their comfortable, safe and peaceable living one amongst another' (II, s. 95). The act of consent is simply what men have to do to get out of an undesirable situation, and for Locke it constituted the sole grounds for political obedience.

Locke is not content to show how legitimate societies might in theory have been constructed. He argues that Rome, Venice and Sparta in fact had their origins in the consent of free and independent men. He cleverly turns Filmer's arguments that government originates from paternal right with the assertion that patriarchial government amounts to government of the father with the consent of the adult children who 'in effect make him the Law-maker, and Governour over all, that remained in Conjunction with his Family' (II, s. 105). Thus Locke is able to conclude 'that all peaceful beginnings of *Government* have been *laid in the Consent of the People*' (II, s. 112). He does not deny of course that many governments have been established by force of arms, he simply denies that such governments have any claim to obedience from their subjects 'till their Rulers put them under such a Frame of Government, as they willingly, and of choice consent to' (II, s. 192). Moreover it is not sufficient for Locke that men should at some time in the dim and distant past have consented or be presumed to have consented to the establishment of a particular form of government. Consent must be renewed in each generation for a man '*cannot* by any *Compact* whatsoever, bind *his Children* or Posterity' (II, s. 116).

READING

John Locke, *The Second Treatise of Government*, Chs. I, II, III and VIII.

M. Seliger, *The Liberal Politics of John Locke* (1968), Part One, Ch. III; Part Two, Ch. VII.

John W. Yolton (Ed.), *John Locke: Problems and Perspectives; A Collection of New Essays* (1969), Hans Aarslett, 'The state of nature and the nature of man'.

3. ROUSSEAU

Rousseau's political writings have been the subject of greater dispute and conflicting interpretation than almost any other political theorist. To different critics he appears as the most virulent exponent of extreme individualism and the great protagonist of collectivism; the finest apostle of true democracy and the spiritual father of totalitarianism; the incarnation of the spirit of revolution and the advocate of caution and conservation; the optimistic herald of a new era and the pessimist who sees no hope for mankind. While some have tried to tie Rousseau down with a neat label of their own choice, others have portrayed him as a walking mass of contradictions, reflecting in his writings the troubles and doubts of his own unstable mental state. But while incongruities do exist there is an underlying unity and consistency about his writings viewed as a whole. Rousseau never changed his basic conceptions about the relationship of man and society, although his particular treatment of the theme varied according to the occasion and his own purpose.

Rousseau himself tells of the sudden revelation which came to him on a summer's day on the road to Vincennes in 1749 as

> swarms of lively ideas presented themselves to me at once with a force and confusion that threw me into an inexpressible turmoil . . . Oh Sir, if I could ever have written one fourth of what I had seen and felt under that tree, with what clarity I should have revealed all the contradictions of the social system! With what force I should have exposed all the abuses of our institutions! With what ease I should have shown

that man is naturally good, and that it is through these institutions alone that men become bad.[1]

Rousseau is essentially a moralist concerned with redeeming men from their follies and from the ill-effects of their social environment. His principal political work, *The Social Contract*, is more aptly described by its sub-title, *Principles of Political Right*; for it is with the principles which should be given effect to, not those most commonly appealed to, that Rousseau deals. He attacks the Dutch jurist, Hugo Grotius, because the latter's 'characteristic method of reasoning is always to offer fact as a proof of right',[2] which is the reverse of what is required – one 'must know what ought to be in order to judge what is'.[3] Rousseau's approach to the nature of man is akin to that of Aristotle, who derived his conception of man's nature in terms of what he had it in him to become under optimum conditions, rather than from the actual character of the typical man. Rousseau's natural man is man as he might be, not man as he is, but since the potential can arise only from the actual it is possible by introspection and self-experience to gain knowledge of the realizable self. In one of his later works, *Rousseau Judge of Jean Jacques*, Rousseau claims that 'it was necessary that one man should paint his own portrait to show us, in this manner, the natural man and if the author had not been just as singular as his books, he would not have written them'.[4] Introspection revealed to Rousseau the existence in men of two basic forces or feelings which he calls *amour de soi* (enlightened self-interest) and *amour-propre* (selfish-interest). The second is a degenerate form of the first and reveals itself as self-advancement at the expense of others. *Amour de soi*, on the other hand, while at root it expresses simply the urge to survive, is the source of all that is worthwhile in life, all that gives real and lasting satisfaction both to oneself and to others.

The nature and relationship of these two natural forces in men is explored by Rousseau in the second of his discources *On the Origin of Inequality* (published in 1755). Rousseau does not treat the problem

1. Letter to Malesherbes, 12 January 1762, quoted by Ernst Cassirer in *The Question of Jean Jacques Rousseau*, edited by Peter Gay, New York, 1954, pp. 46–7.
2. Jean Jacques Rousseau, *The Social Contract*, translated and introduced by Maurice Cranston, Penguin Books, 1968, Bk. I, Ch. 2, p. 51.
3. Jean Jacques Rousseau, *Émile or Education*, translated by Barbara Foxley, Everyman's Library edition, 1930, p. 422.
4. Quoted by Cassirer, op. cit., p. 51.

historically but hypothetically, being more concerned 'to explain the
nature of things than to ascertain their actual origin'.[1] His method is to
strip from man 'all the supernatural gifts he may have received, and all
the artificial faculties he can have acquired only by a long process' and
to view him in the raw 'just as he must have come from the hands of
nature' (ibid., p. 163). In this way it may be possible to throw some
light on what was the form of society best suited to man's needs and
purposes. In developing his conception of the state of nature 'which
no longer exists, perhaps never did exist and probably never will exist'
(ibid., p. 155), Rousseau attacks the way the concept has been handled
by earlier writers who have 'transferred to the state of nature ideas
which were acquired in society; so that in speaking of savages, they
described the social man' (ibid., p. 161). In an unpublished fragment
The State of War, written at about the same time, Rousseau makes a
sharp and effective attack on Hobbes's conception of the state of nature
which ascribes to natural man vices and passions which he could only
have developed under close settled conditions of social life. But if
Rousseau rejects Hobbes's portrayal of natural man as selfish and pug-
nacious, he equally rejects Locke's picture of him as a sociable moral
being. Rousseau's natural man is not a man of reason with full awareness of what the law of nature requires of him, but a timid, solitary,
indolent being concerned only to satisfy his basic needs for food, sleep
and sexual satisfaction. These appetites are easily gratified for primitive
man and give rise neither to a state of war nor a state of settled social
living.

Natural man, according to Rousseau, is moved by two instincts or
faculties, self-preservation and compassion. These he shares with other
living creatures but it is only in man that they assume a distinctive form.
The faculty of self-preservation is the original of *amour de soi*, but
whereas in other creatures this faculty is purely instinctive, in man it is
subject to his will. 'Nature lays her commands on every animal, and the
brute obeys her voice. Man receives the same impulsion, but at the
same time knows himself at liberty to acquiesce or resist' (*Inequality*,
p. 170). The other shared faculty of compassion is for Rousseau man's
'only natural virtue', tempering and restraining the urge for self-preservation, where this operates at the expense of others, and exciting
concern and pity for the plight of fellow creatures. Compassion, like

1. *Inequality*, p. 161, in Jean Jacques Rousseau, *The Social Contract and Discourses*, translated with introduction by G. D. H. Cole, Everyman's Library
   edition, 1946.

self-preservation, is a pre-rational instinct but from it have sprung all the social virtues of generosity, clemency, humanity, benevolence and friendship. Compassion has the power to transform *amour de soi* from a self-regarding simple desire for self-preservation, without reference to others, into a positive social virtue so that each man comes to identify himself with the whole human species. Such a development could not have taken place had man not been possessed of a quality distinguishing him from all other creatures, the capacity for self-improvement 'which by the help of circumstances, gradually developes all the rest of our faculties' (ibid., p. 170). The assumption of such an innate drive for self-improvement is necessary to Rousseau's thesis to explain how man could ever have developed from the self-sufficient, amoral creature that he was into the dependent confused guilt-ridden creature that he is. It required the conjunction over long ages of the internal drive for self-improvement with the external spur of necessity, in particular the pressure of an increasing population on natural food resources, to bring about the gradual change of natural man into rational man.

The state of nature for Rousseau is not a static condition, but a long drawn out period of gradual, but accelerating change which culminates in the establishment of settled civil societies. Within this period Rousseau distinguishes a number of stages. The first important changes in man's natural condition arise from increasing social intercourse and contact with his fellows which resulted from an increase in numbers.

> Taught by experience that the love of well-being is the sole motive of human actions, he found himself in a position to distinguish the few cases, in which mutual interest might justify him in relying upon the assistance of his fellows; and also the still fewer cases in which a conflict of interests might give cause to suspect them (ibid., p. 194).

From these first loose temporary associations there emerges 'the epoch of a first revolution' which introduces on the one hand settled family life, the source of 'the finest feelings known to humanity, conjugal love and paternal affection', and on the other the rudiments of property and a real sense of ownership, 'in itself the source of a thousand quarrels and conflicts' (ibid., p. 195). But initially the evils resulting from proprietorship are outweighted by the benefits of a simple settled social existence. Man is no longer a silent, wandering, joyless creature but a social being finding pleasure in others' company and aware of the need to refrain from doing injury to them. 'Placed by nature,' Rousseau tells us, 'at an equal distance from the stupidity of brutes and the fatal ingenuity of

civilised man' – 'this period of expansion of the human faculties . . .
must have been the happiest and most stable of epochs' (ibid., p. 198).

But alas it does not last. The fatal gap between *amour de soi* and
amour propre has been opened up with the institution of property and
men come more and more to seek to satisfy not their wants but their
ambition to surpass their fellows. 'In a word, there arose rivalry and
competition on the one hand, and conflicting interests on the other,
together with a secret desire on both of profiting at the expense of
others' (ibid., p. 203). The end comes when the bitter conflict of
interests results in every man being concerned to protect what is his
own and to grasp what is another's. It is a Hobbesian state of war but
between men who are presumed to have already passed through the
first stage of primitive society and to have developed the kind of social
relationship to be found in Locke's state of nature.

> Thus as the most powerful or the most miserable considered their
> might or misery as a kind of right to the possessions of others, equiva-
> lent, in their opinion, to that of property, the destruction of equality
> was attended by the most terrible disorders. Usurpations by the rich,
> robbery by the poor, and the unbridled passions of both, suppressed
> the cries of natural compassion and the still feeble voice of justice, and
> filled men with avarice, ambition and vice (ibid., p. 203).

The answer to this chaotic state is found by the rich and corrupt,
who by persuading the poor and wretched that the establishment of
political institutions will guarantee peace and justice for all, secured
their own position as a permanent class of the wealthy. 'All ran headlong
to their chains, in hopes of securing their liberty; for they had just wit
enough to perceive the advantages of political institutions, without experience enough to enable them to foresee the dangers' (ibid., p. 205).
The upshot is what J. H. Broome has aptly termed 'the anti-social
contract',[1] which by establishing political society on the basis of the
selfish interest (*amour propre*) of the rich, instead of the self-interest
(*amour de soi*) of all, opens the road which leads to tyranny.

It is important to note that Rousseau does not see the first form of
political society as tyrannical, even though it authorizes and perpetuates
the divisions between rich and poor. On the contrary he regards political
society as consisting at first 'merely of a few general conventions, which
every member bound himself to observe, and for the performance of

1. J. H. Broome, *Rousseau: A Study of His Thought*, 1963.

covenants the whole body went security to each individual' (ibid., pp. 207-8). It is the very weakness of such arrangements which induces men to take the next step of appointing magistrates to administer the law. It is only where the magistrates become arbitrary hereditary rulers who treat their subjects as mere possessions that tyranny reigns and the last stage of inequality is reached with the dominance of one man's will over the wills of all other men. But for Rousseau the most objectionable feature of the social tyranny he saw all around him was not the oppression itself, but the willingness with which men wore their chains or their sheer inability to recognize their own servitude. 'We cannot,' he argues, 'from the servility of nations already enslaved, judge of the natural disposition of mankind for or against slavery; we should go by the prodigious efforts of every free people to save itself from oppression – it is not for slaves to argue about liberty' (ibid., p. 209).

The importance of the *Discourse on the Origin of Inequality* is to be found not in the particulars of the explanation which Rousseau gives of the human condition, but in the force of the indictment. Man has been corrupted by society but since his nature is malleable he is not past redemption. A return to the primitive condition is not only impossible but undesirable; since it is not society as such which is at fault but the degenerate forms which most societies have assumed over time. There are examples to be found of states which indicate the way in which men can live as free citizens, states like Ancient Rome and Sparta and the Geneva of his own time. In *The Social Contract* Rousseau attempts to show how a society might be constructed which enables each of its members to develop his own individual personality in ways which harmonize with the needs and interests of the community. In *Émile* he describes how the natural personality of a child might, even in a corrupt society, be nurtured and developed by a wise tutor to produce a self-reliant creative free being instead of a creature of fashion and convention.[1] But even in a corrupt society the true man of Rousseau's imagination has social duties. He must make the public good his own and be prepared 'to sacrifice his own interest to the common weal' (*Émile*, p. 437). But in the ideal society the state itself would undertake

---

1. The cloying effect of fashion and convention is the theme of Rousseau's first major writing *A Discourse on the Arts and Sciences*, 1750. 'We no longer dare seem,' he wrote 'what we really are, but lie under a perpetual restraint; in the meantime the herd of men, which we call society, all act under the same circumstances exactly alike, unless very particular and powerful motives prevent them.' Everyman's Library edition, op. cit., p. 122.

the education of its citizens along the lines laid down by Émile's tutor. Then one might produce a golden age of free men in a free society.

Neither *The Social Contract* nor *Émile* are prescriptions to cure society of its ills; they are rather visions of what might one day be. Their importance for Rousseau lies in their providing a standard by which one might judge existing social institutions and an objective to which one should aim in schemes of reform. Rousseau never doubted the validity of the fundamental conceptions which he developed in these two major works: what he did doubt was whether the goals were even realizable as far as most existing societies were concerned. When given the opportunity to produce schemes of reform, as in the cases of Corsica and Poland, he outlined moderate proposals firmly based on what he regarded as the positive features of the existing social fabric. These proposals (discussed in Chapter 6, section iii), while they differ in many particulars from those put forward in *The Social Contract*, are not in contradiction to the spirit of that work. The dramatic act of total alienation of self to the community (the true social contract), which Rousseau requires as the prerequisite for the creation of his ideal society, can never in practice be realized; if for no other reason than that it requires a degree of public spiritedness which can be acquired only through the experience of living in the free creative society which it is the purpose of the social contract to make possible. The ideal has to give way to the realizable, but it remains as the inspiration of what is to be realized.

READING

J. J. Rousseau, *A Discourse on the Origin of Inequality*, Everyman's Library.

J. H. Broome, *Rousseau: A Study of His Thought*, Ch. 3.

John W. Chapman, *Rousseau: Totalitarian or Liberal?*, New York, 1956, Ch. 1.

M. Cranston, Introduction to *The Social Contract*, Penguin Books.

4. BENTHAM AND MILL

One hundred and twenty-five years separate the birth of Jeremy Bentham, the founder of the English school of utilitarianism, from the death of John Stuart Mill, who is variously regarded as the last teacher of the original school and as its unwitting gravedigger.[1] In these sections on Bentham and Mill it is proposed to examine Bentham's views and then to see how far J. S. Mill differs from him or adds something new. While utilitarianism is a disarmingly simple doctrine, as embodied in the principle that pleasure-seeking and pain-avoidance are the main-springs of human action, both its formulation and implications have been subject to widely differing interpretation and criticism. The great assault on utilitarianism made by the English idealist thinkers in the last quarter of the nineteenth century was that pleasure for pleasure's sake was unacceptable as a principle of conduct whether applied by an individual to his own satisfactions or the satisfactions of all. The former doctrine, 'utilitarianism proper' as T. H. Green called it,[2] was associated with Jeremy Bentham and the latter, modern utilitarianism, with that of John Stuart Mill. In the eyes of the idealists both suffered from the same fundamental defect that they regarded society as simply an aggregation of individuals, each one of whom was called to exercise his own personal judgement as to what would bring about the realization of the greatest pleasure for himself or all sentient beings.[3] The purpose of the idealists was to return the abstract individual pleasure seeker into the society of which he was a part, and apart from which he had no being.

Is it correct to regard Bentham as the portrayer of man as a self-seeking, pleasure-guided individual, whether considered in the natural or the social state? Did he see society as an external force whose activities should be kept to the minimum necessary to enable men to live peaceably together? The fundamental principle which underlies all

1. John Stuart Mill (1806–1873) was the son of James Mill, the loyal disciple and friend of Jeremy Bentham (1748–1832). James brought up his son in strict conformity with utilitarian principles. See J. S. Mill, *Autobiography*, 1873, available in the World's Classics series.
2. T. H. Green, *Lectures on the Principles of Political Obligation* (delivered in 1879), reprinted from Green's Philosophical Works, Vol. II, 1917, p. 43.
3. See F. H. Bradley, *Ethical Studies*, 1876, Oxford Paperbacks, 1962, Essay III, 'Pleasure for Pleasure's Sake'.

Bentham's writings is the principle of utility which he uses both descriptively and prescriptively. In the descriptive sense the principle
states that men's actions are prompted by the desire to secure pleasure
and avoid pain. In the prescriptive sense it asserts that this desire is in
itself good for all men and that consequently all actions or propositions
should be judged by whether they tend to augment the happiness of all
members of the community concerned.[1] Bentham proceeds to discuss
how the tendency of any action to promote or retard the interests of the
community may be calculated by reference to its intensity, duration,
certainty or uncertainty, propinquity or remoteness, fecundity (i.e.
chance of its being followed by sensations of the same kind), or purity
(i.e. chance of its not being followed by sensations of the opposite kind),
extent (i.e. number of persons affected). Ideally one would proceed by
calculating the total of the values of the various pains and pleasures
produced or likely to be produced on each individual in turn by the
act in question. One would then add up all the pains of those affected
and all the pleasures and according to whether there was an overall
balance of pleasure or pain the act concerned would have shown itself to
have either a generally good or a generally evil tendency. Bentham recognizes, however, that this ideal could not always be adhered to. 'It is
not to be expected that this process should be strictly pursued previously
to every moral judgement, or to every legislative or judicial operation.
It may, however, be always kept in view: & as near as the process actually
pursued on these occasions approaches to it, so near will such process
approach to the character of an exact one.'[2] He accepts that the sensations of pleasure and pain are personal to the individual who experiences
them and that they cannot therefore strictly be compared; but he argues
'this addibility of the happiness of different subjects . . . is a postulation
. . . without which all political reasonings are at a stand.'[3] Legislators
and judges have to make decisions and in Bentham's view their decisions
will be much less prone to error and partiality if they approach their
tasks in the way he suggests.

Bentham proceeds to give what he claims to be a complete list of
fourteen simple pleasures and twelve simple pains; in the sense that any

1. See Chapter 2, section 4, for a discussion of utility as a prescriptive principle.
2. Jeremy Bentham, *An Introduction to the Principles of Morals and Legislation*,
   1789, reprinted in Blackwell's Political Texts with *A Fragment on Government*, ed. W. Harrison, 1948, p. 153.
3. Quoted by Mary Mack in *Jeremy Bentham: An Odyssey of Ideas 1748–1792*,
   1962, p. 244.

sensation of pleasure or pain if analysed would be found to conform to one or more of these categories. Only benevolence and malevolence amongst the categories are 'extra-regarding', in that they 'suppose the existence of some pleasure or pain of some other person to which the pleasure or pain of the person in question has regard' (*Principles of Morals and Legislation*, p. 162). That is not to say that self-regarding pleasures and pains may not result from other people's actions or that they may not have effects on others. Bentham also emphasized that the same cause may give rise not only to different degrees, but different kinds of pleasure and pain in different people and he lists the various circumstances influencing an individual's sensibility to pleasure and pain. Some of these circumstances are matters over which neither the person affected nor anyone else has any control, such as physical and intellectual power, temperament, age, sex and race. Others are circumstances which are to a large extent under the individual's own direction (religious profession, occupation, firmness of mind); some are the result of the interaction of personal and social factors (moral and sympathetic sensibility, sympathy and antipathy); while others are social circumstances such as education and government which are capable of being altered. These circumstances are for Bentham important considerations to be taken into account by legislators and judges when determining the form and degree of punishment to be applied to particular offences and offenders. What the discussion of these considerations also reveals is the importance which Bentham attached in judging men's actions, to factors other than these uppermost in the mind of the agent. He was far from denying or overlooking the impact of custom and habit on human actions. Where he differs from writers like Blackstone and Burke is in their insistence that prescription was the embodiment of wisdom. On the contrary, Bentham wrote, 'It is under the dominion of usage, custom, precedent that the existing abuses have sprung up and continue.'[1]

Contrary to common belief, Bentham does not view men as hedonistic calculating machines who unerringly choose the most pleasurable paths. On the contrary he sees men as constantly following paths which result in unhappiness both for themselves and for others. Bentham's aim as a utilitarian is above all to show how the external circumstances affecting human behaviour might be made more conducive to the maximization

---

1. Jeremy Bentham, *Handbook of Political Fallacies*, revised and edited by Harold A. Larrabee, Harper Torchbooks, New York, 1962, p. 233.

of satisfaction for all societies' members. To this end the legislator should encourage the sentiment of benevolence and proscribe everything that serves as an incitement to cruelty. 'Men must be freed from fear and oppression, before they can be taught to love each other.'[1] In Bentham's view men are the products of society and can be altered and improved by society, 'let us blame establishments, which alone, and not individuals, are justly blameable: for individuals are what the laws have made them'.[2]

In his best-known work, *Principles of Morals and Legislation*, Bentham is primarily interested in the consequences of men's actions, rather than the circumstances which give rise to them, for it is with the former that legislators and judges have to deal immediately at any point in time. The impact of circumstance is important for determining what reforms in law and institutions are necessary and what punishments should be meted out to those who break the law; but it is the consequences of actions which alone are important in deciding what actions merit judicial punishment. The emphasis on the consequences of action, rather than the aims and purposes of the actor, is a necessary requirement of the doctrine of utility, which judges of actions in terms of their effect on human happiness. It also in Bentham's eyes has the merit of practicality, for consequences are public and assessable while purposes are private and difficult to scrutinize. Bentham's discussion of the problem is based on a distinction he makes between a man's motives and his intentions. 'A man's intentions then on any occasion may be styled good or bad with reference either to the consequences of the act, or with reference to his motives' (*Principles of Morals and Legislation*, p. 205), but since the goodness or badness of the consequences depend on the circumstances, a man can only be held to intend the consequences when he is aware of all the relevant circumstances affecting that consequence. Motives, on the other hand, are for Bentham, the midwives of intentions. 'A motive ... is ... any thing whatsoever, which, by influencing the will of a sensitive being, is supposed to serve as a means of determining him to act, or voluntarily to forbear to act' (ibid., p. 215). The motive for any act is always 'some pleasure, which the act in question is expected to be a means of continuing or producing: some pain which it is expected to be a means of discontinuing or preventing'. Conse-

---

1. Jeremy Bentham, *Theory of Legislation*, edited and translated into French by Etienne Dumont and translated back into English by R. Hildreth, 7th edition, 1891, p. 429.
2. Bentham in 1790. Quoted by Mary Mack in op. cit., p. 325.

quently 'there is no such thing as any sort of motive that is in itself a bad one' (ibid., p. 218). The same motive may give rise to good or bad intentions: sexual desire may stimulate an intention of marriage or of seduction. It is only possible, therefore, to speak of a good or bad motive by reference to the effects to which it gives rise in each particular instance. Motives may be classified, however, with regard to the tendency which they appear to have to unite the interests of the actor with, or dissociate them from, those of other members of the community. That is to say they can be classified in terms of the prescriptive principle of utility.

Bentham distinguishes three categories of motive: *social, dissocial* and *self-regarding*. Of the *social* motives, good will is the only *purely social* one, for it alone coincides with the dictates of utility which 'are neither more nor less than the dictates of the most extensive and enlightened (that is *well-advised*) benevolence' (p. 236). The *semi-social* motives are love of reputation, desire of amity and religion; the *dissocial*, displeasure; the *self-regarding*, physical desire, pecuniary interest, love of power and self-preservation. It is primarily to the *self-regarding* motives that the legislator must directly appeal in his attempt to ensure men's conformity to rules by use of the political sanction of punishment. This does not mean however that 'strength and direction' should not be given to the 'influence of the moral sanction'[1] by seeking to persuade men to act in conformity with the *social* and *semi-social* motives which normally work to the public advantage.

In the brief sketch of Bentham which John Stuart Mill (1806–73) published in 1838, six years after Bentham's death, Mill criticizes Bentham's limited conception of human nature for ignoring such important features as desire for perfection, sense of honour, love of beauty, respect for order, devotion to power, the passion of loving and the promptings of conscience.[2] The only disinterested motive which Bentham recognized, according to J. S. Mill, was sympathy or benevolence and this was weak and of limited application. 'Accordingly Bentham's idea of

---

1. A sanction for Bentham 'is a source of obligatory powers or *motives*: that is, of *pains* and pleasures' (*Principles of Morals*, Ch. III s.2, footnote p. 147). He distinguishes four sources or categories of sanction – *physical sanctions* which stem from the ordinary course of nature; *political sanctions* from authorized judges or magistrates; *moral* or *popular sanctions* from public or group pressures; and *religious sanctions* from the hand of a superior religious being.
2. *Mill on Bentham and Coleridge*, with an introduction by F. R. Leavis, 1950, pp. 66–8.

the world is that of a collection of persons pursuing each his separate interest or pleasure, and the prevention of whom from jostling one another more than is unavoidable, may be attempted by hopes and fears derived from three sources – the law, religion and public opinion' (ibid., p. 70). This portrayal of Bentham's system, while it has the merit of highlighting some of the limitations of his approach, is overdrawn and misdirected. As we have seen Bentham set great store on the encouragement of the natural sentiment of benevolence which he saw in large measure as 'the produce of culture, the fruit of education' (*Theory of Legislation*, p. 427). Given guidance men, in Bentham's view, will come to realize the true connection between their own interest and those of their fellows. Optimistically he looks forward to the time when all men will say with Fénelon 'I prefer my family to myself, my country to my family, mankind to my country' (ibid., p. 431) – a positive conception very different from Mill's negative portrayal. Bentham's whole emphasis is on influencing and improving men with a view to increasing the sum total of human happiness, rather than with showing individuals what each must do to attain personal satisfaction.

Young John Stuart Mill, brought up by his father from birth in accordance with strict utilitarian purposes, was deeply concerned, however, with his own happiness, which he was unable to find in the pursuit of pleasure. Towards the end of his life he wrote of his feelings at the age of sixteen,

> I never, indeed, wavered in the conviction that happiness is the test of all rules of conduct, and the end of life. But I now thought that this end was only to be attained by not making it the direct end. Those only are happy (I thought) who have their minds fixed on some object other than their own happiness; on the happiness of others, on the improvement of mankind, even on some art or pursuit, followed not as a means, but as itself an ideal end. Aiming thus at something else, they find happiness by the way.... Ask yourself whether you are happy, and you cease to be so. The only chance is to treat not happiness but some end external to it, as the purpose of life. Let your self-consciousness, your scrutiny, your self-interrogation, exhaust itself on that; and if otherwise fortunately circumstanced you will inhale happiness with the air you breathe, without dwelling on it or thinking about it, without either forestalling it in imagination, or putting it to flight by fatal questioning. This theory now became the basis of my philosophy of life.[1]

1. John Stuart Mill, *Autobiography*, 1873. World Classics edition, 1924, pp. 120–1.

Expressed in this way it is apparent that John Stuart Mill was quite justified in continuing to regard himself as a utilitarian. Mill was not rejecting happiness as the end or purpose of life, but attempting to resolve the paradox of how to achieve a happiness which vanishes as one pursues it. Nor is there necessarily anything in his formulation to which Bentham would have been likely to raise violent objection. As Mill himself points out in his autobiography, the happiness of others and the improvement of mankind were for utilitarians generally 'the greatest and surest sources of happiness', nor would Bentham have objected to a man committing himself to some art or pursuit as an end in itself if it led to happiness. Ethics was for Bentham 'the art of directing men's actions to the production of the greatest possible quantity of happiness' and if it could be shown that for most men this required that they make some object an end in itself, then this was for them a valid rule of the art.

The other modification which John Stuart Mill introduces into utilitarianism is his distinction between higher and lower pleasures. 'Of two pleasures, if there be one to which all or almost all who have experience of both give a decided preference, irrespective of any feeling of moral obligation to prefer it, that is the more desirable pleasure'.[1] According to Mill those who have experienced both the pleasures of the lower senses and the pleasures of the intellect give overwhelming preference to the latter as a far richer source of happiness; even though that happiness may result in less self-satisfaction and contentment. This capacity for nobler feelings exists in all persons but is easily stunted and destroyed. 'Men lose their high aspirations as they lose their intellectual tastes, because they have not time or opportunity for indulging them; and they addict themselves to inferior pleasures, not because they deliberately prefer them, but because they are either the only ones to which they have access, or the only ones which they are any longer capable of enjoying' (*Utilitarianism*, p. 10). The cultivation of the higher pleasures is to be justified in utilitarian terms because the nobility of character it engenders contributes greatly to the general happiness of mankind. That Bentham himself preferred Mill's higher pleasures his whole life is a testament to. At the same time he accepted that each man formed his own conception of pleasure. 'That is pleasure which a man's judgment, aided by his memory, recommends and recognizes to his feelings *as* pleasures'.[2] Bentham does not require push-pin and poetry to be

1. John Stuart Mill, *Utilitarianism*, 1863: Everyman's Library edition, 1910, p. 8.
2. Quoted by Mack in op. cit., p. 222.

regarded as of equal value as individual pursuits, but simply that they must be so regarded for the computation purposes of legislators and judges. But it is when Bentham discusses the indirect means available for furthering the public good that he comes closest to John Stuart Mill. Bentham calls for social action to weaken dangerous and gross desires by encouraging 'every innocent amusement which human art can invent' (*Theory of Legislation*, p. 376), and he lists them in order of refinement from gardening at the bottom to the cultivation of the arts, sciences and literature at the top. 'Happy the people,' he writes, 'which is seen to elevate itself above gross and brutal vices, to cultivate elegance of manners, the pleasures of society, the embellishment of gardens, the fine arts, the sciences, public amusements, the exercises of the understanding' (ibid., p. 380). It would appear that there is a difference of emphasis and purpose rather than a difference of principle between Bentham and Mill with regard to distinguishing higher from lower pleasures. There is no reason to doubt that Bentham would accept Mill's insistence that utilitarianism 'could only attain its end by the general cultivation of nobleness of character' (*Utilitarianism*, p. 11); but his own interest lay in achieving that end through social action, rather than through the 'internal culture of the individual', to use Mill's own phrase (*Autobiography*, p. 121).

Mills's fundamental adherence to the basic principles of utilitarianism and his difference from Bentham in emphasis is brought out most clearly perhaps in the closing passage of the revised edition of *A System of Logic*, published one year before his death.

> ... the cultivation of an ideal nobleness of will and conduct, should be to individual human beings an end, to which the specific pursuit either of their own happiness or of that of others (except so far as included in that idea) should, in any case of conflict, give way. But I hold that the very question, what constitutes this elevation of character, is itself to be decided by reference to happiness as the standard. The character itself should be, to the individual, a paramount end, simply because the existence of this ideal nobleness of character, or of a near approach to it, in any abundance, would go further than all things else towards making human life happy; both in the comparatively humble sense, of pleasure and freedom from pain, and in the higher meaning, of rendering life, not what it now is almost universally, puerile and insignificant – but such as human beings with highly developed faculties can care to have.[1]

1. Ninth edition, p. 556.

READING

Jeremy Bentham, *An Introduction to the Principles of Morals and Legislation*, Chs. I–X.

John Stuart Mill, *Utilitarianism*, Chs. I–IV.

Mary Mack, *Jeremy Bentham: An Odyssey of Ideas, 1748–1792*, Chs. 5 and 6.

R. J. Halliday, 'Some Recent Interpretations of John Stuart Mill' in *Mill: A Collection of Critical Essays*, ed. J. B. Schneewind, Modern Studies in Philosophy, 1969.

5. HEGEL

George Wilhelm Friedrich Hegel (1770–1831) is perhaps the least read of all the major political theorists. Although the importance and distinctiveness of his contribution is widely recognized, the great difficulty of Hegel's style and subject matter has deterred most students (and not a few teachers) from tackling his works. The difficulty is increased for the student of political theory in that Hegel's political conceptions cannot be understood without reference to the general philosophic system of which they form a part. It is necessary, therefore, to attempt to give a brief survey of Hegel's philosophical approach, before proceeding.[1]

Hegel shared with the philosophers of the Enlightenment an optimism and confidence in man's power to mould his own destiny, which he presents in the form of a philosophy of the development of Spirit. The key to Hegel's approach is his belief that the universe can only be understood as a whole in process of evolution towards a necessary end. Nothing can be grasped and comprehended in terms of the characteristics it exhibits by itself at any specific point in time. It must be seen as what it is in process of becoming within a setting which both influences

---

1. Students may perhaps be persuaded by the aura surrounding the author's revolutionary writings to read Part I of Herbert Marcuse's book *Reason and Revolution*, 2nd edition, 1954, on 'The Foundation of Hegel's Philosophy'. More recent accounts of Hegel's philosophy are to be found in J. N. Findlay, *Hegel: a Re-examination*, 1958, and Walter Kaufmann, *Hegel: Reinterpretation, Texts, and Commentary*, 1965.

it and is influenced by it – not in any random or accidental sense, but as part of a rational overall conception. So for Hegel the Concept of a thing is its destined fulfilled end within the composite whole, as distinct from the form it takes considered in isolation in space and time. Truth is not absolute knowledge of finite separate facts, but the understanding of the Concept in its process of development, an understanding which it is the task of the Hegelian philosophic system to provide; not by displacing earlier philosophic formulations but by fulfilling the partial and potential truths contained in them.

In the preface to his most important work, *Phenomenology of the Spirit*, Hegel writes:

> Opinion considers the opposition of what is true and false quite rigid, and, confronted with a philosophical system, it expects agreement or contradiction. And in an explanation of such a system, opinion still expects to find one or the other. It does not comprehend the difference of the philosophical systems in terms of the progressive development of the truth, but sees only the contradiction in this difference. The bud disappears as the blossom bursts forth, and one could say that the former is refuted by the latter. In the same way, the fruit declares the blossom to be a false existence of the plant, and the fruit supplants the blossom as the truth of the plant. These forms do not only differ, they also displace each other because they are incompatible. Their fluid nature, however, makes them, at the same time, elements of an organic unity in which they not only do not conflict, but in which one is as necessary as the other; and it is only this equal necessity that constitutes the life of the whole.[1]

The world for Hegel is a world of the Spirit, not in the sense that he regards the external world as the product or reflection of mind, but in the sense that nature exists to provide the cradle for the emergence of mind. Although nature is prior to mind in time it logically entails the notion of mind, which it is its purpose to produce. Thus mind or Spirit is immanent in the universe from the start. It finds its expression in man as consciousness, purposive activity directed to the achievement of certain ends; and then as self-consciousness, consciousness of oneself

---

1. Kaufmann, op. cit., 'The Preface to the Phenomenology: Translation', p. 370. This passage brings out the so-called 'dialectical' nature of Hegel's philosophy; but as Kaufmann points out (s.37 'Dialectic') what we have in Hegel is not a strictly adhered to method of exposition or prediction, but a 'vision of the world, of man, and of history which emphasises development through conflict, the moving power of human passions, which produces wholly unintended results, and the irony of sudden reversals' (p. 174).

as a conscious purposive creature. But while Spirit is revealed in, and acts through, the minds of separate individual men, each concerned with their own particular and often conflicting ends, it is itself the universal Concept destined to realize itself as the Absolute Idea where each separate mind will be fully conscious of itself as part of the universal process. Individual minds are not conceived of as being merged in some collective consciousness but as attaining a common understanding of that process, whilst making their own distinctive contributions to its furtherance. The conception has nothing in common with that of a new race of men all imbued with the same aims and ideas, fulfilling some purpose externally imposed on them. Richness and diversity are for Hegel of the very stuff of the Spirit, a richness displayed in art and religion, but above all in philosophy. These provide the necessary framework of unity within which alone the diversity may manifest itself. A man cannot attain to consciousness of his self except within such a framework of reference.

> Consequently, until and unless spirit inherently completes itself, completes itself as a world-spirit, it cannot reach its completion as self-conscious spirit. The content of religion, therefore, expresses earlier in time than (philosophical) science what spirit is; but this science alone is the perfect form in which spirit truly knows itself. The process of carrying forward this form of knowledge of itself is the task which spirit accomplishes as actual History.[1]

History, however, cannot be viewed simply as a kaleidoscope of successive events, it must be comprehended and its truth drawn from it. What 'actually' takes place is not what appears on the surface at the time, but the event understood in terms of its effects in space and time. 'The true is the whole. But the whole is the essence perfecting itself through its development. Of the absolute it should be said that it is essentially result, that it is only in the end what it is in truth; and precisely in this consists its nature: to be actual, subject, or that which becomes itself.'[2] For Hegel the essence of a thing or process is its potentiality, what it has it in itself to become. Actuality is the process of realizing that potentiality, a process which itself takes the form of conflict and

1. G. W. F. Hegel, *Phenomenology of Mind*, translated by J. B. Baillie, revised 2nd edition, 1949, p. 801. Kaufmann argues convincingly, op. cit. pp. 160–1, that the German word *Geist* is better translated as *Spirit* than as *Mind*. I have therefore referred to the *Phenomenology of Spirit* except in regard to citations from Baillie's translation of the work.
2. Kaufmann, op. cit., p. 390.

contradiction, both inwardly and outwardly. 'Contradiction is the root of all movement and life, and it is only in so far as it contains a Contradiction that anything moves and has impulse and activity.'[1] The essence in achieving its inherent potentialities negates itself and becomes Actuality. The inherent potentialities are the reality, which when fulfilled are actualized. Thus the real world is not the observed world of appearances but the world as it is in process of becoming, a process which for Hegel was rational, that is taking place in accordance with the logical inherent process laid bare by Hegelian philosophy. It is the process which is the Reality, not the immediate reality of appearance at any point in time. It is only in the sense that 'what is' is in process of becoming what it potentially is in the overall process of development, that it can be regarded as 'what ought to be'.

Hegel does not take the view that men must accept that everything is for the best in the best of all possible worlds. On the contrary it is man's destiny to mould the world. In this process he is engaged in a conscious struggle not only with the forces of nature but with social institutions and forms which have outlived their usefulness and which require transformation. Human intervention is a necessary condition for the realization of the latent possibilities inherent in the world. It is only through the interaction of things with one another in the process of development that the potentialities can be realized. Consequently only some possibilities are in fact realized. An acorn can only begin to realize its potentiality to be an oak if it falls on to soil. If it falls on rock and is eaten by a squirrel it will of necessity never realize its oak-tree potentiality, but instead its potentiality as a sustainer of life for certain living creatures. Which one of the wide but finite number of possible alternatives will be realized will be determined by the particular circumstances of each case; circumstances which are themselves the outcome of the realization of particular contingencies and possibilities in the past. What happens at any point in time necessarily happens only in the sense that the totality of what has developed into what now is, and is in process of becoming what it now is not, is itself the necessary consequence of everything actually realized out of the range of inherent possibilities in the past. 'The principle of *Development* involves also the existence of a latent germ of being – a capacity or potentiality striving to realize itself. This formal conception finds actual existence in Spirit;

1. *Hegel's Science of Logic*, translated by W. H. Johnston and L. G. Struthers, 1929, Vol. II, p. 67.

which has the History of the World for its theatre, its possession, and the sphere of its realization'.[1]

Although it is only in relation to the history of the world that any individual can comprehend himself or be comprehended, it is simpler and more logical to start one's analysis of man in the restricted personal social setting in which he finds himself, before proceeding to extend the analysis into his relationship with an ever-widening circle which ultimately embraces the whole world as it evolves through space and time. Man, civilized man, is characterized by self-conscious will, which contains two elements. The first is

> the element of pure indeterminacy or that pure reflection of the ego into itself which involves the dissipation of every restriction and every content either immediately presented by nature, by needs, desires, and impulses, or given and determined by any means whatever. This is the unrestricted infinity of absolute abstraction or universality, the pure thought of oneself.[2]

This unrestricted possibility of abstraction is only one side of the will – the other is realization or particularization 'the transition from undifferentiated indeterminacy to the differentiation, determination and positing of a determinacy as a content and object' (ibid., p. 22). The individual will is free precisely so far as it realizes itself in self-conscious action which both expresses and comprehends the universality of the human mind.

> Here is the point at which it becomes clear that it is only as thinking intelligence that the will is genuinely a will and free. The slave does now know his essence, his infinity, his freedom; he does not know himself as human in essence; and he lacks this knowledge of himself because he does not think himself. This self consciousness which apprehends itself through thinking as essentially human, and thereby frees itself from the contingent and the false, is the principle of right, morality, and all ethical life (ibid., p. 30).

Man realizes and expresses his will in the objective world which through its social institutions provides the opportunities necessary for the particularization of his will within a universal framework of social duties, instead of as caprice or appetite. For Hegel social institutions fulfil ethical not socializing roles; their purpose is not simply one of integrating the individual into the wider community, but of doing so in such a

1. G. W. F. Hegel, *Lectures on the Philosophy of History*, translated from the 3rd German edition by J. Sibree, 1890, p. 57.
2. *Hegel's Philosophy of Right*, translated with notes by T. M. Knox, 1952, p. 21.

way that the individual realizes himself as a full self-conscious deter-
minate being. In consequence what Hegel has to say regarding the
institutions of the family, civil society and the state refers to the ethical
role which such institutions ought to play. It does not follow that in
any particular instance they will fulfil this role, though it seems clear
that Hegel believes that they have an inherent tendency to do so. 'When
the existing world of freedom has become faithless to the will of better
men, that will fails to find itself in the duties there recognized and must
try to find in the ideal world of the inner life alone the harmony which
actuality has lost' (ibid., p. 92).

The unit within which the individual finds immediately both the
opportunity to give expression to his will, as a self-conscious person,
and a moral framework of reference for its expression which accords with
the overall development of mankind itself, is the family. 'The family,
as the immediate substantiality of mind, is specially characterized by
love, which is mind's feeling of its own unity. Hence in a family, one's
frame of mind is to have self-consciousness of one's individuality within
this unity as the absolute essence of oneself, with the result that one is
in it not as an independent person but as a member' (ibid., p. 110). In
Philosophy of Right Hegel discusses three phases of the family – marriage, family capital, and education of the children, followed by the
family's dissolution. Each phase is inter-related to the next and can be
understood only in the context of the inevitable end of the family –
dissolution through death of the parents and regeneration in new families
created by the offspring. From another angle it can be argued that the
disintegration of the family is necessary if men are not to be confined
within the limited unreflective natural ethical form of life which the
family provides. This aspect is emphasized by Hegel in the section of
Phenomenology of the Spirit which deals with the family. Here he stresses
that the true ethical element of family life is to be found not in the
sentiment or love existing between the individual members but 'in the
relation of the individual member of the family to the *entire* family as
the real substance, so that the purpose of his action and the content of
his actuality are taken from this substance, are derived solely from the
family life' (op. cit., p. 469). To satisfy the needs and purposes of the
family the father is forced to go outside it, into the community where he
enters into new and more complex relationships which serve wider and
higher objects and needs than those of the family. 'The husband is sent
forth by the spirit of the family into the life of the community, and finds
there his self-conscious reality. Just as the family thereby finds in the

community its universal substance and subsistence, conversely the community finds in the family the formal element of its own realization . . .' (ibid., p. 478).

In civil society men are concerned with the gratification of their own many and various desires, but since these desires are held in common by large numbers of men and can be realized only through joint action, individual desire gives rise to interdependence and the recognition of that interdependence. 'In the course of the actual attainment of selfish ends – an attainment conditioned in this way by universality – there is formed a system of complete interdependence, wherein the livelihood, happiness, and legal status of one man is interwoven with the livelihood, happiness, and rights of all' (*Philosophy of Right*, p. 123). This is seen most clearly in the economic sphere, where men find it necessary, if they are to satisfy the increasing range of wants conjured up by the will, to work not as individual producers, but as units in a production process whose ultimate rationale is the replacement of man-power by machine power. 'When men are thus dependent on one another and reciprocally related to one another in their work and the satisfaction of their needs, subjective self-seeking turns into a contribution to the satisfaction of the needs of everyone else' (ibid., p. 129).

In consequence of their varying wants and differing capacities and circumstances, men become members of distinct classes engaged in a particular kind of economic activity. The agricultural class, which includes all who work on the land, finds its satisfaction in a life largely dependent on the measured regularity of the processes of nature and requiring little in the way of reflection and assertion of will. In contrast the business class, which embraces capitalists, traders and workers, is required to use both foresight and intelligence in mastering and adapting its materials. This class throws up from within it a wide range of associations or Corporations of members engaged in a particular pursuit or trade, each devoted to the furtherance of its particular interests but providing for its members dignity, recognition and consciousness of ends outside themselves, as well as security and satisfaction. But just because the purpose of the Corporation is restricted and finite it needs to be subject to the surveillance of the public authority, whose members form the third class in the community – the universal class of civil servants whose responsibility is to see to the general needs and purposes of the community, in so far as these are not adequately catered for through corporate and class activity. Important as the public authority is, Hegel does not conceive of it regulating every aspect of life. In *The*

German Constitution, written approximately twenty years before *Philosophy of Right*, Hegel wrote

> If the general public authority demands from the individual only what is necessary for itself, and if it restricts accordingly the arrangements for ensuring the performance of this minimum, then beyond this point it can permit the living freedom and the individual will of the citizens, and even leave considerable scope to the latter. Similarly the public authority, concentrated necessarily at the centre, in the government, is regarded by the individuals at the periphery with a less jaundiced eye when it demands what it regards as necessary and what everyone can see *is* indispensable for the whole.[1]

He specifically rejects theories which presuppose that the state is a machine which imparts movement to all the rest of society or 'that all institutions implicit in the nature of a society should proceed from the supreme public authority and be regulated, commanded, overseen, and conducted by it' (ibid., p. 161). The appointed function of the public authority is restricted to the maintenance of security and authority both at home and abroad. Hegel's view as to the specific functions which the public authority should undertake changed and came to include in *Philosophy of Right* and other later writings, the provision of education, administration of justice and the relief of the poor; but his general position regarding the need to limit the range of public activity remained unaltered.

It is clear that Hegel's conception of civil society necessarily involves and leads up to the notion of the state itself; just as his notion of the family involves both civil society and the state. The concept of the state is for Hegel much deeper than that of civil society and is not to be confused with the specific role of the public authority in any state at any time.

> If the state is confused with civil society, and if its specific end is laid down as the security and protection of property and personal freedom, then the interests of the individuals as such become the ultimate end of their association, and it follows that membership of the state is something optional. But the state's relation to the individual is quite different from this. Since the state is mind objectified, it is only as one of its members that the individual himself has objectivity, genuine individuality, and an ethical life. Unification pure and simple is the

1. *Hegel's Political Writings*, translated by T. M. Knox with an introductory essay by Z. A. Pelczynski, 1964, pp. 154-5.

true content and aim of the individual, and the individual's destiny is the living of a universal life (*Philosophy of Right*, p. 156).

The concept of the state, as distinct from the form of particular states, is absolutely rational in that it is the embodiment of the Spirit. The state realizes its purpose when its members are conscious of themselves as its members and aware of the distinctive part each should play in the whole scheme of things. The universal end which the state embodies will only prevail through the positive co-operation of knowing individuals who will their private interests in the light of, and in conscious conformity with, the state's universal end. This is the Idea of the state. Particular states will depart to a greater or lesser extent from this Idea, but every state will realize the Idea to some degree. 'The state is no ideal work of art; it stands on earth and so in the sphere of caprice, chance, and error, and bad behaviour may disfigure it in many respects. But the ugliest of men, or a criminal, or an invalid, or a cripple, is still always a living man.'[1] By the state Hegel means not the structure of the framework of government, which he refers to as 'the strictly political state' (ibid., p. 163), but the totality of the life of the members of a community in so far as their activities forward the realization of the goal of the conscious identification of all individuals with the life and needs of the communal whole. Thus the state embraces the institutions of civil society and the family in that it ensures that these institutions fulfil their true purpose within the whole and are not restricted to narrow particular ends, – which in themselves are often conflicting or even destructive. 'The state, therefore, knows what it wills and knows it in its universality, i.e. as something thought. Hence it works and acts by reference to consciously adopted ends, known principles, and laws which are not merely implicit but are actually present to consciousness; and further, it acts with precise knowledge of existing conditions and circumstances, inasmuch as its actions have a bearing on these' (ibid., p. 165).

READING

Herbert Marcuse, *Reason and Revolution: Hegel and the Rise of Social Theory*, Chs. 4 and 5.

1. ibid., p. 279. This quotation is taken from one of the additions to the original manuscript made by Dr E. Gans from notes taken at Hegel's lectures. The status of such additions is open to question. See Kaufmann, op. cit., s. 52 and 53.

John Plamenatz, *Man and Society*, Vol. II, Ch. 3, 'The Social and Political
Philosophy of Hegel', pp. 129–202.

G. W. F. Hegel, 'The Preface to the Phenomenology', with commentary, in
Hegel by Walter Kaufmann. This is far from easy reading.

6. MARX AND ENGELS

Karl Marx (1818–83) and Frederick Engels (1820–95) collaborated together over a period of forty years to produce the books, pamphlets,
articles and letters which constitute the basic ingredients of Marxist
teaching. However much the various self-styled Marxist groups and
sects may dispute amongst themselves as to whether Kautsky, Plekhanov,
Lenin, Luxemburg, Trotsky, Stalin, Mao Tse-tung or even Castro,
should be regarded as Marxists, they all accept Marx and Engels as the
founders of 'scientific socialism' and all seek to demonstrate the conformity of their own views, and those of their adopted mentors, with
the teachings of the two grand masters. The nature of the doctrine
which Marx and Engels expounded involved them in dealing with a
very wide range of questions in very different ways. As early as 1845
Marx wrote 'The philosophers have only *interpreted* the world, in
various ways; the point, however, is to *change* it'.[1] and in consequence
one finds that a large part of the writings of Marx and Engels are directed
to analysing the immediate political situation and propounding what
action should be taken by the working class to further its aims and
interests. The unity of theoretical analysis and political action is the
keynote both of the doctrine of Marxism itself and of the lives of its
founders. At Marx's graveside Engels, while claiming that Marx had
discovered the laws of evolution in human history and, in particular,
the special law of development of capitalism, insisted that Marx was

> before all else a revolutionary. His real mission in life was to contribute
> in one way or another to the overthrow of capitalist society and of the

1. Karl Marx: *Theses on Feuerbach* reprinted in *Marx and Engels: Basic Writings
on Politics and Philosophy*, edited by L. S. Feuer, Fontana Library, 1969, p. 286.
This is perhaps the best of the cheap paperback editions of the writings of
Marx and Engels and has been used wherever possible in the text. References
are given to Feuer, op. cit.

state institutions which it had brought into being, to contribute to the liberation of the present-day proletariat, which *he* was the first to make conscious of its own position and its needs, of the conditions under which it could win its emancipation.[1]

As Marx himself attested, the most important influences on the development of his thinking were the writings of Friedrich Hegel and his critic Ludwig Feuerbach. His early writings show Marx coming to grips with Hegelian philosophy and seeking to wrest from it what was consistent with the humanist doctrine which he was to build. In a letter to his father in 1837 he explained how, 'setting out from idealism – I hit upon seeking the Idea in the real itself'[2] and in 1844 he drafted a critique of Hegelian philosophy.[3] In this work Marx stresses the great positive contribution which Hegel made in conceiving 'the self-development of man as a process' in which self-conscious man overcomes his sense of alienation from the external world by projecting himself into the world. In this process man becomes what he has it in him to become 'as the result of his *own work*' (p. 321). But while Hegel sees labour as the essence of man, the only labour he recognizes is abstract mental labour. 'The *human quality* of nature, of nature produced through history, and of man's products appear in their being *products* of abstract spirit and hence phases of *mind, thought-entities*' (ibid., p. 320). Man's alienation from the external world cannot be overcome by 'transcending' the objectivity of that world through abstract thought. It is not man as self-consciousness but man as objective being who is alienated from a world which resists his attempts to make it his own. Moreover it is not only or even primarily, natural objects but social institutions which are resistant to men's needs. He can overcome the alienation of the real world only by changing that world in fact not in abstract thought. For Hegel 'private property as *thought* is transcended in the *thought* of morality' –

---

1. Reprinted in Karl Marx *Selected Works in Two Volumes*, Vol. I, p. 17. Marx – Engels – Lenin Institute Moscow under the editorship of V. Adoratsky. English edition London, 1942. Hereinafter referred to as *Karl Marx Selected Works*.

2. Reprinted in *Writings of the Young Marx on Philosophy and Society*, translated and edited by Loyd D. Easton and Kurt H. Guddat, Anchor Books, U.S.A. 1967, p. 46. References are given to Easton and Guddat, op. cit.

3. *Critique of Hegel's Dialectic and Philosophy in General* was first published in Moscow, 1932, with other manuscripts under the title *Economic and Philosophic Manuscripts of 1844*, by the Institute of Marxism-Leninism which issued an English translation in 1959. I have used the translation in Easton & Guddat, op. cit.

'this transcendence in thought which leaves its object intact in actuality believes it has actually overcome it' (ibid., pp. 330–1); but for Marx the transcendence of private property requires 'the destruction of the *alienated* character of the objective world, by the transcendence of the objective world in its alienated existence'. The transcendence is communism, 'the vindication of actual human life as man's property, the emergence of practical humanism' (ibid., p. 331).[1]

In the previous year, 1843, Marx had completed a critical analysis of Hegel's treatment of the state in *Philosophy of Right*.[2] In this work Marx challenges Hegel's underlying conception that the family and civil society derive their existence and purpose from the state as the actualization of the ethical Idea. On the contrary Marx insists that the state exists only as political power divorced from society. In order to become actual members of the state, as distinct from members of society, its members must take over political power. 'The drive of *civil society* to become political or to make *political* society *actual* is evident as a drive toward participation in *legislative power* as *universal* as possible' (p. 199). Though Marx speaks in terms of the need for the 'universalization of voting' it is clear that he is not simply thinking in terms of franchise reform, but of the complete transformation of society. A few months later Marx proclaims his faith that in Germany at least the only class capable of bringing about the emancipation of society is the proletariat. The Hegelian conception of the modern state in abstraction from actual man represents for Marx the reality of modern alienated society; an alienation which can only be overcome by political means if one class in society by virtue of its special position is able to present itself as the liberating force against those who are society's oppressors. Germany, however, lacks both a class of oppressors and a class of liberators. In consequence, German emancipation must await the formation of a new class,

> a class with *radical chains*, a class in civil society that is not of civil society, a class that is the dissolution of all classes, a sphere of society,

1. Like Hegel, (see footnote 1. p. 28 above) Marx does not use the oft-quoted triadic form of the dialectic (thesis – antithesis – synthesis) to expound his analysis and assertions. What he takes over from Hegel is the 'dialectical' conception of development in nature and man through conflict and contradiction, a conception which he radically transforms in content (see above). The triadic framework of the dialectic popularized by Fichte and Schelling is used by Engels in a number of his writings and in particular in *Dialectics of Nature* published after Marx's death.

2. *Critique of Hegel's philosophy of the state*, printed in Easton and Guddat, op. cit.

having a universal character because of its universal suffering and claiming no *particular* right because no *particular wrong* but *unqualified wrong* is perpetrated on it; a sphere that can invoke no *traditional* title but only a *human* title, which does not partially oppose the consequences but totally opposes the premises of the German political system; a sphere, finally, that cannot emancipate itself without emancipating itself from all the other spheres of society, thereby emancipating them; a sphere, in short, that is the *complete loss* of humanity and can only redeem itself through the *total redemption of humanity*. This dissolution of society as a particular class is the *proletariat*.[1]

In *The Holy Family*, written in collaboration with Engels at the end of 1844 and published in the next year, Marx returns to the same theme and insists that it is urgent and compelling need that drives the proletariat to revolt, not concern for humanity or awareness of its historic role. 'It is not a question,' he writes, 'of what this or that proletarian or even the whole proletariat momentarily *imagines* to be the aim. It is a question of *what* the proletariat *is* and what it *consequently* is historically compelled to do.'[2] The second fruit of the collaboration of Marx and Engels was *The German Ideology*, a vast, arid, polemic written in 1845–6 and directed against Feuerbach and other of the Young Hegelians. Although not published in their lifetimes *The German Ideology* contains within it all the essential features of the theory of historical materialism so brilliantly portrayed two years later in *The Communist Manifesto*. Man begins to distinguish himself from the animals when he produces his means of subsistence instead of taking it from nature. In the production of food man develops himself. 'As individuals express their life, so they are. What they are, therefore, coincides with what they produce, with *what* they produce and *how* they produce. The nature of individuals thus depends on the material conditions which determine their production.'[3]

Marx argues that the development of the productive forces or means of production is determined by the progressive development of the division of labour, a division which gives rise to different forms of ownership. He outlines these stages of development from simple tribal ownership of tools and implements to modern large-scale industry

1. *Towards the Critique of Hegel's Philosophy of Law: Introduction* Easton and Guddat, op. cit., pp. 262–3. (*Philosophie des Rechts* is here translated as *Philosophy of Law* instead of *Philosophy of Right*.)
2. Easton and Guddat, op. cit., p. 368.
3. *The German Ideology*, first published in Moscow, 1932, Easton and Guddat, op. cit., p. 409.

where a highly developed differentiation of skills and roles is accompanied by the concentration of ownership in the hands of a small ruling group. The nature of the productive process at any particular period determines the social and political relations which men enter into. The history of the division of labour is the history of the emergence and dominance of private property over communal property and of the various forms which such property took and the economic and social relations to which it gave rise. In classical society the typical relationship is that between slave and master, in feudal society between serf and landowner and in industrial society between 'free' propertyless worker and capitalist. The means of production of wealth, which under primitive conditions were either possessed individually by everyone or possessed communally, have now become alienated from the great majority of the members of the community – 'opposing the productive forces, there is a majority of the individuals from whom these forces have been wrested away and who have become abstract individuals deprived of all real life content (p. 466). The alienation of the majority can only be overcome by the appropriation by the excluded class of 'the existing totality of productive forces', an appropriation which under conditions of capitalism is necessary 'not merely to achieve self-activity but to secure their very existence'. But whereas all previous revolutionary appropriations of the instruments of production by the oppressed classes resulted in these instruments becoming their own private property, while 'they themselves remained subject to the division of labour and their own instrument of production'; in the appropriation by the proletariat the instruments of production 'must be subservient to each individual and the property of all' (p. 467). This transformation of the instruments of production into the servants of men can only take place through revolution, but revolution only becomes feasible and not simply desirable, when the necessary conditions exist. These are, on the one hand the development of the productive forces to the stage where they 'are no longer productive forces but rather destructive ones' (p. 430); and on the other the creation of mass communist consciousness of the need for fundamental change which could 'only take place in a practical movement, in a *revolution*' (p. 431). These developments, moreover, are conceived in international rather than national terms (pp. 427–8).

Finally one should note how, in *The German Ideology*, Marx and Engels develop a theory of the consciousness of man which can be put to service in their conception of the class struggle. Men do not develop their ideas in abstraction, they do not think and theorize apart from the world in which they live. 'Rather, men who develop their material production and their material relationships alter their thinking along with their real existence. Consciousness does not determine life, but life determines consciousness' (p. 415). Since the most important fact about 'the material relationships' of men are the class relationships which they necessarily enter into at each stage in the development of the division of labour and the forces of production, it follows that the ideas of any period reflect this relationship. 'In every epoch the ideas of the ruling class are the ruling ideas, that is, the class that is the ruling *material* power of society is at the same time its ruling *intellectual* power' (p. 438). These ideas though expressed in a universal form as the common interest and concern of all members of society, in fact express the interest and concerns of the ruling class alone. Against them must be set revolutionary ideas, the ideas of the class which has in part at least become conscious of the class nature of the society in which it lives. Just as Marx and Engels portray the dominant ideas of an epoch as the ideas of its ruling class so they declare the state to be 'nothing more than the form of organization which the bourgeois by necessity adopts for both internal and external purposes as a mutual guarantee of their property and interests' (p. 470).

What was lacking in *The German Ideology* was any discussion of the way in which the capitalist economic system worked and any demonstration of the assertion made in *The German Ideology* that at a certain stage in the development of society the productive forces cease to be productive. It was not until 1847 that Marx produced his first important economic work, a series of lectures delivered at the German Worker's Club in Brussels [1] and *The Poverty of Philosophy*, a sharp attack on the French socialist Proudhon's book *Philosophy of Poverty*. In the lectures Marx argued that wages (i.e. the price of labour) are determined by the cost

1. These lectures were published in a revised form in 1849 in the *Neue Rheinische Zeitung*, of which Marx was editor, and later in pamphlet form under the title *Wage-Labour and Capital*. The pamphlet was reissued for sale in a special workers' edition in 1891 and Engels altered the text to take account of changes in Marx's economic thinking after 1849. It is this amended text which is the one now available. In his introduction to the 1891 edition Engels wrote 'My alterations all turn on one point. According to the original the worker sells his *labour* to the capitalist for wages: according to the present text he sells his labour *power*' (*Karl Marx Selected Works*, Vol. I, p. 243). See Chapter V Section 6, pp. 216–18 below, for a discussion of Marx's labour theory of value.

of the existence and reproduction of the worker, but that the labour purchased by the capitalist produces value in excess of its price. This surplus value is the source of both productive capital and profits. But the greater the growth of productive capital the greater the division of labour and the application of machinery; and in consequence the greater the competition amongst workers for the reduced number of jobs available and the lower their wages. On the other hand the greater the output of consumer goods the more extensive the crises of over-production to which the system becomes subject. In *The Poverty of Philosophy* Marx criticized Proudhon for failing to see the inherent and necessary class nature of the capitalist economic system. He develops the analysis of the nature of capitalism begun in *The German Ideology* and argues that the bourgeois economic system produces wealth under conditions which result in the creation of poverty and of the class of the poor, the modern proletariat. He takes issue with those socialists who call on the workers to desist from trade union and strike activity on the grounds that it is impossible for the workers to raise their real wages under capitalism. Marx stresses that it is above all 'the maintenance of wages, this common interest which they have against their boss unites them in a common thought of resistance'. It is precisely in the struggles in support of its wages that this mass of workers 'becomes united, and constitutes itself as a class for itself. The interests it defends become class interests'.[1] Marx concludes: 'the antagonism between the proletariat and the bourgeoisie is a struggle of class against class, a struggle which carried to its highest expression is a total revolution'.[2]

At the end of 1847 in an atmosphere charged with the expectation of revolution in Europe, Marx and Engels were commissioned by the London centre of the small but dedicated Communist League to compose a definite statement of its beliefs and aims. The result was the most celebrated and dramatic political document of all time, *The Manifesto of the Communist Party*, whose bold challenge has rung down the years.

> The communists disdain to conceal their views and aims. They openly declare that their ends can be obtained only by the forcible overthrow of all existing social conditions. Let the ruling class tremble at a com-

1. K. Marx, *The Poverty of Philosophy*, edited by C. P. Dutt and V. Chattopadhyaya, Martin Lawrence, London, n.d., p. 145.
2. ibid., p. 147.

munistic revolution. The proletarians have nothing to lose but their chains. They have a world to win. Working men of all countries unite![1]

The Manifesto draws together in one short document the ideas and principles which its authors had developed in their earlier writings. The essential features are not new; what is new is the clarity and unity of the whole now presented. Its readers are given an historical explanation of the existing social order, a damning indictment of that order, a prophecy of the inevitable coming of a new Jerusalem on earth, and a call to take part in building the new society by working together to smash the old. Greater emphasis than in their earlier writings is placed both on the revolutionary role which the bourgeoisie has played in developing the means of production and in simplifying all human relations by reducing them to a callous cash nexus; and on the internal weaknesses and contradictions of capitalism. The bourgeoisie is compelled to revolutionize constantly the means of production, only to be faced with ever-recurring, ever-deepening crises of over-production.

> And how does the bourgeoisie get over these crises? On the one hand, by enforced destruction of a mass of productive forces; on the other, by the conquest of new markets, and by the more thorough exploitation of the old ones. That is to say, by paving the way for more extensive and more destructive crises, and by diminishing the means whereby crises are prevented ... But not only has the bourgeoisie forged the weapons that bring death to itself; it has also called into existence the men who are to wield those weapons – the modern working class – the proletarians (p. 55).

The growing competition between individual capitalists, the recurring crises of capitalism, makes the worker's wage subject to ever greater fluctuations, at the same time as he is subject to ever greater exploitation in the shape of prolonged working hours and an intensification of the work process. He is driven into conflict with the bourgeoisie, at first as an individual facing an employer, but increasingly as a member of the working class against the capitalist class. The experiences gained in these conflicts lead to the creation of an ever-expanding union of workers bound together by the nightmare prospect of increasing degradation and pauperism.

> And here it becomes evident that the bourgeoisie is unfit any longer to be the ruling class in society, and to impose its conditions of existence upon society as an overriding law. It is unfit to rule because it is

1. *The Manifesto of the Communist Party*, in Feuer, op. cit., p. 82.

incompetent to assure an existence to its slave within his slavery, because it cannot help letting him sink into such a state that it has to feed him instead of being fed by him. Society can no longer live under the bourgeoisie: in other words, its existence is no longer compatible with society (p. 61).

The most distinctive and striking section of the *Manifesto* is that devoted to discussing the fundamental principles of communism as seen by Marx and Engels. They insist that these are not based on abstract ideas or moral principles but 'merely express, in general terms, actual relations springing from an existing class struggle, from a historical movement going on under our very eyes' (p. 62). The programme they put forward in the name of communism is (i) the abolition of bourgeois private property 'under which the labourer lives merely to increase capital, and is allowed to live only in so far as the interest of the ruling class requires it' (p. 63); (ii) abolition of the bourgeois family based on private gain whose complement is that 'all family ties among the proletarians are torn asunder and their children transformed into simple articles of commerce and instruments of labour' (p. 66); (iii) the abolition of countries and nationality for 'as the antagonism between classes within the nation vanishes, the hostility of one nation to another will come to an end' (p. 68).

In order to bring about the overthrow of capitalism the proletariat must organize itself as a class and prepare to make itself the ruling class. By sweeping away the old conditions of production based on the private exploitation of capital it will 'have swept away the conditions for the existence of class antagonisms and of classes generally, and will thereby have abolished its own supremacy as a class. In place of the old bourgeois society, with its classes and class antagonisms, we shall have an association in which the free development of each is the condition for the free development of all' (ibid., p. 70).[1]

1. In 1852 Marx wrote to G. Weydemeyer: 'no credit is due to me for discovering the existence of classes in modern society nor yet the struggle between them. Long before me bourgeois historians had described the historical development of this class struggle and bourgeois economists the economic anatomy of the classes. What I did that was new was to prove: (1) that the *existence of classes* is only bound up with *particular, historic phases in the development of production*: (2) that the class struggle necessarily leads to the *dictatorship of the proletariat*: (3) that this dictatorship itself only constitutes the transition to the *abolition of all classes* and to a *classless society*.' *K. Marx and F. Engels Selected Correspondence 1846-1895*, translated by Dona Torr from the Russian edition edited by V. Adoratsky, London, 1936, p. 57.

READING

K. Marx and F. Engels, *Manifesto of the Communist Party*; F. Engels, *Socialism: Utopian and Scientific*. These are both included in Marx and Engels, *Basic Writings on Politics and Philosophy*, edited by Lewis S. Feuer.

K. Marx and F. Engels, *The German Ideology*. Extracts in Loyd D. Easton and Kurt Guddat, *Writings of the Young Marx on Philosophy and Society*.

C. Wright Mills, *The Marxists*. Chs. 4–6, Pelican Books, 1963.

APPENDIX

The following celebrated account of Marx's theory of historical development appeared in the preface which he wrote to his work *A Contribution to the Critique of Political Economy* which appeared in 1859. The conclusions set out below were, he wrote, those at which he arrived during his stay in Brussels between 1845 and 1848 'and which, once reached, continued to serve as the leading thread in my studies'.

In the social production which men carry on they enter into definite relations that are indispensable and independent of their will; these relations of production correspond to a definite stage of development of their material powers of production. The sum total of these relations of production constitutes the economic structure of society – the real foundation, on which rise legal and political superstructures and to which correspond definite forms of social consciousness. The mode of production in material life determines the general character of the social, political, and spiritual processes of life. It is not the consciousness of men that determines their existence, but, on the contrary, their social existence determines their consciousness. At a certain stage of their development the material forces of production in society come into conflict with the existing relations of production, or – what is but a legal expression for the same thing – with the property relations within which they had been at work before. From forms of development of the forces of production these relations turn into their fetters. Then comes the period of social revolution. With the change of the economic foundation the entire immense superstructure is more or less rapidly transformed. In considering such transformations the distinction should always be made between the material transformation of the economic conditions of production, which can be determined with the precision of natural science, and the legal, political, religious, aesthetic, or philosophic – in short, ideological – forms in which men become conscious of this conflict and fight it out. Just as our opinion of an individual is not based on what he thinks of himself, so can we not judge such a period of transformation by its own consciousness; on the contrary, this consciousness must rather be explained from the contradictions of material life, from the existing conflict between the social forces of production and the relations of production. No social order ever disappears before all the productive forces for which there is room in it have been developed, and new, higher relations of production never appear before the material conditions of their existence have matured in the womb of the old society. Therefore mankind always takes up only such problems as it can solve, since, looking at the matter more closely, we will always find that the problem itself arises only when the material conditions necessary for its solution already exist or are at least in the process of formation. In broad outlines we can designate the Asiatic, the ancient, the feudal, and the modern bourgeois methods of production as so many epochs in the progress of the economic formation of society. The bourgeois relations of production are the last antagonistic form of the social process of production – antagonistic not in the sense of individual antagonism, but of one arising from conditions surrounding the life of individuals in society; at the same time the productive forces developing in the womb of bourgeois society create the material conditions for the solution of that antagonism. This social formation constitutes, therefore, the closing chapter of the prehistoric stage of human society. (Translated from the 2nd German edition by N. I. Stone, Charles H. Kerr and Company, 1904, and reprinted in *Marx and Engels: Basic Writings on Politics and Philosophy*, edited by Lewis S. Feuer, pp. 84–5.)

CHAPTER 2

Morality and Religion

1. HOBBES

In recent years theorists have attacked the traditional view of Hobbes as the first major philosopher[1] to make a sharp break with medieval thought grounded on the Christian conception of natural law. The traditional view was that Hobbes derived his theory of politics solely from the presentation of man as a rational being motivated by self-interest. The new view is most clearly expressed by Professor Warrender, who writes:

> Hobbes's theory of political society is based upon a theory of duty, and his theory of duty belongs essentially to the natural law tradition. The laws of nature are eternal and unchangeable and, as the commands of God, they oblige all men who reason properly, and so arrive at a belief in an omnipotent being whose subjects they are.[1]

It is proposed in this section to examine this view briefly by seeing what Hobbes has to say about morals and religion in *Leviathan*. Two important introductory points should be noted. First, it is apparent that there are a number of passages in Hobbes's writings which are capable of interpretation in the way that Warrender and others suggest. What has to be decided is their place in his scheme as a whole, remembering that writers are not always consistent and sometimes use arguments to buttress their conclusions, which they themselves do not accept. The second point is that the new view of Hobbes is one which would have been completely unrecognizable to all his contemporaries, friend and foe alike. As Quentin Skinner has skilfully argued, the Warrender thesis turns Hobbes into an incredible bungler 'presenting a traditional type of Natural Law theory of politics in a manner so convoluted that it was everywhere taken for the work of a complete utilitarian', who despite his

1. Howard Warrender, *The Political Philosophy of Hobbes*, 1957, p. 322. See also F. C. Hood, *The Divine Philosophy of Thomas Hobbes*, 1964: 'Hobbes's morality is traditional and Christian' (p. 13).

terror of being arraigned for heterodoxy 'never once attempted either to disown the alarmingly radical critics who cited his authority, or to disarm his innumerable critics by pointing out their misconception of his intentions'.[1]

The problem of whether, or to what extent, Hobbes takes up the traditional Christian view in his account of Natural Law can best be approached by looking at the classic expression given to it by St Thomas Aquinas. Natural Law for St Thomas is 'nothing else than the participation of the eternal law in rational creatures'.[2]

> The order of the precepts of the natural law corresponds to the order of our natural inclinations. For there is in man a natural and initial inclination to good which he has in common with all substances; in so far as every substance seeks its own preservation according to its own nature. Corresponding to this inclination, the natural law contains all that makes for the preservation of human life, and all that is opposed to its dissolution.

Secondly,

> there pertains to the natural law all those instincts, which nature has taught all animals, such as sexual relationship, the rearing of offspring, and the like. Thirdly, there is in man a certain inclination to good, corresponding to his rational nature: and this inclination is proper to man alone. So man has a natural inclination to know the truth about God and to live in society. In this respect there come under the natural law, all actions connected with such inclinations: namely that a man should avoid ignorance, that he must not give offence to others with whom he must associate and all actions of like nature.[3]

Natural Law provides, as far as its general first principles are concerned, 'a norm of right conduct' binding on all men and known to all men through reason: although in particular cases it can admit of exceptions both with regard to rightness and to knowability.[4]

If one examines St Thomas Aquinas' conception of natural law one finds that it has both descriptive and prescriptive elements. The precepts of natural law are derived from the natural inclinations which men have; partly in common with and partly as distinctive from other crea-

---

1. Quentin Skinner, 'The Ideological Content of Hobbes's Political Thought', *Historical Journal*, IX, 3, 1966.
2. *Summa Theologica*, Prima Secundae Qu. 91 Art. 2, in Aquinas, *Selected Political Writings*, edited by A. P. D'Entrèves and translated by J. G. Dawson, 1959, p. 115.
3. ibid., Qu. 94 Art.2 p. 123.
4. ibid., Qu. 94 Art.4 p. 125.

tures. Consequently in this sense they are descriptive and explanatory of the way men actually do behave – laws of nature in the scientific rather than the moral sense. But for man the laws are prescriptive because as a rational creature he is able to frustrate or redirect these natural inclinations to his own purposes. The two elements are united through God, the source of man's natural inclinations and of his reason. Reason is held in high regard, not because it permits men to control their own actions and live their own lives, but as the instrument of participation in divine providence which enables men to distinguish good from evil. It is only because reason is God-directed that it can be relied on to provide a standard of moral conduct for men who do not have the benefit of Christian revelation and teaching.

How does this compare with the views expressed by Hobbes? The most striking difference is that whereas Aquinas starts with God and derives reason and natural law from the divine providence and purpose, Hobbes starts, as we have seen (Chapter 1, section 1, above), with certain basic propositions about the nature of man, which he seems to have regarded as self-evident truths. Each man is driven by the desire for power and the fear of death to seek his own personal satisfaction. It is only because the consequences of unrestricted individual self-assertion are so disadvantageous that men's reason suggests articles of peace to restrain the natural tendency to self-destruction. Hobbes's account of the laws of nature as rules of individual self-preservation is not based on any conception of man as a creature of God; but this is not to say that no place can be found for God within it. On the contrary Hobbes speaks of God as 'the Author' of the Law of Nature (*Leviathan*, p. 178). Does he mean to suggest, however, that men are required to carry out the laws of nature *because* they have been ordained by God or is this an additional reason which applies only to those who believe in God? In other words does Hobbes write as a committed Christian accepting the role of natural law as set out by Aquinas, or does he write as a man concerned to demonstrate that sufficient reasons for these principles can be shown whether God exists or not? The answer must surely be that, although God is the cornerstone of Thomist teaching, not only may he be omitted from the Hobbesian picture without materially altering its message, but that Hobbes himself does just this. He opens Part III of *Leviathan* 'Of a Christian Common-Wealth' with these words

I have derived the Rights of Soveraigne Power, and the duty of Subjects hitherto, from the Principles of Nature onely; such as Experience has found true, or Consent (concerning the use of words) has made so;

that is to say, from the nature of Man, known to us by Experience, and
from Definitions (of such words as are Essentiall to all Politicall
reasoning) universally agreed on. But in that I am next to handle,
which is the Nature and Rights of a CHRISTIAN COMMON-
WEALTH, whereof there dependeth much upon Supernaturall Revelations of the Will of God; the ground of my Discourse must be, not
only the Naturall Word of God, but also the Propheticall (p. 199).

Hobbes is clearly concerned to show how belief in Christian teaching
affects the views that he claims to have already established on a purely
secular basis. The words of the Christian Scriptures, in so far as they
differ from the Laws of Nature are 'legible to all men that have the use
of naturall reason' and are not binding on any 'to whom God hath not
supernaturally revealed, that they are his, nor that those that published
them, were sent by him' (p. 209). Unless Hobbes can establish this he
is unable to provide a sure foundation for a state where all irrespective
of belief are required to obey the sovereign.

The only point remaining to be considered is whether Hobbes regarded his laws of nature as moral principles which were binding in
some sense other than that they were conducive to individual self-
preservation. Hobbes certainly speaks of the laws as 'Morall Vertues'
'Immutable and Eternall' which 'bind to a desire they should take place'
(p. 82), but only in the sense that all men accept the laws as 'the meanes
of peaceable, sociable and comfortable living' (p. 83). They are binding
for Hobbes in a prudential rather then a moral sense, for it follows
from the nature of man as he had described and deduced it, that unless
men give effect to these laws they will suffer the horrors of war and the
fears of sudden death. Peace is the object of the laws of nature and peace
is the necessary means to continued existence and the satisfaction of
desires.[1] What is less clear is whether the laws can be regarded as
binding on each man simply because they are in his own interest or
whether because they are necessary for men as a whole. That is to say
do they have a claim on me for observance arising out of the common
good as distinct from my own good? It must, I think, be allowed that
Hobbes is unclear as to whether a man can ever have an overriding
obligation to obey the natural law where it conflicts with his own
interest. At two points where he does touch on the question he solves
it to his own satisfaction by arguing in effect that it can never be in an
individual's interest not to desire the fulfilment of the natural law under

1. For a fuller discussion of this point, see M. M. Goldsmith, *Hobbes's Science
of Politics*, 1966, Ch. 4.

conditions where others fulfil it – conditions which, as we have seen, he believed could be realized only in a Commonwealth ruled by a Sovereign. Thus he writes, respecting man's natural condition, 'he that having sufficient Security, that others shall observe the same Lawes towards him, observes them not himselfe, seeketh not Peace, but War; *and consequently the destruction of his Nature by Violence*' (p. 82, my italics). Similarly he rebuts 'the Foole' who argues that it cannot be contrary to reason for a man to break the natural law requiring the keeping of promises if the breach is to his own advantage, by insisting that such a man will either be cast out of society and perish, or if not he will remain simply through the errors of other men – a situation which he could not reasonably have foreseen or relied upon. Consequently not to keep covenants is held by Hobbes to be 'against the reason of his preservation' (p. 76). Hobbes's argument is a thin one. A man's selfish ends may clearly be advanced even within the framework of the law at the expense of other members of the community, without any threat to his own existence. Hobbes's position can only be effectively maintained if one accepts a notion of self-interest in terms either of some higher self (as in Christian teaching) or of the interest of the community as a whole (as with Rousseau). But Hobbes does not take up either of these positions. He attempts to deal with the problem on the basis of his conception of individual rational self-interest. Men are required by reason to obey natural laws because their observance is the condition of self-preservation, not because the laws are ordained by God or are for the good of the community. Reason or revelation may show that the natural laws are commands of God or that their observance is conducive to the preservation of the human species; but these are contingent reasons, not sufficient or even necessary reasons, for the observance of natural laws.

Hobbes finds the 'natural seed of Religion' in man's curiosity which leads him to seek the causes of events 'till of necessity he must come to this thought at last, that there is some cause, whereof there is no former cause, but is eternall, which it is men call God' (p. 53). This seed has been nourished by two sorts of men, one according to their own invention and the other according to God's revelation, 'but both sorts have done it, with a purpose to make those men that relyed on them, the more apt to Obedience, Lawes, Peace, Charity and civill Society' (p. 57). The fruits of revelation are not available to those 'to whom God hath not supernaturally revealed that they are his, nor that those that published them were sent by him' (p. 209). Such persons have no obligation to obey the dictates of religion except in so far as they are required by reason or by command of the sovereign. Man's reason, Hobbes tells us, discloses the divine law as requiring simply the fulfilment of the laws of nature and the honouring and worship of God as the embodiment of 'Irresistible Power'. A breach of the natural law leads inevitably to punishment here on earth, as a natural consequence of the act itself; intemperance for example gives rise to disease. Observance of the natural law is conducive to the preservation of man's life on earth, not 'to the attaining of an eternal felicity after death', for there can be no natural knowledge of man's estate after his demise (p. 76). The lesson which reason teaches is that God is best honoured by obedience to the laws of nature, laws which Hobbes has already established as dictates of worldly self-interest.

In his discussions of a Christian Commonwealth, Hobbes seeks to show that acceptance of Christian Scriptures and Revelation need not make (indeed for his purposes must not be allowed to make) any fundamental difference to the principles he has already established. Thus he argues,

> Seeing then our Saviour, and his Apostles, left not new Lawes to oblige us in this world, but new Doctrine to prepare us for the next; the Books of the New Testament, which contain that Doctrine, untill obedience to them was commanded, by them that God had given power to on earth to be Legislators, were not obligatory Canons, that is, Laws, but onely good, and safe advice, for the direction of sinners in the way of salvation, which every man might take, and refuse at his owne perill, without injustice (p. 284).

The doctrines of Christ do not add anything to or alter in any way men's obligations to the civil law. Hobbes's purpose is made plain in the manner in which he deals with the crucial question of what is to happen when a Christian receives a command from his ruler which in his eyes conflicts with God's will. He starts by accepting the traditional view that a man ought to obey the command of God rather than the command of his lawful sovereign, but he then proceeds to so qualify and interpret this position as to make it inapplicable and irrelevant in practice. He makes a sharp distinction between what is and what not necessary to salvation and insists that obedience to the commands of the sovereign is required of Christians in all things except where obedience would lead to 'the forfeiture of life Eternall'. But, Hobbes continues, 'All that is NECESSARY *to Salvation* is contained in two Vertues, *Faith in*

Christ,[1] and *Obedience to Laws*' (p. 319). The laws to be obeyed are the laws of the earthly sovereign and the laws of nature 'whereof the principall is, that we should not violate our Faith, that is, a commandment to obey our Civil Soveraigns' (p. 320). Hobbes is thus able to conclude that 'it is not hard to reconcile our Obedience to God, with our Obedience to the Civil Soveraign; who is either Christian or Infidel' (p. 328). For the Christian sovereign allows men to believe that *Jesus is the Christ* and requires obedience to all his civil laws 'in which also are contained all the Laws of Nature'; while the Infidel Sovereign, to whom obedience is required by the Laws of nature and the counsels of Christ and the Apostles, will not be 'so unreasonable' as to kill or persecute a subject 'that waiteth for the second comming of Christ, after the present world shall bee burnt, and intendeth then to obey him (which is the intent of beleeving that Jesus is the Christ), and in the mean time thinketh himself bound to obey the Laws of that Infidel King' (p. 328). Since no king could prevent a man believing in Christ, it followed that no man ever had excuse for not obeying his king.

One of Hobbes's main objects in *Leviathan* is to avoid any conflict of authority and for this reason he insists that the sovereign power cannot be divided and that no alternative sources of authority must be allowed to exist. The most dangerous alternative sources of authority in seventeenth century Europe were the Christian Churches, claiming obedience to their spiritual commands in the name of God. Hobbes could not in the climate of the time, deny God's authority (nor is there any real reason to believe that he wished to do so), but he could ensure that God's authority was not used by the churches to undermine the authority of the secular ruler. He does this by denying that Christ and the Apostles ever claimed or had any powers to command men to do anything contrary to the civil law and by redefining a Church as '*A Company of men professing Christian Religion, united in the person of*

1. What Hobbes understands by faith in Christ is best seen in his *De Cive*, XVIII, quoted by William B. Glover, 'God and Thomas Hobbes', *Hobbes Studies*, edited by K. C. Brown, 1965, p. 154. 'These words, Jesus is the Christ, do signify that Jesus was that person, whom God had promised by his prophets should come into the world to establish his kingdom; that is to say, that Jesus is the Son of God, God, the creator of heaven and earth, born of a virgin, dying for the sins of them who should believe in him; that he was Christ, that is to say a king; that he revived (for else he were not like to reign) to judge the world, and to reward everyone according to his works, for otherwise he cannot be a king; also that men shall rise again, for otherwise they are not like to come to judgment.'

one Soveraign'. For unless the head of the state is also the head of the church 'there must needs follow Faction, and Civil war in the Common-wealth, between the *Church* and *State* – and (which is more) in every Christian man's own brest, between the *Christian* and the *Man'* (p. 252). Hobbes is far more interested in preventing a conflict of conscience than with seeing that men act according to conscience, and one way of ensuring this is to show that conscience, reason and revelation all require obedience to the sovereign. In so far, of course, as the sovereign himself embodies Christian teaching in the civil law, obedience to that teaching is required; but because of the sovereign's powers of command not because of the doctrine itself. Hobbes even insists that the Apostles of the Church themselves were permitted to teach Christian Doctrine only 'so far forth, as no precedent Law, to which they were obliged to yeeld obedience, was to the contrary' (p. 285). He denies that a sovereign could be guilty of heresy, '*For Hæresie is nothing else, but a private opinion, obstinately maintained, contrary to the opinion which the Publique Person* (that is to say, the Representant of the Commonwealth) *hath commanded to be taught'* (p. 316). A sovereign can not, of course, command men's beliefs but he can command their actions in all things as long as he retains the sovereign power.

READING

Hobbes, *Leviathan*, Chs. 22, 23 39, and 43.

2. LOCKE

In the *Essay Concerning Human Understanding* (1690), Locke makes the bold assertion that the principles of morality are capable of rational demonstration 'wherein I doubt not but from self-evident propositions, by necessary consequences, as incontestable as those in mathematics, the measures of right and wrong might be made out, to any that will apply himself with the same indifference and attention to the one as he

does to the other of these sciences'. Locke fails to recognize the fundamental distinction between a science whose properties expressed logical
relationships and a study whose propositions express obligation. Locke
gives two examples of moral propositions which he claims are as certain
as any demonstration in Euclid. The second of these is 'No government
allows absolute liberty'; the idea of government being the establishment of society upon certain rules or laws which require conformity to
them; and the idea of absolute liberty being for any one to do whatever
he pleases.[1] Three points can be made about this example. Firstly, the
proposition is not watertight (if it were it would be tautological), for
one might without contradiction on the basis of the definitions of
government and absolute liberty used say that 'a government could
allow absolute liberty to its subjects if none of them wanted to do what
the government did not want them to do, or if all of them wanted to do
what the government wanted them to do'. Secondly, the definitions
used by Locke are not the only ones which might be used. For example
if absolute liberty is defined as obedience to the state or service to the
community, the proposition 'no government allows absolute liberty'
would not be meaningful. It is the very definition of basic concepts and
terms which is a matter of dispute in moral and political theory. There
is *no* self-evidently 'correct' definition of liberty or government. Different conceptions are more or less useful or relevant for different purposes. Thirdly, if one examines the proposition 'No government allows
absolute liberty', it is apparent that it is not a moral proposition at all.
It does not lay down any obligations or make any evaluation. It is,
or rather is claimed to be, a universal truth in the sense of a universally
valid conclusion from the defined premises; but because these premises
are themselves thought to be self-evidently true propositions about
social man, the conclusion is held to be universal factual truth about the
external world. But it does not follow, of course, that because 'no
government allows absolute liberty' absolute liberty ought not to be
allowed or encouraged or applauded. To produce a moral proposition
we must introduce a judgement of value into our statements of fact or

1. John Locke, *Essay Concerning Human Understanding*, Bk. IV, Ch. 3, section
18. Everyman's Library edition (abridged). Euclidean propositions were, of
course, seen by Locke and other thinkers of his time to embody absolute, not
relative or conditional truths. There was for Locke no question of Euclid
having selected certain basic premises or having made certain suppositions
and consequently no conception that other constructions and consequently
'truths' were possible using different premises or suppositions.

our definitions and such judgements cannot be demonstrated or established in a mathematical sense.

It is not surprising, therefore, that although Locke on a number of occasions claims that moral principles can be conclusively demonstrated he never attempts to make good that claim himself. In an unpublished paper *Of Ethick in General*, which he had originally intended to add to the *Essay Concerning Human Understanding*, Locke promises to 'establish morality, therefore, upon its proper basis' by showing 'that there are certain rules, certain dictates, which it is his (i.e. God's) will all men should conform their actions to, and that this will of his is sufficiently promulgated and made known to all mankind';[1] but there the paper abruptly ends. Von Leyden has pointed to the existence of two separate and conflicting strands in Locke's ethical thinking, absolutism and hedonism. The former finds its most complete expression in his earlier writings on natural law and the latter in the *Essay Concerning Human Understanding*. In the last of his eight *Essays on the Law of Nature* Locke attacks both the doctrine that there is no law of nature because all men 'are driven by innate impulse to seek their own interests', and that 'the basis of natural law is each man's own interest' in that its observance leads always to what is useful and advantageous. Locke insists that each person's own interest cannot be the standard of what is right and what is wrong and he distinguishes sharply between the utility or profit which may accrue from doing what is right from making utility itself the standards of morality: 'the rightness of an action does not depend on its utility; on the contrary; its utility is a result of its rightness'.[2]

But in the celebrated *Essay Concerning Human Understanding* he expressed himself in words which might have been written by Jeremy Bentham himself, the father of English utilitarianism.

> Things then are good or evil, only in reference to pleasure or pain. That we call *good*, which is apt to cause or increase pleasure or diminish pain in us; or else to procure or preserve us the possession of any good or absence of any evil. And, on the contrary, we name that *evil* which is apt to produce or increase any pain, or diminish any pleasure in us: or else to procure us any evil, or deprive us of any good (Bk. II, Ch. XX s.2).

1. Quoted by Von Leyden, op. cit., p. 70.
2. Essays on the Law of Nature, VIII: 'Is Every Man's Own Interest the Basis of the Law of Nature? No', Von Leyden, op. cit., pp. 205–15. For a contrary view, see Hans Aarsleff, 'The State of Nature and the Nature of Man' in *John Locke: Problems and Perspectives*, edited by J. W. Yolton, 1969.

Locke attempts to reconcile this hedonist approach with his assertion of absolute moral principles through the notion of God as the punisher after death of those who break his laws. 'When infinite happiness is put into one scale, against infinite misery in the other. . . . Must it not be a most manifest wrong judgement that does not presently see to which side, in this case, the preference is to be given' (Bk. II Ch. XXI, s. 70). Evil is the result of wrong judgement, of men revelling in the forbidden fruits of this world, without thought or heed of the retribution which will follow in the next. (*Moral good and evil* then is only *the conformity or disagreement of our voluntary actions to some law, whereby good or evil is drawn on us, from the will and power of the law-maker*' (Bk. II, Ch. XXVIII, s. 5). The 'only true touchstone of moral rectitude' he tells us is the divine law, in which was included both the law of nature and God's revealed law.

In spite of Locke's insistence that his purpose in writing the *Essay Concerning Human Understanding* was not 'to treat of the grounds of true morality' but 'only to show whence men had moral ideas, and what they are',[1] the general impact of the *Essay* was to raise doubts as to whether Locke had not undermined the traditional grounds for belief in absolute moral principles, while failing to provide the rational demonstration of their validity which he claimed was possible. While Locke accepted that certain issues were matters of faith or revelation and therefore 'above reason', he insisted '*Nothing that is contrary to, and inconsistent with, the clear and self-evident dictates of reason, has a right to be urged or assented to as a matter of faith, wherein reason hath nothing to do*' (Bk. IV, Ch. XVIII, ss. 7–10). Richard Ashcraft in his essay 'Faith and Knowledge in Locke's Philosophy',[2] argues that Locke's acceptance in the *Essay Concerning Human Understanding* (Bk. IV, Ch. XVIII, s. 8) of the superiority of revelation to reason in those fields where certainty of knowledge is not ascertainable, is a fundamental concession to revelation since Locke admits that there are very few things of which men can be certain (Bk. IV, Ch. XIV, ss. 1 & 2). What Professor Ashcraft overlooks is Locke's insistence that reason not revelation must be the judge of what is certain and that reason is to determine the validity of any claim to divine authority. 'Whatever God hath revealed is certainly true: no doubt can be made of it. This is the proper object of faith: but whether it be a *divine* revelation or no, reason must judge; which can

1. Letter to James Tyrrell, quoted by Von Leyden op. cit., p. 76.
2. Richard Ashcraft, 'Faith and Knowledge in Locke's Philosophy', in *John Locke: Problems and Perspectives*.

never permit the mind to reject a greater evidence to embrace what is less evident, nor allow it to entertain probability in opposition to knowledge and certainty' (Bk. IV, Ch. XVIII, s. 10).

As an ardent Christian, Locke was distressed by the assertions that the *Essay Concerning Human Understanding* undermined both religion and morality by grounding them on the shifting sands of reason. He himself saw no incompatibility between his Christian beliefs and the argument of the *Essay*; and would no doubt have been prepared at any time in his life to give the assurance contained in his published letter to the Bishop of Worcester in 1697 to 'condemn and quit any opinion of mine, as soon as I am shown that it is contrary to any revelation in the Holy Scripture'.[1] What Locke failed to see, or to accept, was that others might, on the basis of the principles of the *Essay*, legitimately question the divinity of Scriptural revelation itself in terms of rationality. The fundamental assertion in the *Essay* that *'no proposition can be received for divine revelation, or obtain the assent due to all such, if it be contradictory to our clear intuitive knowledge'* (Bk. IV, Ch. XVIII, s. 5), cannot be strictly maintained alongside an unquestioned acceptance of the divine authority of the Scriptures, since the former requires that one would, in principle, be prepared to deny authority to a Scriptural text. Indeed the very notion of 'proving' the validity of Scriptural texts in terms of their rationality was anathema to traditional Christian thinking, even if every text were shown to have passed the test.

In 1695 in *The Reasonableness of Christianity* Locke admits that 'human reason unassisted' had 'never from unquestionable principles, by clear deductions, made out an entire body of the "law of nature"' and in a letter to his friend William Molyneux a year later he excuses reason (and therefore himself as its disciple) from undertaking the task 'since she may find man's duty clearer and easier in revelation than in herself'.[2] Yet only a few years earlier in the most influential of his works, the *Second Treatise of Government* (1690) Locke used the notion of natural laws 'intelligible and plain to the rational creature' to provide a basis for determining when men might justifiably revolt against established rule. By providing a rational basis for revolt, without reference to the authority of any Church and independent of (although buttressed by) Scriptural texts, Locke unwittingly played an important part in turning the Christian political tradition of natural law into the secular tradition of natural rights, and in changing the emphasis from obligation

1. Quoted in ibid., p. 223.
2. Quoted in ibid., p. 219.

and submission to authority, to the assertion of rights and the questioning of claims to authority.

The natural state of men Locke tells us is 'a *State of perfect Freedom* to order their Actions, and dispose of their Possessions, and Persons as they think fit, within the bounds of the Law of Nature, without asking leave, or depending upon the Will of any other Man' (II, s. 4). Reason teaches man the rules which must be observed if the state of perfect freedom is to be maintained. It teaches him that since all men share in the same nature and have the same faculties all have equal claims to mutual respect.

> Every one as he is *bound to preserve himself*, and not to quit his Station wilfully; so by the like reason when his own Preservation comes not in competition, ought he, as much as he can, *to preserve the rest of Mankind*, and may not unless it be to do Justice on an Offender, take away, or impair the life, or what tends to the Preservation of the Life, the Liberty, Health, Limb or Goods of another (II, s. 6).

It will be noticed that Locke insists that men have a positive duty to help their fellows as well as negative duties to refrain from interference with them. It is left to each man to judge for himself the extent both of his obligations to others and of his own rights. If he thinks that his rights under the Law of Nature have been infringed he is entitled to punish the transgressor; for in the state of nature everyone necessarily has the right to defend his rights under that Law. As to what the law itself teaches, though Locke gives a number of examples, he declines 'to enter here into the particulars' while insisting that 'it is certain there is such a Law, and that too, as intelligible and plain to a rational Creature and a Studier of that Law, as the positive Laws of Common-wealths, nay possibly plainer' (II, s. 12). Indeed the positive laws of Commonwealths must themselves conform to the Law of Nature which serves as the fundamental guide for all men's actions both within and without society. 'Thus the Law of Nature stands as an Eternal Rule to all Men, *Legislators* as well as others. The *Rules* that they make for other Mens Actions, must, as well as their own and other Mens Actions, be conformable to the Law of Nature, i.e. to the Will of God' (II, s. 135). Moreover since the law of nature requires men to preserve themselves they may not put themselves under the absolute arbitrary control of any ruler, for this would give the ruler the power of life and death.

> Despotical Power is an Absolute, Arbitrary Power one Man has over another, to take away his Life, whenever he pleases. This is a power, which neither Nature gives, for it has made no such distinction between

one Man and another; nor Compact can convey, for Man not having such an Arbitrary Power over his own Life, cannot give another Man such a Power over it (II, s. 172).

The emphasis on reason rather than authority as the guide to truth is to be found in *A Letter Concerning Toleration* composed in 1667.[1] Men he insists must save their own souls. 'Liberty of conscience is every man's natural right' (p. 156). Since only God himself can determine which is the true faith men must be guided by 'the light of their own reason' and 'the dictates of their own consciences' (p. 128), not the will of their rulers in matters of religion. That is not to say that Locke regards what a man believes as a matter of no concern; on the contrary nothing earthly can compare in importance with the fate of his eternal soul. What Locke denies is that that fate is the concern of the civil authorities or that any one Church can establish a clear claim to possess the monopoly of the way to salvation. 'No man by nature is bound unto any particular church or sect, but every one joins himself voluntarily to that society in which he believes he has found that profession and worship which is truely acceptable to God' (p. 129). Locke wishes to break completely with the traditions of both the medieval world and of the Reformation which had forged close links between the realms of the civil and ecclesiastical authorities. Instead of the unity of Christendom and the Reformation principle *cuius regio eius religio* (i.e. taking one's religion from one's ruler), Locke declares

> the church itself is a thing absolutely separate and distinct from the commonwealth. The boundaries on both sides are fixed and immovable. He jumbles heaven and earth together, the things most remote and opposite, who mixes these two societies, which are in their original, end, business, and in everything perfectly distinct and infinitely different from each other (p. 135).

The responsibility of the civil ruler is to secure for his subjects 'the just possession of these things belonging to this life' (p. 126). He has no concern with the care of men's souls because there are no grounds for holding that God has given any man authority 'to compel any one to his religion. Nor can any such power be vested in the magistrate by the consent of the people, because no man can so far abandon the care of his own salvation as blindly to leave to the choice of any other, whether prince or subject, to prescribe to him what faiths or worship he shall

1. John Locke, *The Second Treatise of Government and a Letter Concerning Toleration*, edited by J. W. Gough, 1946, p. 156.

embrace' (p. 127). The sanctions available to the civil power are useless for purposes of salvation, for while laws and punishments are capable of getting men to conform to outward forms of worship and to profess articles of faith, they cannot produce that 'inward persuasion of the mind, without which nothing can be acceptable to God' (p. 127). The role of the civil authority in matters of religion should be restricted to seeing that the ordinary civil laws are kept and that no church teaches doctrines which stand 'condemned by the judgement of all mankind' in that they 'manifestly undermine the foundations of society' (p. 154).[1]

READING

John Locke, *A Letter Concerning Toleration.*

Richard I. Aaron, *John Locke*, 1955, Part III, Ch. 1, Moral Philosophy.

John Locke, *Essays on the Law of Nature*, edited by W. Von Leyden. Introduction, Chs. V and VI.

J. W. Yolton (Editor), *John Locke: Problems and Perspectives*; Hans Aarsleff 'The state of nature and the nature of man in Locke', Richard Ashcraft 'Faith and Knowledge in Locke's Philosophy'.

1. This view contrasts sharply with that put forward by Locke only seven years previously in his *Two Tracts on Government*, edited by Philip Abrams, 1967, where he writes 'Grant the people once free and unlimited in the exercise of their religion and where will they stop, where will they themselves bound it, and will it not be religion to destroy all that are not of their profession' (p. 159) and that 'a liberty for tender consciences was the first inlet to all those confusions and unheard of and destructive opinions that overspread this nation, (p. 160). For these practical, not doctrinal reasons, he then held it necessary that 'the supreme magistrate of every nation what way soever created, must necessarily have an absolute and arbitrary power over all the indifferent actions of his people' (p. 175), i.e. over all those matters where the law of nature and divine revelation do not require specific obedience to God's will. Indifferent things including such matters as the form and manner of Christian worship.

3. ROUSSEAU

In his *Confessions* Rousseau declares that the great practical moral lesson which men have to learn is to avoid those situations of life which bring our duties into conflict with our interests. This principle can be seen as underlying in different ways the treatment of the subject matter of his two most important works *Émile* and *The Social Contract*. In the former his aim is to show how a child might be guided to become a man free in the recognition of necessity and with desires attuned to his fully developed powers. In the latter Rousseau shows what form society must take if personal interests and social duties are to coincide. The two conceptions reinforce one another and each requires the other for its own full success.

Rousseau sees natural man as an amoral creature without any conception of right or wrong, good or evil. Morality for Rousseau is thus the result of society not its cause. Man's interests in the natural state are self-directed because natural man is self-sufficient. The only extra-directed feeling which he shows is compassion or pity at the suffering of others. This, however, is presented by Rousseau less as a moral feeling of concern for others than an innate tendency for men to identify themselves with those who suffer. It gives rise, he tells us, not to the sublime maxim of rational justice '*Do to others as you would have them do unto you*', but to the less perfect but more useful maxim of natural goodness '*Do good to yourself with as little evil as possible to others*' (*Inequality*, p. 185). This maxim is essentially self-directed and negative, requiring men to refrain from doing harm to others in seeking their own preservation, rather than to actively seek their good. Nevertheless the primeval feeling of compassion is seen by Rousseau as the source of all social virtues. In the state of nature itself, compassion 'supplies the place of laws, morals and virtues, with the advantage that none are tempted to disobey its gentle voice' (p. 184). It is because men's actions are guided by this innate capacity for compassion that Rousseau speaks of men as 'naturally good'; in the sense that the sympathy and imagination of natural man prevent him from harming other creatures; not in the sense that he chooses as a responsible rational being to act in conformity with understood and accepted principles of right behaviour. Rousseau's natural man is guided neither by the light of true reason nor by the revelations of God and Divine Scripture.

It is in the sense of 'a rule prescribed to a moral being, that is to say intelligent, free, and considered in his relations to other beings (p. 156), that Rousseau attacks traditional conceptions of natural law. Such conceptions make the mistake of imposing on natural man a set of moral rules which he was quite incapable of formulating or understanding in terms of the knowledge he had. In a section of the first draft of *The Social Contract* omitted from the final version, Rousseau argues that the notions of natural law as the law of reason 'only begin to develop when the prior development of passions renders all its precepts powerless'.[1] He does not reject the notion of natural law itself, but the conception that natural man could have been guided in his actions by rationally deduced rules of conduct. Rousseau finds the origin of 'the rules of natural right' in 'the agreement and combination which the understanding is able to establish between the two principles of self-preservation and compassion existing in man 'prior to reason', but which 'our reason is afterwards obliged to establish on other foundations' (*Inequality*, p. 157). Thus what Rousseau provides is a picture of the gradual evolution of rudimentary rules of conduct which natural man adheres to, but without any conception of their existence as rules and consequently without any obligation to obey them. In course of time the intuitively understood relationship between self-preservation and compassion becomes articulated in the moral maxim 'Do good to yourself with as little evil as possible to others'.

It is not until man has 'insensibly acquired some gross ideas of mutual undertakings and of the advantages of fulfilling them' (p. 194), until 'morality began to appear in human actions' (p. 198), and property 'gave rise to the first rules of justice – to secure each man his own' (p. 201), that the need for and feasibility of organized political society could arise. Thus the notion of a social contract is not conceived by Rousseau in terms of primitive man but of man after 'a multitude of ages', driven by his bitter experiences of the problems of social living into seeking security and peace 'by subjecting equally the powerful and the weak to the observance of reciprocal obligations' (p. 205). The man presented by Rousseau in *A Discourse on the Origin of Inequality* as ripe for the confidence trick perpetrated by the rich on the poor, had already developed a sense of obligation to carry out agreements made, based on an understanding of mutual advantage.

1. Quoted by C. E. Vaughan, *The Political Writings of Jean Jacques Rousseau*, 1915, Vol. I, p. 449.

In *The Social Contract* the slow unfolding historical drama of man's evolution from the primitive to the civil state is replaced by a fable showing how primitive man on the edge of the abyss of physical extinction might have saved both his existence and his freedom. In consequence the very act of effecting the social contract is shown as bringing about

> a remarkable change in man; it puts justice as a rule of conduct in the place of instinct, and gives his actions the moral quality they previously lacked. It is only then, when the voice of duty has taken the place of physical impulse, and right that of desire, that man, who has hitherto thought only of himself, finds himself compelled to act on other principles, and to consult his reason rather than study his inclinations (*The Social Contract*, Bk. I, Ch. 8, p. 64).

The difficulty about this fable presentation of what was for Rousseau a hypothetical and abstract problem is that it makes the transformation of man a miracle. How could such 'a narrow stupid animal' ever have determined upon such an intellectually sophisticated and mutually beneficial form of social contract and how could he ever have been induced to keep its terms? The former difficulty is met partially at least, if one inserts the more realistic evolutionary hypothesis used in *A Discourse on the Origin of Inequality*, but the latter is more fundamental. That Rousseau himself was not unaware of this weakness in his argument can be seen from an undated fragment he wrote: 'How can we count on the promises which nothing can force the contracting parties to make good, and which, when the interest that makes them acceptable changes, they will inevitably desire to break?'.[1] The weakness is not peculiar to Rousseau, however. It is common to all social contract theories which must rely on a combination of self-interest and an acceptance of a moral obligation to keep one's promises to explain both the act of compact and its initial observance. The difference between Rousseau and most other contract theorists is that he makes clear in *A Discourse on the Origin of Inequality* his belief that the notion of an obligation to keep promises arises only very slowly out of the experience of social living.

The social contract itself plays a less important role in Rousseau's political thinking than with Hobbes or Locke. It does not provide the reason why the members who have instituted a political society should obey its laws, nor do its terms indicate what laws are valid and what

1. Quoted by C. E. Vaughan, op. cit., Vol. I, p. 444.

are not. The contract is simply the chosen instrument for bringing civil society into being. Moreover, while Rousseau in *The Social Contract* presents the contract as a miracle opening the way to social freedom (instead of a fraud as in the *Discourse on Inequality*), he recognizes that the miracle may misfire and his social freedom be so abused as to 'lower him to something worse than what he had left' (Bk. I, Ch. 8, p. 65). The social compact can fulfil its purpose only if the society which it instituted is guided by the general will of the community. It is the general will not the social contract which is the vital core of Rousseau's political thinking. Indeed in *A Discourse on Political Economy*, where Rousseau outlines the ideas later developed in *The Social Contract* there is no reference to the notion of compact. 'The body politic,' he writes,

> therefore, is also a moral being possessed of a will; and this general will, which tends always to the preservation and welfare of the whole and of every part, and is the source of the laws, constitutes for all the members of the State, in their relations to one another and to it, the rule of what is just or unjust (*Political Economy*, pp. 236–7).

The same principle holds good in *The Social Contract*. It is the general will, not the nature of the original contract, which is the guide to action. The social contract is protrayed by Rousseau as a necessary condition for the realization of a society in which the general will is to be the motive force; but where the act of compact is itself the first expression of the general will. It is the general will not the form and content of the contract which is sovereign and consequently it is possible for the general will to revoke the terms of the original compact (*Social Contract*, Bk. III, Ch. 18).

While the general will originates from the socializing of self-interest (*amour de soi*) under the influence of compassion and in opposition to narrow selfish interest (*amour propre*), it would be wrong to posit an absolute coincidence between *amour de soi* and the general will. The general will is concerned with what is good for the community as a whole and not with purely individual pursuits. While the general will, as the will for the common good, has an absolute claim in respect of all matters pertaining to the general welfare, it has no interest in private matters. Rousseau wrote:

> we have to consider besides the public person those private persons who comprise it (i.e. the state) and whose life and liberty is naturally independent of it. Here we have to distinguish clearly between the respective rights of the citizens and of the sovereign, and distinguish

between the duties which the citizens have as subjects from the natural rights which they ought to enjoy as men (Bk. II, Ch. 4, p. 74).

Since the general will cannot by its nature impose upon the subjects anything useless to the community or applicable only to a segment of it, it follows that many aspects of life would be free from communal control; even though the sovereign itself is judge of what impositions are necessary. In these areas the individual might act as he himself thought fit. We may gain some idea of how Rousseau thought a person should act in his private life by referring to *Émile*. He does not suggest that Émile should devote himself solely to furthering the interests of others; on the contrary he insists that 'self-love is always good, always in accordance with the order of nature. The preservation of our own life is specially entrusted to each one of us, and our first care is, and must be to watch over our own life' (*Émile*, p. 174). What a man must learn to do is not to abandon self-love (*amour de soi*), but to extend it to others, which requires, not simply refraining from injuring them, but promoting their happiness. Rousseau's basic moral teaching is that a man should fulfil his social obligations in accordance with the general will and develop his own capacities and abilities to the full.

The general will, as the embodiment of social morality, has overriding claims against the particular wills of the individual members of a community. For although all men at heart 'always love what is good or what they think good', they often go wrong in judging what is good. Rousseau, therefore, in *The Social Contract* introduces two authorities whose concern it will be to uphold the rule of what is good. The first of these is the censor who is to preserve popular and customary morality 'by preventing opinions from being corrupted, by preserving their integrity with wise rulings, and sometimes even by settling points on which opinion is uncertain' (*Social Contract*, Bk. IV, Ch. 7, p. 175). While the censor upholds the morality which the law sustains, the legislator or law-giver, is concerned with the formation of the laws themselves and the moulding of opinion.

Whoever ventures on the enterprise of setting up a people must be ready, shall we say, to change human nature, to transform each individual, who by himself is entirely complete and solitary, into a part of a much greater whole, from which that same individual will then receive, in a sense, his life and his being. The founder of nations must weaken the structure of man in order to fortify it, to replace the physical and independent existence we have all received from nature with a moral and communal existence. In a word each man must be stripped of his own powers, and given powers which are external to him, and which he cannot use without the help of others' (Bk. II, Ch. 7, pp. 84–5).

The legislator is to protect men from their baser selves and help them to develop such a sense of community and public interest that eventually the office will become largely redundant. He is assumed to be the embodiment of the general will and unless he is such a true embodiment he cannot fulfil the role which Rousseau lays down for him. His position is in many ways parallel to that of the tutor in *Émile* and that book contains one passage which brings out very clearly the conflict between the higher and lower self which it is the function of both legislator and tutor to resolve. Émile on reaching manhood pleads with his tutor 'I mean to obey your laws, I shall ever do so, that is my steadfast purpose; if I ever disobey you, it will be against my will; make me free by guarding me against the passions which do me violence; do not let me become their slave; compel me to be my own master and to obey, not my senses but my reason' (*Émile*, p. 290). Since the legislator is to possess no executive powers and his legislative authority is purely advisory, Rousseau insists that he must have recourse to God if he is to persuade men to abandon their immediate partial interests. By putting forward his own ideas as the commands of God the legislator will be able to get his own way.

Rousseau's views on religion are set out in the profession of faith of the Savoyard vicar in *Émile* and in the chapter on Civil Religion in *The Social Contract*. In the former Rousseau expresses his belief in the existence of God as the creator of the universe and his rejection of the mechanistic materialism of the *Philosophes*. His faith is not Christian for it categorically repudiates the doctrines of original sin and redemption through Christ. 'Has he (God) not given me conscience that I may love the right, reason that I may perceive it, and freedom that I may choose it? If I do evil I have no excuse; I do it of my own free will' (*Émile*, p. 257). The true tenets of this natural religion have, in Rousseau's eyes, been corrupted as men have claimed direct knowledge of God through revelation, and as they have come to require outward observance of particular forms of worship, instead of the simple service of a sincere heart and true conscience. The multiplicity of faiths and sects is for Rousseau a clear indication of degeneration, for how is a man to know how to serve God if every group claims infallibility and prophesies damnation for all who follow any path but their own? In spite of these sentiments, however, Rousseau allows that all religions are 'wholesome institutions' where they have their reason 'in the country, the government, the genius of the people, or in other local causes which make one preferable to another in a given time or place' (*Émile*, p. 272).

The theme is taken up and developed along rather different lines in *The Social Contract*. Rousseau distinguishes two main forms which religion takes in relation to society. The first, natural religion, epitomized in the simple precepts of the Christian Gospels without rites or cults, makes all men children of one God. Its great weakness is its very universality and other-worldliness, since 'far from attaching the hearts of the citizens to the state, this religion detaches them from it as from all other things of this world' (*Social Contract*, Bk. IV, Ch. 8, p. 182). The second form, civil religion, has no such defects since its dogmas and rites are specific requirements of faith for all who live within the boundaries of the state. It suffers from a deeper ill, from the lies and errors compounded in its doctrines and the intolerance which stems from exclusiveness and contempt for other beliefs.[1] In the model state Rousseau proposes to combine the positive features of both these forms in order to provide a religion which will promote the well-being and harmony of the community. Under his scheme each person would be bound by a 'purely civil' profession of faith in the tenets of natural religion, viz. 'the existence of an omnipotent, intelligent, benevolent divinity that foresees and provides; the life to come; the happiness of the just; the punishment of sinners' (Bk. IV, Ch. 8, p. 186). The only novel features are the incorporation as a religious dogma of 'the sanctity of the social contract and the law' which make the observance of civil requirements a spiritual duty; and the proscription of intolerance. In Rousseau's view the observation of these dogmas by all men is necessary for the fulfilment of their social and moral duties in the community. Those who refuse to profess them should be banished and those who profess but publicly break them should be put to death, since the dogmas are a minimum requirement of citizenship.

Whereas in the corrupt society depicted in *Émile* the individual must learn to rely solely on his own individual conscience, in the ideal society of *The Social Contract* individual conscience must conform to the general conscience in all matters which concern the commonweal. Outside of such matters 'everyone may hold whatever opinions he pleases, without the sovereign having any business to take cognizance

---

1. The third form in which men are subject to two sets of rulers, the civil and the ecclesiastical, is dismissed by Rousseau as worthless because it destroys social unity.

of them' (Bk. IV, Ch. 8, p. 185). Consequently although the tenets of Rousseau's civil religion look very restrictive they would in principle permit men of every religious faith and creed, Christian and non-Christian alike, to live together on terms of equality and harmony; since the terms themselves require the express prohibition of religious intolerance and of doctrines 'contrary to the duties of the citizen' (ibid. p. 187). Rousseau does not establish a separate religion at all. The only features of his civil religion not common to virtually all Western faiths are those which require observance of the sanctity of the social contract and the law, and the tolerance of other beliefs. These two 'dogmas' are crucial, for without them religious belief is liable to become a source of weakness instead of strength in the community; either through a church setting itself up as an alternative source of authority to the civil power or engaging in religious strife or even war against its rivals. Rousseau would use the civil power to enforce religious toleration or to drive out those who obstinately persist that 'Outside the church there is no salvation'.

READING

J. J. Rousseau, *The Social Contract*, Bk. I, Chs. 6–8; Bk. II, Chs. 1–4, 6–7, Bk. IV, Chs. 7–8.

J. H. Broome, *Rousseau: A Study of His Thoughts*, Chs. 4 and 5.

E. Cassirer, *The Question of Jean Jacques Rousseau*, New York, 1954.

4. BENTHAM AND MILL

Bentham opens his best-known work, *An Introduction to the Principles of Morals and Legislation*, with the following words:

> Nature has placed mankind under the governance of two sovereign masters, *pain* and *pleasure*. It is for them alone to point out what we ought to do, as well as to determine what we shall do. On the one hand the standard of right and wrong, on the other the chain of causes and effects, are fastened to their throne. They govern us in all we do, in all we say, in all we think: every effort we can make to throw off our subjection, will serve but to demonstrate and confirm it. In words a man

may pretend to abjure their empire: but in reality he will remain subject to it all the while. The *principle of utility* recognizes this subjection, and assumes it for the foundation of that system, the object of which is to rear the fabric of felicity by the hands of reason and of law. Systems which attempt to question it, deal in sounds instead of senses, in caprice instead of reason, in darkness instead of light (p. 125).

This oft-quoted passage has been the source of more confusion and disagreement than any other in Bentham's writings. Considered in isolation it apparently asserts that pain and pleasure determine in fact how all men actually do behave and also how they ought to behave. But if all action is the consequence of necessary responses and reactions to pain and pleasure stimuli, then no question of prescriptive behaviour would seem to arise. Even if men have conceptions of how they ought to behave, such conceptions will themselves be derived from prior experiences of pleasure and pain and be applied only in so far as they have been found conducive to producing pleasure or alleviating pain. The claim, however, which Bentham makes on behalf of utility is that it is irrelevant 'whether a sentiment question can be originally conceived from any other source than a view of utility' and whether such a sentiment 'in point of *right* – can properly be justified on any other ground by a person addressing himself to the community' (Ch. II, s. 15, p. 142, my italics). Utilitarianism in Bentham's eyes provides both a subjective explanation of the way men behave, in terms of their responses to pain and pleasure and an objective standard of social action in terms of the principle of utility[1] or greatest happiness principle[2] 'which states the greatest happiness of all those whose interest is in question, as being the right and proper and universally desirable, end of human action: of

1. Bentham was well aware that he used the term utility both descriptively and prescriptively. In 1816 he wrote, 'The ... phrase principle of utility is ... employed in two difference senses: the *exegetic* or *explanatory*, and the *Deontological* or *Censorial*.' Quoted by Mary Mack, op. cit., p. 224.
2. The principle of the greatest happiness of the greatest number is ambiguous. The two extremes would be (a) the greatest total amount of happiness irrespective of its distribution, and (b) the greatest happiness of the majority, irrespective of the minority. Thus an action which resulted in giving twelve persons two units of pleasure and seven people three units of pain would be unacceptable under (a) and acceptable under (b). Bentham's own position is itself not unambiguous but for the most part he appears to adhere to (a), with the proviso that since the distribution of pains and pleasures will itself affect the calculation one is to make, as well as the total of the calculation, both directly and indirectly, it will normally be the majority who will in fact benefit from a decision in accordance with (a).

human action in every situation, and in particular in that of a functionary or set of functionaries exercising the powers of Government' (Ch. I, s. I, p. 125). If only the interest of an individual is in question with respect to any action of his, then that action will conform to the principle of utility if it adds to the sum total of his pleasures or diminishes the sum total of his pains. If, however, the action affects others then it must be calculated with reference to the pleasure and pain of those affected and ultimately of the whole community. Bentham sees no conflict in principle between the interest of the individual and the community because to him the interest of the community is simply 'the sum of the interests of the several persons who compose it' (p. 126), and because he is prepared to accept negative conformity to the utility principle (i.e. action which does no harm) as adequate (Ch. I, s. 10, p. 127). It would appear from this that the greatest happiness principle was for Bentham the only right guide for all human conduct and that it should be used both by the individual himself, and by legislators to determine which of the various actions which men found pleasure in should be discouraged or prevented – it being assumed that all actions were motivated by the desire for pleasure.

If one turns, however, to *The Handbook of Political Fallacies* (published in 1824 but mostly written much earlier) Bentham is found taking up a quite different stand. He accepts that the best that 'the most public spirited man' (i.e. 'the most virtuous of men') can do is 'to bring the public interest (meaning his own personal share in it) as often as possible into coincidence, and as seldom as possible into repugnance with his private interests' (p. 230). This in itself might mean no more than that the greatest happiness principle, expressed as the advancement of the public interest, was an ideal or aspirant standard of morality which few could hope to live up to (as with the Christian code of forgiving one's enemies and turning the other cheek). But Bentham goes on to say that

in this natural and general predominance of personal interest over every variety of more extensive interest, there is no just cause for regret. Why? Because upon this predominance depends the existence of the species and of every individual belonging to it. Suppose for a moment the opposite state of things – in which everyone should prefer the public interest to his own – and the necessary consequences would be no less ridiculous in idea than disastrous and destructive in reality (p. 230).

What follows from this is far from clear. If the survival of the species depends on the predominance of private over public interest in what

sense can 'the most public spirited man' be 'the most virtuous of men'?
Does Bentham perhaps assume that a leaven of public spiritedness is
necessary to temper the normal and necessary self-interestedness of the
majority of men? He certainly assumes that the great majority will act
in accordance with self-interest, as understood in terms of expectations
of pleasure seeking and pain avoidance, and that this will in most cases
produce more good than harm. 'Society is so constituted that, in labour-
ing for our particular good, we labour also for the good of the whole.
We cannot augment our own means of enjoyment without augmenting
also the means of others' (*Theory of Legislation*, p. 53). Harm, however,
there will be and Bentham holds it to be the business of government to
reduce it to the minimum possible through the judicious use of reward
and punishment. But governments also have longer term responsibilities
to educate men so that their behaviour becomes grounded more 'on
enlarged and sympathetic than on narrow and self-regarding affections,
and accordingly, upon the whole, more comfortable to the dictates of
utility' (*Morals and Legislation*, p. 183).

It would appear, therefore, that while Bentham believes that an
impossible situation would be created if all men acted in accordance
with the greatest happiness principle, he holds that, men being inclined
to press their interests without regard or reference to others, it is necessary to promote concern for and protect the interests of others. He
writes,

> But, in order that an individual should perceive this connection between
> the interests of others and his own, he needs an enlightened spirit and
> a heart free from seductive passions. The greater part of men have
> neither sufficient light, sufficient strength of mind, nor sufficient moral
> sensibility to place their honesty above the aid of the laws. The legis-
> lator must supply the feebleness of this natural interest by adding to it
> an artificial interest, more steady and more easily perceived (*Theory
> of Legislation*, p. 64).

But since the law is essentially a negative restraining force it is necessary to supplement its corrective influence on anti-social behaviour

> by the moral or social code – a code which is not written, which exists
> only in opinion, in manners and in habits, and which begins where the
> legislative code finishes. The duties which it prescribes, the services
> which it imposes, under the names of equity, patriotism, courage,
> humanity, generosity, honour, and disinterestedness, do not directly
> borrow the aid of the laws, but derive their force from other sanctions,
> founded upon punishments and rewards. As the duties of this secon-
> dary code have not the imprint of the law, their fulfilment has more

éclat; it is more meritorious; and a superior degree of honour attached to their performance happily makes up for their deficiency in positive force (p.188).

Men who pursue their own ends and desires at the expense of injuring their fellows are not so much evil as ignorant, for by their conduct they deprive themselves of many kinds of pleasure. 'The more enlightened he is, the more clearly will he perceive the connection between his private interest and the interest of the whole' (p. 369). The more enlightened men become the more they will develope a spirit of general benevolence, 'a sweet and calm sentiment which we delight to experience, and which inspires us with a repugnance to the cause of suffering' (p. 64). A man then should seek first his own interest, but in such a way as not to cause pain to others 'for our own interest, well understood, will never leave us without motives to abstain from injuring our fellows' (p. 63). He should practise enlightened benevolence which will both further the pleasures of others and give pleasure to himself. What Bentham is concerned with is the consequences of a man's actions not the intentions of the actor. Consequently it is possible for him to argue both that it would be undesirable that all men should *prefer* other people's interest to their own and that it 'is desirable that on every occasion the course *taken* by every man's conduct should be that which will be in the highest degree conducive to the welfare of the greatest number of those sentient beings in whose welfare it exercises any influence'.[1] In Bentham's view the practical consequences of everyone acting on the former unnatural principle would be calamitous since it would not produce the greatest happiness of all in society, but this is no way invalidates the desirability of securing that the consequences of each man's actions should be such as to further that end. The whole purpose of Bentham's life's work was to show what practical steps could be taken to help realize that goal in the society of his time.

John Stuart Mill follows Bentham in arguing that utilitarianism does not require that men should always act out of regard for the interests of others. He accepts that the sense of moral duty is only one motive and that its role is to act as censor of our other motives not to replace them – 'ninety-nine hundredths of all our actions are done from other motives, and rightly so done, if the rule of duty does not condemn them' (*Utilitarianism*, p. 17). The majority of men are not required to determine their actions by reference to the good of humanity –

---

1. Quoted by Mary Mack, op. cit., pp. 224–5, (my italics).

it is a misapprehension of the utilitarian mode of thought, to conceive it as implying that people should fix their minds upon so wide a generality as the world, or society at large. The great majority of good actions are intended not for the benefit of the world, but for that of individuals, of which the good of the world is made up; and the thoughts of the most virtuous man need not on these occasions travel beyond the particular persons concerned, except so far as is necessary to assure himself that in benefiting them he is not violating the rights, that is, the legitimate and authorised expectations, of any one else.

Mill continues:

> The multiplication of happiness is, according to utilitarian ethics, the object of virtue: the occasions on which any person (except one in a thousand) has it in his power to do this on an extended scale, in other words to be a public benefactor, are but exceptional; and on these occasions alone is he called on to consider public utility; in every other case, private utility, the interest or happiness of some few persons, is all he has to attend to (p. 17).

For Mill the principle of utility as a prescriptive principle of behaviour is capable of being used only on a limited scale. Both in respect of the vast majority of actions carried out from motives other than the sense of duty and the small minority carried out in conformity with that motive, the principle of utility is, for Mill, only directly relevant in a negative sense; in that it indicates what actions ought not to be done. Even here it is not normally the primary general principle of utility which should operate but the more specific secondary principles of justice, with their corresponding rights and duties.[1]

The foundation for the development of utilitarian morality, for Mill as for Bentham, is the natural sentiment in men to be in unity and harmony with their fellows. This sentiment, which leads men to identify their interests with those of others, tends to grow stronger under the impact of civilization, but Mill calls for positive purposive action to accelerate the process.

> If we now suppose this feeling of unity to be taught as a religion, and the whole force of education, of institutions, and of opinion, directed, as it once was in the case of religion, to make every person grow up from infancy surrounded on all sides both by the profession and the practice of it, I think that no one, who can realise this conception, will feel any misgivings about the sufficiency of the ultimate sanction for the Happiness morality (p. 30).

1. For a discussion of Mill's views on justice, see Chapter 3, section 4, below, pp. 120–2.

In the essay on *Utility of Religion*, written a few years previously but not published until a year after his death, Mill develops this conception of what he terms the Religion of Humanity. He concluded that 'the sense of unity with mankind, and a deep feeling for the general good, may be cultivated into a sentiment and a principle capable of fulfilling every important function of religion . . . better than any form whatever of supernaturalism' (3rd edition, 1885, p. 110). It was better because it was disinterested, making no appeal to the rewards and punishments of an after-life; and it was intellectually and morally more satisfying and consistent than religions which preach obedience to a 'perfect' God who condemns generations of men to 'blind partiality, atrocious cruelty and reckless injustice' in this world and the torments of Hell in the next (p. 112). It is interesting to note that during his lifetime Mill permitted himself the luxury of, what was for him, an unusually sharp and forceful attack on current religious conceptions. He wrote 'I will call no being good, who is not what I mean when I apply that epithet to my fellow-creatures; and if such a being should sentence me to hell for not so calling him, to hell I will go' (*Examination of Sir William Hamilton*, 1872 (4th edition), p. 129).

Mill's views on religion seem to differ from those of Bentham as set down in *The Analysis of the Influence of Natural Religion on the Temporal Happiness of Mankind*,[1] although in *Principles of Morals and Legislation* he looks forward not to the replacement of supernatural religions by the Religion of Humanity (i.e. utility) but their reconciliation. 'Happily,' he writes, 'the dictates of religion seem to approach nearer and nearer to a coincidence with those of utility every day' (p. 241).

Maurice Cowling uses Mill's advocacy of the Religion of Humanity as a justification for his portrayal of Mill as a censorious moralist, whose 'object was not to free men, but to convert them, and convert them to a peculiarly exclusive, peculiarly insinuating moral doctrine' (*Mill and Liberalism*, 1963, p. xiii). Cowling claims that Mill hoped to see the supercession of the Christian clergy by a secular 'clerisy' of intellectuals who would, by persuasion and education, bring about a 'spiritual consensus' in the nation on the basis of the Religion of Humanity. He supports this assertion by a quotation from Mill's autobiography in which Mill expresses his agreement with Auguste Comte's view 'that

---

1. Published in 1822 under the pseudonym of 'Philip Beauchamp' which covered the collaboration of Bentham and George Grote. The book is discussed in Leslie Stephen's classic work *The English Utilitarians*, Vol. II, Ch. VIII.

the moral and intellectual ascendancy, once exercised by priests, must in time pass into the hands of philosophers, and will naturally do so when they become sufficiently unanimous, and in other respects worthy to possess it' (*Autobiography*, p. 179). But Cowling omits the succeeding sentences:

> But when he [i.e. Comte] exaggerated this line of thought into a practical system, in which philosophers were to be organized into a kind of corporate hierarchy, invested with almost the same spiritual supremacy (though without any secular power) once possessed by the Catholic Church – it is not surprising, that while as logicians we were nearly at one, as sociologists we could travel together no further.

Comte's religion of Humanity, Mill continued, 'leaves an irresistible conviction that any moral beliefs concurred in by the community generally, may be brought to bear upon the whole conduct and lives of its individual members, with an energy and potency truly alarming to think of' (pp. 180–1). In spite of Cowling's reference to Mill's commitment 'to claim extensive authority for the clerisy' (op. cit., p. 106), Mill himself nowhere uses the phrase. Cowling gives Mill's quotations from Coleridge on the role of the clerisy, as the learned of all professions, as though they expressed Mill's own views. The conclusion which Mill himself draws from Coleridge's assertion that the responsibility of the national church for the advancement of knowledge and the civilization of the community may need to be placed in other hands, is not that a secular clerisy should take over this role, but that Coleridge's words would help to shame the Church into reforming herself and vindicate 'the principle of an endowed class, for the cultivation of learning, and for diffusing its results among the community' (*Mill on Bentham and Coleridge*, op. cit., p. 148). Mill's clerisy is a figment of Cowling's imagination. Cowling is on stronger ground in drawing attention to the contradiction between Mill's championing of individualism on the one hand and his espousal of utilitarian principles on the other. The contradiction is not peculiar to Mill, however, it lies at the heart of all ethical doctrines which assert the intrinsic value of individual free choice, alongside the assertion of what that choice ought to be. It is particularly striking in Mill because of his identification in most people's eyes with the most liberal form of individualism through his plea for diversity and dissent. Yet he writes in *Utilitarianism* words which might almost have been penned by Rousseau:

> As the means of making the nearest approach to this ideal, ('the golden rule of Jesus of Nazareth' – my note) utility would enjoin,

first, that laws and social arrangements should place the happiness, or (as speaking practically it may be called) the interest, of every individual, as nearly as possible in harmony with the interest of the whole; and secondly, that education and opinion, which have so vast a power over human character, should so use that power as to establish in the mind of every individual an indissoluble association between his own happiness and the good of the whole; especially between his own happiness and the practice of such modes of conduct, negative and positive, as regard for the universal happiness prescribes; so that not only he may be unable to conceive the possibility of happiness to himself, consistently with conduct opposed to the general good, but also that a direct impulse to promote the general good may be in every individual one of the habitual motives of action, and the sentiments connected therewith may fill a large and prominent place in every human being's sentient existence (*Utilitarianism*, p. 16).

Mill's conception is not of diversity and dissent as ends in themselves but as means to the achievement of the greatest good of all men considered as individuals.

READING

Jeremy Bentham, *An Introduction to the Principles of Morals and Legislation*, Chs. I, II, VII–XI and XVII.

John Stuart Mill, *Utilitarianism*, Chs. I–IV.

Maurice Cowling, *Mill and Liberalism*. Chs. 4 and 5 are reprinted with slight alterations in *Mill: A Collection of Critical Essays*, ed. J. B. Schneewind.

5. HEGEL

In contrast to most philosophers, Hegel makes a sharp distinction between morality and ethics. He sees morality as being historically and logically a prior and necessary stage in the development of man as an ethical being, consciously identifying himself with the spirit of the universe. Morality for Hegel meant awareness of oneself as a moral agent, responsible for one's own acts. The whole emphasis is on the individual conscious of himself and concerned with his own spiritual development, anxious to live the good life as the life that is good for him. Self-perfection is the whole end of existence. Such a notion, while it marks an advance on simple unreflective acceptance of customary mores and attitudes, suffers from a lack of just that attachment to the world outside the self which customary morality provides. It is the role of ethics to provide this necessary link so that the individual may realize the abstract formal principles of morality which he has personally identified himself with within the framework of institutions and roles provided by a community dedicated to this purpose.

The process whereby an individual passes from the realm of abstract morality to ethical action involves the recognition that his subjective will is part of a universal will and that it needs to be embodied in action; that high-sounding abstract moral principles of duty have no strict meaning until they are applied, even if in an attenuated form. The translating of principles into action necessarily involves not merely giving them reality and objectivity but recognizing their validity and objectivity for others. The principles I adopt for myself have to be principles that are capable of being applied, and which I do in fact apply, to others.

> Since in carrying out my aims I retain my subjectivity during this process of objectifying them I simultaneously supersede the immediacy of this subjectivity as well as its character as this my individual subjectivity. But the external subjectivity which is thus identical with me is the will of others. The will's ground of existence is now subjectivity and the will of others is that existence which I give to my aim and which is at the same time to me an other. The achievement of my aim, therefore, implies this identity of my will with the will of others, it has a positive bearing on the will of others (*Philosophy of Right*, p. 77).

When I act in the external world I am responsible only for the consequences which I intend in the situation as I comprehend it. Thus actions cannot be judged solely in terms of their consequences because some consequences are the result of chance or of the necessarily limited and particular position from which the actor judged the situation. On the other hand intentions cannot be assessed apart from the consequences which necessarily follow from their implementation.

> The consequences, as the shape proper to the action and immanent within it, exhibit nothing but its nature and are simply the action itself; therefore the action can neither disavow nor ignore them. On the other hand, however, among the consequences there is also comprised something interposed from without and introduced by chance, and this is quite unrelated to the nature of the action itself (pp. 80-1).

As far as the actor himself is concerned the fulfilment of his intentions in completed action is a source of satisfaction, satisfaction which Hegel declares to be 'the right' of the subject. He scorns those who see a fundamental antagonism between self-satisfaction and morality and who persist in denigrating the ends which men seek as mere ends of self-gratification. In *Phenomenology of Mind* he writes:

> The moral consciousness cannot renounce happiness and drop this element out of its absolute purpose. The purpose, which is expressed as pure duty, essentially implies retention of individual self-consciousness and maintenance of its claims. Individual conviction and knowledge thereof constituted a fundamental element of morality. This moment in the objectified purpose, in duty fulfilled, is the individual consciousness seeing itself as actually realized. In other words, this moment is that of enjoyment, which thus lies in the very principle of morality, not indeed of morality immediately in the sense of a frame of mind, but in the principle of the *actualization* of morality. Owing to this, however, enjoyment is also involved in morality, as a mood, for morality seeks, not to remain a frame of mind as opposed to action, but to act or realize itself. Thus the purpose, expressed as a whole along with the consciousness of its elements or moments, is that duty fulfilled shall be both a purely moral act and a realized individuality, and that nature, the aspect of individuality in contrast with abstract purpose, shall be one with this purpose (pp. 617-8).

Hegel sharply attacks subjective morality which, denying the possibility of any objective absolute standard of good and evil, makes the individual conscience the sole source of moral authority. To leave morality to the discretion and whim of every man is to deny morality; for any man may claim that his actions, no matter how evil they may seem to others, are acts which he holds to be good. Subjective morality not only upholds the conduct of sincere convinced eccentrics and bigots but makes it possible for the hypocrite to cover his base purposes with the cloak of proclaimed good intentions. Subjective morality is a denial of morality in that it refuses to accept that men have 'a duty to know the good and to be aware of its distinction from evil' –

> But if a good heart, a good intention, a subjective conviction are set forth as the source from which conduct derives its worth, then there is no longer any hypocrisy or immorality at all; for whatever a man does, he can always justify by the reflection on it of good intentions and motives, and by the influence of that conviction that it is good. Thus there is no longer anything absolutely vicious or criminal; and instead of the above-mentioned frank and free, hardened and unperturbed sinner, we have the man who is conscious of being fully justified by

intention and conviction. My good intention in my action and my conviction of its goodness makes it good. We speak of judging and esti-
mating an *action*; but on this principle it is only the intention and
conviction of the agent, his faith, by which he ought to be judged
(*Philosophy of Right*, p. 99).

Subjective morality is simply consistency in one's adherence to what one
believes, irrespective of what is the content and purpose of that belief
and what the consequences which flow or would flow from its being
expressed in action. At one end of the scale subjective morality is simply
a guise for the perpetration of base and selfish desires, while at the
other it assumes the noble form of the 'beautiful soul' which, refusing
to sully itself in the outside world, withdraws into itself to cultivate inner
goodness through contemplation.

All forms of subjective morality are defective because they refuse
to recognize that the very principle of morality is universality, the need
to act with regard to a wider frame of reference than the individual.
There can be no true good which is the good for me alone, but only the
good for all. But the good must not be left at the level of abstraction, it
must be actualized through the particular wills of individuals. It is
through the translation of the abstract idea of good into personal action
in particular situations that the good is realized. The element of truth
in subjective morality is the assertion that the individual has the right
only to give recognition and effect to what his insight or conscience upholds. Hegel bitterly attacks medieval conceptions of morality as
obedience, 'that blind and unconditional compliance which does not
know what it is doing, and whose course of action is a mere groping
about without clear consciousness or intelligence'. True morality is
'an obedience to laws which I recognize as just' (*Philosophy of History*,
p. 396), and requires the conjunction of conscience and reason.

Conscience is the expression of the absolute title of subjective self-
consciousness to know in itself and from within itself what is right and
obligatory, to give recognition only to what it thus knows as good, and
at the same time to maintain that whatever in this way it knows and
wills is in truth right and obligatory. Conscience as this unity of subjective knowing with what is absolute is a sanctuary which it would be
a sacrilege to violate. But whether the conscience of a specific individual corresponds with this Idea of conscience, or whether what it takes
or declares to be good is actually so, is ascertainable only from the
content of the good it seeks to realise. What is right and obligatory is
the absolutely rational element in the will's volitions and therefore it
is not in essence the *particular* property of an individual, and its form

is not that of feeling or any other private (i.e. sensuous) type of know-ing, but essentially that of universals determined by thought i.e. the form of laws and principles. Conscience is therefore subject to the judgement of its truth or falsity, and when it appeals to itself for a decision, it is directly at variance with what it wishes to be, namely the rule for a mode of conduct which is rational, absolutely valid and universal (*Philosophy of Right*, p. 91).

To say that man has a conscience is not to proclaim the goodness of its determination but to assert that he has a capacity for good; but also a capacity for evil. Good and evil have a common root in the self-determination of the will, which arises out of the discovery of self and consciousness of self as a distinct person capable of choice. It is because the full adult, as distinct from the child, lunatic or beast, has trans-cended the level of natural impulsive action and become capable of rational reflection that he finds himself on the verge between good and evil. He is then capable of consciously willing what was formerly the mere expression of impulsive desire and may reject what is rational and universal in favour of what satisfies his natural will. The will is only good in so far as it labours to give effect to what is universally valid, shunning the gratification of self as the criterion of purposive action.

Man, however, does not have to create for himself a world of moral action. He is not left unaided to determine how best the Spirit of rationality can be furthered in the universe. He exists in a world in which the Spirit of Reason is immanent and where it has actualized itself in essence, in social institutions and codes of conduct, as Ethical life.

> The objective ethical order, which comes on the scene in place of good in the abstract, is substance made concrete by subjectivity as infinite form. Hence it posits within itself distinctions whose specific character is thereby determined by the concept, and which endow the ethical order with a stable content independently necessary and sub-sistent in exaltation above subjective opinion and caprice. These dis-tinctions are absolutely valid laws and institutions (p. 105).

Thus Hegel denies the individual conscience the right to determine for itself how it shall act in society. It must take its key from the customs, laws and moral principles upheld by the community and given effect to through the institutions of family, civil society and the state.

What is not clear, however, is whether Hegel holds that the nature and purpose of the actual institutions and laws of any particular com-munity must be taken as binding on the individuals who constitute it;

or how far they are binding only if they themselves conform to the wider and more universal purpose embodied in the realization of the Absolute Idea. The answer would appear to lie along the following lines. It is only through conscious conformity with the laws and institutions of a state that an individual can live an ethical life. These laws provide the individual with a clear indication of what is required of him and he has no valid right to set against the laws the claims of personal conscience. 'In this objective field, the right of insight is invalid as insight into the legal or illegal, *qua* what is recognized as right, and it is restricted to its elementary meaning, i.e. to knowledge in the sense of acquaintance with what is legal and to that extent obligatory' (p. 88). On the other hand Hegel recognizes that there may be times when the actual society in which a man lives fails to provide a suitable area for the particularization of the universal principles of rational conduct, i.e. where the ethical life is impossible. In such circumstances an individual may find it necessary to retreat into himself and realize as best he can the narrow good of 'the beautiful soul'. It seems clear, however, that Hegel regards such circumstances as exceptional. The state must normally be regarded as providing for most people principles of, and the conditions for, living an ethical life in the situation existing. In the Preface to *Philosophy of Right* Hegel writes:

> This book, then, containing as it does the science of the state, is to be nothing other than the endeavour to apprehend and portray the state as something inherently rational. As a work of philosophy, it must be poles apart from an attempt to construct a state as it ought to be. The instruction which it may contain cannot consist in teaching the state what it ought to be; it can only show how the state, the ethical universe, is to be understood (p. 11).

Hegel expresses the same theme on the relationship between 'is' and 'ought' in his other writings. In *Phenomenology of Mind* he holds, 'What is universally valid is also universally effective: what *ought to be*, as a matter of fact, *is* too; and what merely *should* be, and is *not*, has no real truth' (p. 289). In *The German Constitution* he declares,

> For it is not what is that makes us irascible and resentful, but the fact that it is not as it ought to be. But if we recognize that it is as it must be, i.e. that it is not arbitrariness and chance that make it what it is, then we also recognize that it is as it ought to be. Yet it is hard for the ordinary run of men to rise to the habit of trying to recognize necessity and to think it (p. 145).

Finally in *Lectures on the Philosophy of History* he writes, 'The insight then to which . . . philosophy is to lead us, is, that the real world is as it ought to be – that the truly good – the universal divine reason – is not a mere abstraction, but a vital principle capable of realizing itself' (p. 38). Hegel holds that man has a moral duty to the state in which he lives, to identify himself with it, its needs and its aspirations, so that he takes on in his person the character and spirit of the nation to which he belongs. The individual identifies himself with the nation and the nation is identified with the process of world history. Yet conversely it appears that if the existing social and political order in any state frustrates the process of historical development and cramps both the national spirit and the opportunity for individual rational activity, then it stands condemned. Thus Hegel justified the French Revolution as the assertion of the ideas of Right and Reason against the established framework of injustice. Nowhere, however, does Hegel indicate how one is to determine whether an established order has outgrown its purpose and how the Spirit of a Nation is to be gauged or its purposes understood.

In *Philosophy of History* Hegel claims that it is in the sphere of religion that a nation expresses most clearly its moral identity. Hegel's views on religion changed fundamentally in the course of his lifetime. Kaufmann[1] has drawn attention to the fact that in his early writings Hegel ridiculed and attacked Christian teaching and even the person of Christ himself. In his later works Hegel emphasizes the positive role of religion in general and Christianity (especially in its Protestant form) in particular, but he never adopts the attitude of a Christian believer. He interprets the doctrines of Christianity as revealing in figurative and mythical form the essential truths about the nature of the universe, truths which are to be found more adequately and scientifically expressed in his own writings. The ultimate lesson which men will learn from the 'factual Incarnation' of God in Christ and his death on the Cross is the transfiguration of his independent particular existence in the universality of the spirit. The lesson will mean 'the death of the abstraction of Divine being', the recognition 'that God Himself is dead'. 'This harsh utterance is the expression of inmost self-knowledge which has simply self for its content; it is the return of consciousness into the depth of darkness where Ego is nothing but bare identity with Ego, a darkness distinguishing and knowing nothing more outside it' (*Phenomenology of*

1. Kaufmann, *Hegel*, sections 8, 9 and 10.

Mind, pp. 781–2). This cold and abstract destiny which Hegel holds out for man is not the concern of the state in the immediate present, where religion still has a positive role to play.

In *Philosophy of Right*, Hegel insists that it is only in some forms that religion fulfils its proper function, as the embodiment of absolute truth. Where a religion fails to see the divine nature of the role of the state, and tries to make its teaching the sole source of authority, then the life of the community is undermined. The proper role of religion is to concern itself with the inner disposition and attitude of mind of the subjective individual; not to seek to apply these tenets to the outside world, without regard to the special claims and role of the state. In particular it cannot be accepted that the domain of the church embraces the whole field of spiritual and moral life for 'the state is not a mechanism but the rational life of self-conscious freedom, the system of the ethical world' (*Philosophy of Right*, p. 170). Consequently in all matters affecting ethical principles, law and institutions, as distinct from matters of doctrine and faith, the state has its own obligations to fulfil. The state must be prepared to protect objective truth against religious institutions which through their teachings undermine the social order. The proper relationship between state and church is one in which the church recognizes the state and upholds it. In return the state should afford every protection and assistance to the church in the furtherance of its purely religious ends and should require all men to belong to *a* church – '*a* church is all that can be said, because since the content of a man's faith depends on his private ideas, the state cannot interfere with it' (p. 168). Hegel is prepared on these grounds to adopt a tolerant attitude towards the members of sects like Quakers and Anabaptists whose religion requires them to decline to carry out some of the fundamental obligations men have to the state, such as defending it against its enemies; provided that they perform some other service instead. Such persons, however, have no rights of citizenship, because they refuse to carry out a citizen's duties. They can be tolerated only where the state is strong.

READING

Hegel, *Philosophy of Right*, Part II: 'Morality'.

6. MARX AND ENGELS

In *The German Ideology* (written in 1845-6) Marx and Engels set out their conception of the relationship between the ideas and principles which men have and the society in which these ideas and principles are held and expressed. They insist that morality, religion, metaphysics and ideology in general do not have an independent existence, but are developed by man in the process of living in a world where the basis of life is effort and work. 'Men who develop their material production and their material relationships alter their thinking and the products of their thinking along with their real existence.'[1] With the division of labour in the field of production there arises a division between physical and mental labour which makes possible the emergence of theories of theology, philosophy, ethics, etc. Marx and Engels accept that such theories may be critical of, or in opposition to, the existing social order, but only if that order is itself unbalanced, in the sense that it is out of line with the changing economic and productive forces. Marx and Engels remained true to this formulation throughout their lives, although Engels in 1890 thought it necessary to stress that he and Marx had never asserted that the economic forces were the only determining forces but simply 'the *ultimately* determining element in history'. Among the other influences which might preponderate in determining the *form* of historical struggles, but not their outcome, were the ideas and doctrines which men had come to hold.[2]

Engels develops this theme in *Anti-Dühring* (1878) and *Ludwig Feuerbach* (1888). In the former Engels stresses that conceptions of morality, of what constitutes good and bad, have varied enormously from one nation to another and from one age to another. This is because men 'derive their moral ideas in the last resort from the practical relations on which their class position is based – from the economic relations in which they carry on production and exchange'.[3] The three major moralities of modern Europe were Christian feudal morality

1. Easton and Guddat, op. cit., p. 415.
2. Letter from Engels to Bloch reprinted in *Engels: Selected Writings*, edited by W. O. Henderson, Pelican Books, 1967, pp. 333-5. See also letter from Engels to Conrad Schmidt, ibid., pp. 439-45.
3. F. Engels, *Herr Eugen Dühring's Revolution in Science (Anti-Dühring)*, translated by Emile Burns, London, 1934, p. 107.

typical of the aristocracy, the rationalist materialist morality typical of
the enlightened bourgeois, and the proletarian morality of the future.
Each of these moral theories contains elements common to the others
since they were all evolved during different stages of the historical
development of human society under class conditions. Class society
is above all concerned with the protection of property and consequently
all class moralities proclaim the moral law 'Thou shalt not steal'.
'Does this law thereby become an eternal moral law?' asks Engels. 'By
no means. In a society in which the motive for stealing has been done
away with, in which therefore at the most only lunatics would ever steal,
how the teacher of morals would be laughed at who tried solemnly to
proclaim the eternal truth: Thou shalt not steal!'

> We therefore reject every attempt to impose on us any moral dogma
> whatsoever as an eternal, ultimate and forever immutable moral law
> on the pretext that the moral world too has its permanent principles
> which transcend history and the differences between nations. We
> maintain on the contrary that all former moral theories are the product,
> in the last analysis, of the economic stage which society had reached at
> that particular epoch. And as society has hitherto moved in class
> antagonisms, morality was always a class morality; it has either justified
> the domination and the interests of the ruling class, or, as soon as the
> oppressed class has become powerful enough, it has represented the
> revolt against this domination and the future interests of the oppressed.
> That in this process there has been on the whole progress in morality,
> as in all other branches of human knowledge, cannot be doubted. But
> we have not yet passed beyond class morality. A really human morality
> which transcends class antagonisms and their legacies in thought be-
> comes possible only at a stage of society which has not only overcome
> class contradictions but has even forgotten them in practical life (pp.
> 107–8).

In the meantime one must choose between the feudal morality
representing the past, bourgeois morality representing the present and
proletarian morality which, standing for the overthrow of the present,
represents the future.

In *Ludwig Feuerbach* Feuerbach is criticized by Engels for failing
to appreciate that the absolute moral claim of every man to satisfy his
urge to happiness, on condition that he respects equal rights for all
other men, is meaningless under capitalism. The urge towards happiness depends far more on material means than on ideal rights 'and
capitalist production takes care to ensure that the great majority of
those with equal rights shall get only what is essential for bare exis-

tence'.[1] Marxists are concerned not with what motivates an individual to act as he does in his private life but with the driving causes which set in motion whole classes and peoples, producing great historical transformations. These driving causes will have their origin in the material conditions of existence of those concerned, though they themselves may express their own motives in quite other terms.

For Marx and Engels one of the most striking forms in which competing economic classes have seen and presented their underlying interests has been through religion. The Young Hegelians had been distinguished from their master by their rejection of the religious elements in his teaching and their assertion that the true basis of religion is to be found in man's social needs and historical experience. Marx echoed these ideas in one of his own early criticisms of Hegel when he wrote '*Man makes religion*, religion does not make man' – 'Religion is the sigh of the oppressed creature, the heart of a heartless world, as it is the spirit of spiritless conditions. It is the *opium* of the people.'[2] In the same year writing *On the Jewish Question* Marx insists that the political emancipation of men from religious control by the state does not produce human emancipation from religion itself. The democratic bourgeois state expresses 'the *human ground* of Christianity', for 'religion is here the spirit of civil society expressing the separation and withdrawal of man from man' – man 'corrupted by the entire organization of our society, lost and alienated from himself, oppressed by inhuman relations and elements – in a word, man who is not yet an *actual* species-being'.[3] Bourgeois democracy emancipates the state from religion, while leaving men subject to its thrall. Human emancipation requires revolutionizing and socializing the separated elements of life: the transformation of the existing world of atomistic, mutually hostile individuals. In the process of this transformation men will liberate themselves from the realms of religious whim and fancy. In the case of the Jews their religion had, in Marx's view, already become socialized as practical egoism which found fulfilment in money as the alienated essence of man's labour and life which dominates all who worship it. 'The *social* emancipation of the Jew is *the emancipation of society from Judaism*' (ibid., p. 248). Three years later Marx published an equally bitter attack on the social

1. F. Engels, *Ludwig Feuerbach and the End of Classical German Philosophy*, printed in Feuer, op. cit., p. 262.
2. K. Marx, *Towards the Critique of Hegel's Philosophy of Law: Introduction* 1843, Easton and Guddat, op. cit., p. 250.
3. ibid., p. 231.

principles of Christianity, which had justified slavery, glorified serfdom, defended the oppression of the proletariat and vindicated oppression
as Divine punishment for sin or Divine opportunity to receive Grace
through suffering. Christianity preached abasement, submission and
humility to a proletariat which needed courage, pride and self-esteem to
carry out its revolutionary tasks.[1]

Marx devotes little further attention to the problem of religion but
his colleague Engels returns to it in a number of works. The most interesting of these, *On the History of Early Christianity*, was published in
the year before his death and draws surprising parallels between the
early history of Christianity and the early history of the working-class
movement.

> Like the latter, Christianity was originally a movement of oppressed
> people: it first appeared as the religion of slaves and emancipated
> slaves, of poor people deprived of all rights, of peoples subjugated or
> dispersed by Rome. Both Christianity and the workers' socialism
> preach forthcoming salvation from bondage and misery; Christianity
> places this salvation in a life beyond, after death, in heaven; socialism
> places it in this world, in a transformation of society. Both are per-
> secuted and baited, their adherents are despised and made the objects
> of exclusive laws, the former as enemies of the human race, the latter
> as enemies of the state, enemies of religion, the family, social order.
> And in spite of all persecution, nay, even spurred on by it, they forge
> victoriously, irresistibly ahead.[2]

Engels does not accept that religion is necessarily at all times and in all
its forms 'the opium of the people'. On the contrary in *The Peasant War
in Germany* (1850) Engels argued that during the fourteenth and fifteenth
centuries there emerged a clearly defined, plebeian heresy which went far
beyond the burgher heresy of Luther, with its attacks on the wealth and
political power of the church. 'Equality of the children of God' became
a demand for the civil equality of nobleman and peasant, burgher and
plebeian and for the abolition of corvée, ground-rents, taxes and privileges. This movement reached its culminating point in the Peasants'
War of 1525 in Germany when the victorious burgher heresy led by
Luther was confronted by the plebeian heresy of Münzer, who called

1. K. Marx, 'The Communism of the Paper *Rheinischer Beobachter*', 1847,
   excerpt in Feuer, op. cit., pp. 308–10.
2. F. Engels, *On the History of Early Christianity*, reprinted in Feuer, op. cit.,
   p. 209.

for the immediate establishment of the kingdom of God by the abolition of class differences, private property and the arbitrary power of the state.[1] By putting himself at the disposal of the German princes, Luther made German Lutheranism the tool of feudal reaction. Calvinism, the other great Protestant creed, succeeded in establishing a bourgeois republic in Holland devoted to the twin causes of serving God and Mammon.[2]

While Christianity had in its beginnings, and on rare occasions in its subsequent history, played a progressive role, Engels held with Marx that its modern role was wholly reactionary. 'Christianity,' he argued, in *Ludwig Feuerbach*, 'had become incapable for the future of serving any progressive class as the ideological garb of its aspirations. It became more and more the exclusive possession of the ruling classes, and these apply it as a mere means of government, to keep the lower classes within bounds.'[3] Engels supports this claim in the introduction he wrote in 1892 to the first English edition of *Socialism: Utopian and Scientific*. He declares that in England, unlike the Continent, the rise of materialism was associated with the aristocracy, not the bourgeoisie, who remained faithful to the Protestant creeds they had defended against kings and lords. The experience of first the Reign of Terror in France and later the continental revolutions of 1848 convinced the bourgeoisie of the dangers which resulted where the lower orders lost the religious instincts of submission.

If the British bourgeois had been convinced before of the necessity of maintaining the common people in a religious mood, how much more must he feel that necessity after these experiences? Regardless of the sneers of his Continental compeers, he continued to spend thousands and tens of thousands, year after year, upon the evangelization of the lower orders; not content with his own native religious machinery, he appealed to Brother Jonathan, the greatest organizer in existence of religion as a trade, and imported from America revivalism, Moody and Sankey, and the like; and finally he accepted the dangerous aid of the Salvation Army, which revives the propaganda of early Christianity, appeals to the poor as the elect, fights capitalism in a religious way,

1. See excerpts in Feuer, op. cit., pp. 452–75.
2. A short easily accessible criticism of the alleged connection between the Reformation and the rise of the bourgeoisie is to be found in G. R. Elton, *Reformation Europe 1517–1559*, Ch. X, 'Society', pp. 305–18.
3. Feuer, op. cit., pp. 280–81.

and thus fosters an element of early Christian class antagonism, which one day may become troublesome to the well-to-do people who now find the ready money for it.[1]

Marx and Engels insist that what is important about their own doctrine of socialism is that it is secured on a firm foundation of economic fact. It does not represent a moral protest against capitalism but a demonstration that capitalism is a doomed system. Engels makes this point very firmly in *Anti-Dühring* when he writes

> If for the imminent overthrow of the present mode of distribution of the products of labour, with its crying contrasts of want and luxury, starvation and debauchery, we had no better guarantee than the consciousness that this mode of distribution is unjust, and that justice must eventually triumph, we should be in a pretty bad way, and we might have a long time to wait. The mystics of the Middle Ages who dreamed of the coming millennium were already conscious of the injustice of class contradictions.

The guarantee lies in the fact that

> modern large-scale industry has called into being on the one hand a proletariat, a class which for the first time in history can demand the abolition, not of one particular class organization or another or of one particular class privilege or another, but of classes themselves, and which is in such a position that it must carry through this demand on pain of sinking to the level of the Chinese coolie; while this same large-scale industry has on the other hand brought into being, in the bourgeoisie, a class which has the monopoly of all the instruments of production and means of subsistence, but which in each boom period and in each crash that follows on its heels proves that it has become incapable of any longer controlling the productive forces, which have grown beyond its power . . . [so that] if the whole of modern society is not to perish, a revolution of the mode of production and distribution must take place, a revolution which will put an end to all class divisions. On this tangible, material fact which is impressing itself in a more or less clear form, but with invincible necessity, on the minds of the exploited proletarians . . . modern socialism's confidence of victory is founded (pp. 175–7).

1. F. Engels, introduction to the English edition of *Socialism: Utopian and Scientific*, 1892, reprinted in *K. Marx and F. Engels: On Religion*, Moscow, 1955, pp. 308–9. *Socialism: Utopian and Scientific* consists of three chapters from *Anti-Dühring*. The term 'Brother Jonathan' is an earlier version of 'Uncle Sam'. The reference to the Salvation Army fighting capitalism 'in a religious way' conflicts with what Engels had written in *Ludwig Feuerbach* (see above).

What has to be noted about this formulation is that it projects not the inevitability of the victory of socialism but the inevitable collapse of capitalism. The alternative to socialism is the reversion to a Hobbesian-style state of nature. Those who accept this analysis have the choice between seeking to delay the break-up of capitalism by propping up its institutions and ideas and undermining the spread of socialist doctrine and working-class organization among the proletariat or of allying themselves with that class. This is the moral choice which the Marxist doctrine presents, but it is not an open choice. Marx and Engels could not, even if they had so wished, provide a morally neutral picture of capitalist society; their works portray a sympathy with and devotion to the cause of the working class which has little to do with that class's assumed ultimate triumph. Marx's major work *Das Kapital* is an indictment rather than an academic treatise – 'capital' he declaims, 'comes into the world soiled with mire from top to toe, and oozing blood from every pore'.[1] A moral stand against capitalism was not a sufficient condition for being a socialist, but it was a necessary one.

READING

K. Marx, *On the Jewish Question*, L. D. Easton and K. H. Guddat, op. cit., pp. 216–48.

F. Engels, *Ludwig Feuerbach and the End of Classical German Philosophy*, Part III, Feuer, op. cit., pp. 257–64.

F. Engels, *The Peasant War in Germany*, excerpt in Feuer, op. cit., pp. 452–75.

J. Plamenatz, *Man and Society*, Vol. II, Ch. 5, section III, 'What did Marx and Engels Mean by Ideology?', pp. 323–50.

1. K. Marx, *Capital*, translated by Eden and Cedar Paul, Everyman's Library edition, 1933, p. 843. This comprises *Das Kapital*, Volume I, first published in German in 1867.

CHAPTER 3

Law and Political Obligation

1. HOBBES

Hobbes derives his notion of the state of nature not from historical fact, but from the consequences which would flow from leaving men to their natural devices and passions. It is a construction which for Hobbes is necessary, not hypothetical, in the sense that if man has the characteristics which Hobbes ascribes to him, the absence or breakdown of civil authority must lead to the 'state of warre'. It is self-evident, therefore, granted Hobbes's basic terms, that men must live in ordered society if they are to live as men and not as raging beasts. But Hobbes's construction provided a basis not simply for asserting that men need to live under a civil power but what form that power should take: power 'as may be able to defend them from the invasion of Forraigners, and the injuries of one another, and thereby to secure them in such sort, as that by their owne industrie, and by the fruites of the Earth, they may nourish themselves and live contentedly' (p. 89). Hobbes argues that because of men's warring passions the only way to erect such a Common Power is

> to conferre all their power and strength upon One Man, or upon one Assembly of men, that may reduce all their Wills by plurality of voices, unto one Will – and every one to owne, and acknowledge himselfe to be Author of whatsoever he that so beareth their Person, shall Act, or cause to be Acted, in those things which concerne the Common Peace and Safetie; and therein to submit their Wills, every one to his Will, and their Judgements, to his Judgement (p. 89).

Such a state might be instituted in only one of two ways, consent or force, and Hobbes sets out to show that in both cases the institution necessarily gives rise to rights and duties which men are obliged to accept.

Hobbes first proceeds to discuss how an effective Commonwealth might be instituted by consent and lays down strict rules both as to the making of the contract and to its contents. The fundamental rules to be followed are: (i) the contract is not revocable, (ii) the sovereign is not a party to the contract and therefore cannot be arraigned for breach of its terms (though if he fails, or is unable to act as a sovereign the contract lapses), (iii) all who become members of the community established are bound by the terms of establishment whether or not they actually assent to these terms. Hobbes sees that unless such rules are adhered to (or unless men act as though they apply) no contract of the kind required can possibly be made. The terms of the contract are contained in the requirement that the sovereign is 'to be Judge both of the meanes of Peace and Defence; and also of the hindrances and disturbances of the same; and to do whatsoever he shall think necessary to be done – for the preserving of Peace and Security' (pp. 92–3). Thus the sovereign is to be the source of all rules and laws, the judge of all disputes, the censor of opinions, the commander of the armed forces, the appointer of all officials, the fountain of all rewards, honours and punishments. These powers Hobbes writes of as the 'rights' of the sovereign. Hobbes defines a right as 'liberty to do or to forbeare', without interference (p. 66), so that in this sense the rights of the sovereign stem from the unqualified power which has been conferred upon him.

But the sovereign not only has the power to ensure that men do what they have contracted to do, he also has a legitimate claim to their observance of the terms of the covenant renouncing all their rights: save those which from their nature are irrenounceable, such as the right to defend oneself from attack. Hobbes writes:

> And when a man hath in either manner abandoned, or granted away his Right; then is he said to be OBLIGED, or BOUND, not to hinder those, to whom such Right is granted or abandoned, from the benefit of it; and that he OUGHT and it his DUTY, not to make voyd that voluntary act of his own: and that such hindrance is INJUSTICE and INJURY (pp. 67–8).

The concept of obligation which Hobbes introduces here does not depend on the power of the sovereign, for force alone can never create duties; it stems from the third law of nature which requires men to keep their covenants; because the maintenance of society depends on the keeping of covenants and self-preservation is realizable only within society. Men thus have an obligation to obey the sovereign in all that he requires of them because under an instituted Commonwealth they have promised to so obey him.

But once a society has been instituted the keeping of covenants seems to become an obligation in its own right, as Warrender suggests, which I am required to give effect to, even if it does not seem to be to my advantage to do so – though Hobbes, as we have seen, attempts to argue that my real advantage (as understood by reason) as distinct from my apparent advantage, as presented by my passions, will show that the keeping of covenants is always to my advantage. In any case Hobbes strongly insists that a man is required to obey his sovereign in all things because he has authorized him to act for him in all things; except such as are contrary to the purposes of the authorization, i.e. the preservation of the life of each person. Indeed Hobbes goes so far as to argue that because 'he that doth any thing by authority from another, doth therein no injury to him by whose authority he acteth'. The acts of an instituted sovereign can be no injury to any of his Subjects; nor ought he to be by any of them accused of Injustice' (p. 92), for he has been authorized to do whatever he thinks necessary for the well-being of the Commonwealth.

Hobbes then proceeds to deal with Commonwealths established by acquisition. 'And this kind of Dominion, or Soveraignty differeth from Soveraignty by Institution, onely in this, That men who choose their Soveraign, do it for fear of one another, and not of him whom they Institute: But in this case, they subject themselves, to him they are afraid of. In both cases they do it for fear' (p. 104). Submission to a man 'who hath their lives and liberty in his power' amounts to authorization of his actions in just the same way as does conferment of power and rights under instituted sovereignty. The rights and consequences of sovereignty are thus the same in both cases. There is to our eyes something logically odd in equating both free and forced choices as binding authorizations for the acceptance of the decisions of a ruler; but what we have to remember is that, in terms of the hypothetical cases under discussion, there *is* little difference between the alternatives and consequences in each case. The alternative to submission is death, to institution the dreadful 'state of warre'. The instituted and acquired Commonwealth must take exactly the same form if they are to fulfil their role of saving men from themselves and from foreigners. The distinction is one of the origin not of the form of government. Hobbes simply discusses the two ways in which an authoritarian régime with all-embracing powers may be set up. As we have seen in our own time it makes little difference in practice whether men choose to be ruled by a tyrant (as in Hitler's Germany) or whether they have a tyrant forced upon them (as in Stalin's Russia). This is not to suggest that the Hobbesian model state is tyrannical in the sense of being governed in an arbitrary fashion, still less that it is totalitarian.

The essentially constitutional nature of the Hobbesian state is seen in the requirement that the commands of the sovereign must be embodied in civil laws, for it is, he says, of the essence of civil laws 'to be made known, to every man that shall be obliged to obey them, either by word, or writing, or some other act, known to proceed from the Soveraign Authority' (p. 144). Thus for Hobbes a Commonwealth cannot exhibit those characteristics of arbitrary tyranny seen in totalitarian states and in despotisms where the private decrees or whims of the rulers take precedence over declared law. It is true that Hobbes says that the sovereign himself is not subject to the civil law, but this seems to be simply the logical consequence of his position as sovereign. 'For having power to make, and repeale Lawes, he may when he pleaseth, free himselfe from that subjection, by repealing those Lawes that trouble him, and making of new; and consequently he was free before. For he is free, that can be free when he will' (p. 141). There seems no suggestion that the ruler would be entitled to break the laws which he had not repealed or amended, but simply an assertion that he is not bound by the laws because he can repeal or amend if he wills. Again, although custom has no force against the civil law, which can be abolished or interpreted at will by the sovereign, Hobbes argues that his silence gives custom a binding authority. The sovereign's laws in Hobbes' model commonwealth[1] have the fundamental characteristics which distinguish law from arbitrary commands. In particular Hobbes makes the interpretation of the civil law by judges subject to the natural law principle of equity, which requires '*if a man be trusted to judge between man and man – that he deale Equally between them*. For without that, the Controversies of men cannot be determined but by Warre' (11th Law of Nature, p. 80). Hobbes states that no judge may punish the innocent, or give sentence without hearing the evidence and goes so far as to assert that neither a judge appointed by the sovereign, nor the sovereign himself, can make laws that conflict with the principle of equity.

> For though a wrong Sentence given by authority of the Soveraign, if he know and allow it, in such Lawes as are mutable, be a constitution of a new Law – yet in Lawes immutable, such as are the Lawes of

---

1. Model both in the sense of an artificial construction and in the sense of being the best possible state for men as they are; though not an ideal state.

Nature, they are no Lawes to the same. . . . Princes succeed one another; and one Judge passeth, another commeth; nay Heaven and Earth shall passe; but not one tittle of the Law of Nature shall passe; for it is the Eternal Law of God. Therefore all the Sentences of precedent Judges that have ever been, cannot all together make a Law contrary to naturall Equity (p. 147).

He follows this up with the assertion that 'whatsoever is not against the Law of Nature, may be made Law in the name of them that have the Soveraign power' (p. 153).

These expressions give support to the view that here Hobbes is using the notions of natural law in the traditional sense as the standard which determines whether a civil law has the qualities entitling it to be regarded as true and binding law.[1] But the impression is misleading for Hobbes is at pains to stress that because men are blinded by self-love and passion natural law 'is now become of all Laws the most obscure; and has consequently the greatest need of able interpreters' (p. 146). The 'interpretation' is provided at two levels. The primary is by the incorporation of the natural law in the civil law and the secondary by the application of the civil law by judges to particular cases in accordance with the principles of natural equity. Hobbes's formulation of the relationships of natural to civil law is as follows: 'The Law of Nature, and the Civill Law, contain each other, and are of equall extent. For the Lawes of Nature . . . are not properly Lawes, but qualities that dispose men to peace and to obedience. When a Commonwealth is once settled, then are they actually Lawes and not before.'

> The Law of Nature therefore is a part of the Civill Law in all Commonwealths of the world. Reciprocally also, the Civill Law is a part of the Dictates of Nature. For Justice, that is to say, Performance of Covenant, – is a Dictate of the Law of Nature. But every subject in a Common-wealth, hath covenanted to obey the Civill Law (either one with another, as when they assemble to make a common Representative, or with the Representative it selfe one by one, when subdued by the Sword they promise obedience, that they may receive life;) And therefore Obedience to the Civill Law is part also of the Law of Nature. Civill and Naturall Law are not different kinds, but different parts of Law (pp. 141–2).

The effect of these passages, viewed in the context of the whole of *Leviathan*, seems to be that obedience to the civil law is necessitated by the

---

1. See Aquinas, *Selected Political Writings*, pp. 137 and 139 for the traditional treatment of the concept of an unjust law which 'cannot be called a law'.

natural law requirement to keep covenants made; that the civil law must be treated as though it were in accordance with the natural law[1] and interpreted by judges and officials in accordance with the principle of equity; that while a sovereign has authority from the covenant to make any law that he wills, a law may in practice conflict with the natural law. Such a law would be objectively a bad law in that it was contrary to the interests of the Commonwealth, but the sovereign would be accountable to God alone for his failure to carry out the proper duties of his office, 'namely the procuration of *the safety of the people*' (p. 178).

But while a sovereign may not be challenged or disobeyed he may be advised and Hobbes gives his own advice in Chapter XXX. A ruler who wishes to establish a sound commonwealth or avoid a relapse into disorder, should maintain entire all the rights of sovereignty and cause his subjects to be regularly instructed as to the nature and grounds of these rights. A wise sovereign will have regard to the needs of his people. He will administer justice equally between his subjects, provide for those unable to maintain themselves, punish and reward according to deserts and the public interest, and choose good councillors. A sovereign who ignores such advice and seeks to rule in his own interest alone will undermine his office, 'For the good of the Soveraign and People, cannot be separated' (p. 185).

It is important to stress once more that what Hobbes claims to provide us with in *Leviathan* is not a description of how states behave or a picture of an ideal state but a scientific doctrine 'concerning the Constitution, Nature and Right of Soveraigns, and concerning the Duty of Subjects, derived from the Principles of Naturall Reason' (p. 197). For this reason one must be chary of assuming that any particular axiom or conclusion considered by itself is one which Hobbes would argue was applicable and relevant to any state. What he does claim is that experience shows the need for the general application of the basic principles of sovereignty which he has deduced. Consequently he retains the hope 'that one time or other, this writing of mine, may fall into the hands of a Soveraign, who will consider it himselfe . . . and by the

---

1. Hobbes lists as the first of his diseases of the Commonwealth '*that every private man is Judge of Good and Evill actions*', whereas except where the law is silent 'it is manifest, that the measure of Good and Evill actions, is the Civill Law' (p. 172).

exercise of entire Soveraignty, in protecting the Publique teaching of it, convert this Truth of Speculation into the Utility of Practice' (p. 197).

Hobbes, *Leviathan*, Chs. XXVI and XXX.

2. LOCKE

In the *Two Treatises of Government* John Locke demolishes one theory of political obligation based on divine right to replace it by one of his own based on consent. Although the conception that rulers draw their authority from God was a traditional tenet of Christian teaching, it had never been accepted as constituting 'the right divine of kings to govern wrong'. Divine right theory turned kings into absolute monarchs, subject to none of the checks of customary rights and traditional procedures to which medieval rulers had been held subject. The acceptance of such a theory would, in Locke's view, reduce men to the level of slaves and encourage kings to become tyrants. The undermining of the influence of such a doctrine among the small politically active group of English gentry was particularly necessary in the crucial decade 1679–89, if the twin fields of religious and political life were to be protected from first the threat and then the reality of a dedicated proselytizing Catholic king.

Sir Robert Filmer's version of the divine right theory derived the authority of rulers from Adam, who received from God dominion over the whole world. In the *First Treatise* John Locke meets Filmer on his own ground and seeks to show by reference to biblical texts that there are no grounds for the claims which Sir Robert makes. Locke's conclusions are:

1. That *Adam* had not either by natural Right of Fatherhood or by positive Donation from God, any such Authority over his Children, or Dominion over the World as is pretended.
2. That if he had, his Heirs, yet, had no Right to it.
3. That if his Heirs had, there being no Law of Nature nor positive Law of God that determines, which is the Right Heir in all Cases that may arise, the Right of Succession, and consequently of bearing Rule, could not have been certainly determined.

4. That if even that had been determined, yet the knowledge of which is the Eldest Line of *Adam's* Posterity, being so long since utterly lost, that in the Races of Mankind and Families of the World, there remains not to one above another, the least pretence to be the Eldest House, and to have the Right of Inheritance (*Second Treatise*, s. 1).

But having shown to his own satisfaction that no case can be made in scriptural or logical terms for unqualified submission and allegiance to existing rulers as successors to the sovereign title of Adam, Locke needs to demonstrate on what grounds and under what conditions submission to authority is required, and how one is to distinguish rightful authority from mere possession. Locke heatedly repudiates Filmer's assertion (which incidently cuts across Filmer's own argument of the divine source of authority) that *'it skills not which way Kings come by their Power, whether by Election, Donation, Succession, or by any other means; for it is still the Manner of the Government by Supreme Power; that makes them properly Kings, and not the Means of obtaining their Crowns'* (quoted by Locke, I, s. 78). Locke takes it as axiomatic that men need to live under and submit to a government, but not to any government for 'a Man can never be oblig'd in Conscience to submit to any Power, unless he can be satisfied who is the Person, who has a Right to Exercise that Power over him' (I, s. 81). Though this seems to make political obedience a matter of personal conviction and decision, it is clear from the discussion that Locke is not here arguing that a man is entitled to disobey any law or command which he does not believe is right. Further Locke does not hold that a man ought only to obey, or can only justifiably be required to obey, a ruler whom he personally is convinced has a right to command him; but only that the absence of such conviction robs the ruler of moral authority as far as that individual is concerned. He may be required to obey in the general interest or he may himself conform without personal conviction out of regard for the convictions or interests of others.

The theory of political obligation outlined in the *Second Treatise* is centred on the notion of consent, which is itself anchored in the natural law precept that men must keep their promises (II, s. 14). He uses it to explain how the hypothetical natural man of his creation might become the citizen of a Commonwealth.

Men being, as has been said, by Nature, all free, equal, and independent, no one can be put out of this Estate, and subjected to the Political Power of another, without his own *Consent*. The only way whereby any one devests himself of his Natural Liberty, and *puts on the bonds of Civil Society* is by agreeing with other Men to joyn and unite into a

Community, for their comfortable, safe, and peaceable living one amongst another (II, s. 95).

It can be seen that if one presents the issue, as one of rational free and equal men deliberating together about the disadvantages of their natural condition, then consent or force are the only possible alternative methods by which a political community might be established. Since force by itself cannot establish obligation, the only way in which men can create a society which they are all under an obligation to obey is by consent. The conception of 'creating' a political community necessarily involves the notion of consent. Participation in the decision to create *is* an act of consent which morally binds those who make it to adhere to it. Locke recognized of course that most men live in societies which already exist and whose origin is far from clear. This did not, however, make any essential difference to his argument. While he accepts, for example, that the paternalists may well be right in their claim that civil society developed out of the family he insists that the Father in such cases held authority 'not by any *Paternal Right*, but only by the Consent of his Children' (II, s. 74). When Locke writes '*the beginning of Politick Society* depends upon the consent of the Individuals to joyn, into and make one Society' (II, s. 106), he is not insisting that all governments were formed in this way, but simply that this is the only legitimate basis on which they may be founded. We could if we wished, although Locke himself does not do so, ask of any existing form of political society or government 'is this the sort of government or society which free and equal and rational men could conceivably have created of their own free will' and if the answer is 'No' then one might conclude that it fails to meet Locke's consent test of legitimacy.

Locke himself however argues along a different line. He denies both the Filmer thesis that men are born subjects of a prince and '*therefore under the perpetual tye of Subjection and Allegiance*' (II, s. 114) and the Hobbesian claim that an original act of compact binds succeeding generations to submission, for a man '*cannot* by any *Compact* whatsoever, bind *his Children* or Posterity' (II, s. 116). A child is under his father's authority until he comes of age, 'then he is a Free-man, at liberty what Government he will put himself under; what Body Politick he will unite himself to' (II, s. 118). On the other hand a man cannot be left to determine for himself whether he accepts the authority of the government at any time or not. Locke seeks to avoid the twin dangers of tyranny and anarchy by use of the notion of consent. Everyone, he argues, accepts that 'an *express Consent*, of any Man, entring into any Society, makes him a perfect Member of that Society, a Subject of that Government' (II, p. 119). Such a member is subject to the authority and laws of the Society both with regard to his person and his property. Consequently it follows, Locke insists, that anyone else, not being a person who has given express consent, also becomes subject to the authority of the government if 'by inheritance, Purchase, Permission or otherways' he comes to enjoy the property of a member (II, s. 120). The conditions controlling the use of members' possessions are attached to those possessions and are necessarily transferred along with them to any new owner. Such an owner is said by Locke to have given his *tacit consent* to the government as soon as he legitimately comes into possession of the property of one who has *expressly* consented. By extension, whoever enjoys what is available to those who have become members of the community by *express consent* are held to have *tacitly* consented to be subject to the same conditions which bind the members concerned.

> Every Man, that hath any Possession, or Enjoyment, of any part of the Dominions of any Government, doth thereby give his *tacit Consent*, and is as far obliged to Obedience to the Laws of that Government, during such Enjoyment, as any one under it; whether this his Possession be of Land, to him and his Heirs for ever, or a Lodging only for a Week; or whether it be barely travelling freely on the Highway; and in Effect it reaches as far as the very being of any one within the Territories of that Government (II, s. 119).

In consequence the only difference in the position of members of a community and other persons in the community is that the former, having expressly consented, are bound to that community for life while the latter, because their consent is only tacit arising out of the enjoyment of what members enjoy, may quit the community at any time they wish.

> *The Obligation* any one is under, by Virtue of such Enjoyment, *to submit to the Government, begins and ends with the Enjoyment*; so that whenever the Owner, who has given nothing but such *tacit Consent* to the Government, will, by Donation, Sale, or otherwise, quit the said Possession, he is at liberty to go and incorporate himself into any other Commonwealth, or to agree with others to begin a new one, in *vacuis locis*, in any part of the World, they can find free and unpossessed: Whereas he, that has once, by actual Agreement, and any *express* Declaration, given his *Consent* to be of any Commonweal, is perpetually and indispensably obliged to be and remain unalterably a Subject to it, and can never be again in the liberty of the state of Nature; unless by any Calamity, the Government, he was under, comes to be dissolved;

or else by some publick Act cuts him off from being any longer a
Member of it (II, s. 121).

What Locke has done is to use the familiar notion that express consent or compact to enter civil society creates an obligation to obey its
rules, to substantiate the proposition that the same obligation applies to
all who come to reside therein. Unfortunately it is far from clear what
Locke means by express consent and it is important to Locke's theory
that it should be possible to establish this. Firstly, although all inhabitants have the same obligation to obey the government, those who have
given express consent do not possess the right to dispose of their possessions and quit the community and are forced to continue living there,
no matter how distasteful or oppressive the régime has become. On
the other hand, and this is the second point, it would appear that only
those who have expressly consented are members of the community
and therefore eligible to exercise political rights under the constitution
or, in exceptional and extreme circumstances, to take action against
despotic rule. Thirdly it is only on the basis of established express
consent that one can deduce the tacit consent obligations of the remaining members of the community. Fourthly the existence of express
consent is regarded by Locke as a necessary, though not sufficient, condition of legitimate rule.

The brief references which Locke makes to explicit consent are vague
and inconsistent. On the one hand he states quite categorically that
nothing can make a man a subject or member of a commonwealth 'but
his actually entering into it by positive Engagement, and express Promise
and Compact' (II, s. 122), which would restrict membership to those
who had sworn allegiance in some form or other. On the other hand
he argues that the inheritance of land from parents itself involves
'voluntary Submission' to the government of their father's country,
'there being always annexed to the Enjoyment of Land, a Submission
to the Government of that Country, of which that Land is a part' (II,
s. 73). It is this voluntary Submission, 'being given separately in their
turns, as each comes of age' (II, s. 117), which makes sons members of
the same community as their fathers, a submission which may be evaded
only by renouncing the inheritance and emigrating. It is difficult to
determine what Locke meant in these passages. If one looks at the problem in terms of seventeenth century England, specific acts of submission
on reaching adulthood were not required either by those who stood to
inherit or those who inherited their father's land. On the other hand

oaths of allegiance were required from all those wishing to hold any public office and might be required of anyone else. If one takes the narrow position that only those were members of the community who specifically made 'positive Engagement, and express Promise and Compact' (II, s. 122), then membership of the English Commonwealth in 1689 would have been restricted to the small group of professed Anglicans holding public office.[1] If one adds to this category all those adults who stand to benefit from the inheritance of their parents' land (a loose reading of II, ss. 73 and 117), one widens the category of membership at the expense of undermining the notion of express consent; while still excluding the 'lower orders' (servants, labourers, apprentices, vagrants, etc.) who become lumped in the same civic category as resident friendly aliens.[2] But in terms of English law as it stood then and stands now all those born in England were English subjects and owed allegiance to the person of the sovereign. Locke's notion of express consent can only be made to accord with the legal position (a position which was customarily understood and accepted) if one interprets it as the negative conditional consent which all those who might be required to take an oath of allegiance are regarded as having given if they had not taken the opportunity to quit the community on reaching adulthood. This weak diluted form of explicit consent is, however, sufficient for Locke's purposes, and enables one to establish the four points mentioned above; although at the expense of making the right to emigrate the sole basis of the distinction in terms of consent between legitimate and illegitimate rule.[3]

Although the act of express consent binds a man to be the permanent subject of the Commonwealth in which he lives, the burden of this bond is less onerous than might at first appear, because Locke's conception of

1. Forty-shilling freeholders in the counties might, as electors, also have been covered since such electors were primarily jurors at the country courts, in which capacity they would have been required to swear a judicial oath embracing allegiance.
2. It is possible, though rather unlikely, that Locke read the requirement embodied in English law at the time that no aliens were eligible to own land in England, as meaning that only those who owned land, or were in line of inheritance to it, were subjects of the sovereign. It was possible for the king to accord an alien the status of denison which would give him and his heirs the right to own land. (W. S. Holdsworth, *History of English Law*, Vol. IX, pp. 76–7, 1926).
3. A stimulating discussion of the problem is to be found in Ch. 10, 'The Creation of the Legitimate Polity', of John Dunn's *The Political Thought of John Locke*, 1969.

obligation for all subjects is conditional not absolute. Locke excludes absolute monarchy altogether from his category of civil societies entitled to obedience, for arbitrary power is not only inconsistent with the ends of Society and Government but with the laws of nature themselves. Consequently consent, whether express or tacit, cannot legitimize it. 'For a man, not having the Power of his own Life, *cannot*, by Compact, or his own Consent, *enslave himself* to any one, nor put himself under the Absolute, Arbitrary Power of another' (II, s. 23). By absolute arbitrary rule Locke meant rule without settled standing laws by one who combined in his person all the powers of the legislative, executive and judicial arms of government (II, ss. 91 and 137. It follows that men are justified in taking such steps as are necessary to preserve themselves from or rid themselves of absolute arbitrary rule (II. s. 149). Indeed it might be argued that since Locke insists that men have no right to give such power over themselves to another (since they are themselves bound by the law of nature to preserve themselves) they have not merely a right but a duty to resist or overthrow absolute arbitrary rule. 'Men can never be secure from Tyranny, if there be no means to escape it, till they are perfectly under it: And therefore it is, that they have not only a Right to get out of it, but to prevent it' (II, s. 220).

In developing his case for resistance to tyranny Locke repudiates Hobbes's thesis that disobedience and revolt threaten a return to the state of nature and stresses the distinction between the *Dissolution of the Society* and the *Dissolution of the Government*. Locke clearly sees that it is the form of government under which men are to live not the existence of political society, which is at stake in a rebellion. Almost the only way in which the latter may be dissolved is from without by conquest. Conquest itself, Locke insists, can create no right of dominion, unless the conqueror's adversary was himself the original aggressor. But even in these circumstances the conqueror has an absolute claim to obedience only from those who 'actually assisted, concurr'd, or consented to that unjust force' (II, s. 179). This claim does not extend to their descendants or those forced to submit and promise allegiance to the conqueror.

> For the first *Conqueror never having had a Title to the Land* of that Country, the People who are Descendants of, or claim under those, who were forced to submit to the Yoke of a Government by constraint, have always a Right to shake it off, and free themselves from the Usurpation, or Tyranny, which the Sword hath brought in upon them, till their Rulers put them under such a Frame of Government, as they willingly, and of choice consent to (II, s. 192).

What applies in the case of foreign conquerors is also applicable, in Locke's view, to usurpers and tyrants. Usurpation is an unlawful change in the person of the ruler, tyranny is the exercise of political power beyond the bounds permitted by the law and the constitution for the personal advantage of the tyrant; consequently whereas the rule of a usurper may be legitimized by freely given consent, tyranny is the misuse of power by either a lawful or an unlawful ruler and as such can never be legitimized.

Locke is careful to make clear the point that it is only when and where a prince has exceeded his authority that he may be rightfully resisted. A man is not entitled to 'appeal to Heaven' against his ruler (i.e. oppose him with force) simply because he is aggrieved at not having been rightly dealt with – this would 'unhinge and overturn all Polities, and instead of Government and Order, leave nothing but Anarchy and Confusion' (II, s. 203). An appeal to Heaven is never justified as long as there remains an appeal to law through independent and unbiased courts. Though all men have the right of resistance to manifest acts of tyranny, the exercise of this right will not, Locke argues, threaten the existence of the government unless

> these illegal acts have extended to the Majority of the People; or if the Mischief and Oppression has light only on some few, but in such Cases, as the Precedent, and Consequences seem to threaten all, and they are perswaded in their Consciences, that their Laws, and with them their Estates, Liberties, and Lives are in danger, and perhaps their Religion too (II, s. 209).

In Locke's view a man is absolved from the obligation of obedience to any authority in the state which fails to act in accordance with the purposes and powers for which it was created.

If any arm of government exceeds its authority, or invades the basic natural rights and liberties of its citizens or fails to carry out effectively its responsibilities, then for Locke the whole structure of government is dissolved and power reverts to the people 'For all *Power given with trust* for the attaining an *end*, being limited by that end, whenever that *end* is manifestly neglected, or opposed, the *trust* must necessarily be *forfeited*, and the Power devolve into the hands of those that gave it, who may place it anew where they shall think best for their safety and security' (II, s. 149). It is clear from this that when Locke says in the same section that 'this Power of the People can never take place till the Government be dissolved', he is referring both to acts which directly dissolve the government (e.g. the delivery of the country into the hands of a

foreign prince, II, s. 217, or the neglect and abandonment of duties
such that the laws cannot be executed, II, s. 219) and acts which indirectly dissolve it through a forfeiture of trust which absolves men from
allegiance. Locke sees the executive as the main source of oppression and
misrule in political communities and instances hindering or by-passing
the legislature, altering the electoral system or interfering with free
elections as acts which entitle the withdrawal of allegiance. He accepts,
however, that a popularly elected legislature too may forfeit its authority.
'The *Legislative acts against the Trust* reposed in them, when they endeavour to invade the Property of the Subject, and to make themselves, or any
part of the Community, Masters, or Arbitrary Disposers of the Lives,
Liberties, or Fortunes of the People' (II, s. 221). In all such cases the
responsibility for any consequent rebellion which may break out is on
the heads of those who failed in their responsibilities.

> The end of Government is the good of Mankind, and which is *best
> for Mankind*, that the People should be always expos'd to the boundless
> will of Tyranny, or that the Rulers should be sometimes liable to be
> oppos'd, when they grow exorbitant in the use of their Power, and
> imploy it for the destruction, and not the preservation of the Properties
> of their People ? (II, s. 229).

READING

John Locke, *Second Treatise of Government*, Chs. XVI–XIX.

John Plamenatz, *Man and Society*, Vol. I, Ch. 6, section iii, 'Locke's Conception
of Society and of Consent'.

M. Seliger, *The Liberal Politics of John Locke*, Ch. 9, 'Individual Consent'.

John Dunn, *The Political Thought of John Locke*, Ch. 10   'The Creation of the
Legitimate Polity'.

3. ROUSSEAU

Rousseau explains in *Émile* (p. 422) that his interest lies in 'the principles
of political law' which ought to underlie the organization of the state,
not with 'the positive laws of settled governments' which were the concern of 'the illustrious Montesquieu' in *The Spirit of the Laws*. Law

for Rousseau can never be simply the command of him who has the power to ensure compliance to his will, for 'might does not make right' and the duty of obedience is owed only to legitimate powers' (*Social Contract*, Bk. I, Ch. 3, p. 53). For Rousseau there is a fundamental incompatibility between being a full human being and being subject to the unquestioned and unlimited commands of another. The subject of a despot, no less than the master's slave, is an abject creature and such complete dependence of one man on another morally corrupts both parties. Rousseau argues that men can have no obligation to those who claim absolute authority over them, because the notion of obligation cannot exist in the complete absence of rights. A man can owe an obligation only in so far as he is free to determine whether he will meet it.

> To renounce freedom is to renounce one's humanity, one's rights as a man and equally one's duties. There is no possible *quid pro quo* for one who renounces everything; indeed such renunciation is contrary to man's very nature; for if you take away all freedom of the will, you strip a man's actions of all moral significance. Finally, any covenant which stipulated absolute dominion for one party and absolute obedience for the other would be illogical and nugatory. Is it not evident that he who is entitled to demand everything owes nothing? And does not the single fact of there being no reciprocity, no mutual obligation, nullify the act? For what right can my slave have against me? If everything he has belongs to me, his right is *my* right, and it would be nonsense to speak of my having a right *against* myself (Bk. I, Ch. 4, p. 55).

Slaves are consequently under no moral obligation to obey their masters. They have no duty of obedience though they may be forced to act as though they had.

In *The Social Contract* Rousseau argues that private citizens are not bound to obey a ruler who ceases to administer the state in accordance with the law and usurps the law-making power (Bk. III, Ch. 10, p. 133). He makes the same point in *A Discourse on Political Economy* when he insists that the social relationship between ruler and subjects precludes rulers from setting themselves above the law without forfeiture of allegiance, 'for nobody is bound by any obligation to one who claims that he is under no obligation to others' (*Political Economy*, p. 241). Rousseau follows Locke in his condemnation of absolute and arbitrary rule as contrary to nature and in the insistence that life and liberty are essential gifts of nature 'of which it is at least doubtful whether any have a right to divest themselves' (*Inequality*, p. 211). Unlike Locke, however,

Rousseau does not proclaim an unequivocal right of rebellion against arbitrary rule. Indeed he does not even go so far as to say that men have a right to disobey a tyrannical ruler; he simply asserts that men have no specific moral obligations to obey such a prince. Popular insurrections are seen by Rousseau as an inevitable consequence of the 'excessive corruption' of despotism, rather than as the rightful expression of reason in revolt. He will go no further than to admit that the deposition of a tyrant 'is as lawful an act as those by which he disposed, the day before, of the lives and liberties of his subjects' (p. 219).

Rousseau's failure to proclaim a right of rebellion in his published works might of course have been simply a consequence of the conditions under which they were written. Rousseau suffered severely from censorship – *The Social Contract* was publicly burnt in his home state of Geneva which issued an order for his arrest, and *Émile* was banned by the French authorities. It is clear, however, from his unpublished writings and his letters that Rousseau had a horror of revolution and civil wars. Though he accepts that revolutions may occasionally result in the replacement of tyranny by constitutional rule, they are, in his view, more likely to bring about the collapse of civil society altogether (*Social Contract*, Bk. II, Ch. 8). So far indeed is he from being an apostle of revolution that he calls on Émile to love and protect his native land, even though its laws and institutions serve private instead of public interests. Except under conditions of despotism a man has an obligation to carry out any duties which the state may call on him to fulfil (*Émile*, pp. 437–9).

It does not come as a surprise therefore to find Rousseau making the sentiments of patriotism and nationalism the key to his proposals for constitutional reforms in Poland and Corsica. It was precisely because the inhabitants of each of these two countries were aware and proud of their distinctiveness as a separate people that he saw hope for their future. There was no question for Rousseau of directly applying the theoretical conceptions of *The Social Contract* to these communities, but of building on the particular positive features in each from which a truly free state might ultimately be developed. Rousseau, therefore, proposed to the Poles a system of government which 'with little fundamental change in your laws, seems to me to be capable of bringing patriotism and its attendant virtues to the highest point of intensity'.[1] If Poles can come to love their country before anything else they will

1. *The Government of Poland*, in *Rousseau's Political Writings*, translated and edited by F. Watkins (1953), p. 169.

obey the laws not because of the attendant penalties, but because they 'rest on the inward assent of their will'. To mould men in this manner is the task of education which 'must give souls a national formation, and direct their opinions and tastes in such a way that they will be patriotic by inclination, by passion, by necessity' (p. 176).

Rousseau is not irrevocably committed, however, to nationalist principles, if by nationalism we mean the assertion of the unqualified right of all nation states to maintain their separate existence without recognition of any wider obligations. In *A Discourse on Political Economy*, he postulates the existence of a universal general will of all mankind – 'the great city of the world becomes the body politic, whose general will is always the law of nature, and of which the different States and peoples are individual members' (p. 237). In *Émile* he outlines a scheme of inquiry into suprastate relations and organization which may well have been partially executed in the sixteen destroyed chapters of his *Fragment on Federation*. He writes,

> We shall inquire whether too much or too little has not been accomplished in the matter of social institutions: whether individuals who are subject to law and to men, while societies preserve the independence of nature, are not exposed to the ills of both conditions without the advantages of either . . . Is it not this partial and imperfect association which gives rise to tyranny and war? – Finally we will inquire how men seek to get rid of these difficulties by means of leagues and confederations, which leave each state its own master in internal affairs, while they arm it against any unjust aggression . . . The Abbé de Saint-Pierre suggests an association of all the states of Europe to maintain perpetual peace among themselves. Is this association practicable, and supposing that it were established, would it be likely to last? (*Émile*, p. 430).[1]

Rousseau always adhered firmly to the views set out clearly in *The State of War* (c. 1755) that no state is ever justified in embarking on war to acquire territory or spoils, but only to protect its right to an independent existence.[2] The nationalism which Rousseau espouses is never aggressive.

1. Six years earlier Rousseau produced short abstracts and a criticism of two of the writings of the Abbé de Saint-Pierre. His preliminary conclusion was that although the Abbé's scheme was in the general interest, the bitter opposition of particular interests (i.e. individual rulers) would be so strong that the immediate consequences of the dreadful and violent revolution which would be required to bring it about would outweigh the long term advantages. See *Jugement sur la Paix perpétuelle*, C. E. Vaughan, op. cit., Vol. I, p. 396.
2. C. E. Vaughan, op. cit., Vol. I, pp. 291-2.

In *The Social Contract* Rousseau is not directly concerned with inculcating the spirit of national distinctiveness and superiority but with the inward sense of being members of a community. The principles which he discusses are those which are necessary for the creation of any real community of free men; though later in the book he emphasizes the importance of having regard to the particular features and qualities existing in a people in determining the nature of its constitution and laws (Bk. II, Ch. 11). The only truly free community for Rousseau is one in which 'each individual, while uniting himself with the others, obeys no one but himself, and remains as free as before' (Bk. I, Ch. 6, p. 60). This formulation is only possible on the assumption that man is a creature divided against himself, with a higher moral will which he would obey if only he were not constantly ensnared by the selfish passions of his base will. Essentially what Rousseau does is to secularize and socialize the traditional Christian presentation of the conflict in the hearts of men between God and the Devil. God appears stripped of his divine apparel as the general will, the will for the common good of the community, which resides in all men, while the Devil appears as the narrow, particular, sensual self. Just as the Christian argued in terms of Christian values, that all men were under a strict moral obligation to obey God 'whose service is perfect freedom',[1] Rousseau insisted that all men have an absolute duty to obey the dictates of the general will. In submitting himself to the general will a man obeys nobody but himself, for his own higher self is a personal embodiment of the general will. If, however, he resists the general will; if, that is, his base and sensual self prevails over his higher self, then he may be compelled to comply, 'which means nothing other than that he shall be forced to be free; for this is the condition which, by giving each citizen to the nation, secures him against all personal dependence' (*Social Contract*, Bk. I, Ch. 7, p. 64).

It is only by positing the existence in all men of a common will which is always rightful and always directed to the common good that Rousseau is able to show how men might be free in political society. If we concede or assume the existence of such a common will there still remain the problems of how that will is to express itself and how it is to be distinguished from other wills. The answer to the first problem is that since the general will resides in all it must be expressed by all – 'the general

---

1. *The Book of Common Prayer* (Church of England), second collect of the Order for Morning Prayer.

will, to be truly what it is, must be general in its purpose as well as in its nature, that is it should spring from all and apply to all' (Bk. II, Ch. 4, p. 75). The act of the whole people decreeing in the common interest for the whole people is what Rousseau terms law. In contrast Rousseau declaims in *Émile*: 'In vain do we seek freedom under the power of the laws. The laws! Where is there any law? Where is there any respect for law? Under the name of the law you have everywhere seen the rule of self-interest and human passion' (p. 437), and he informs the Poles that in Europe 'if we have laws, it is solely for the purpose of teaching us to obey our masters well, to keep our hands out of other people's pockets, and to give a great deal of money to public scoundrels'.[1] It is to law in the former sense only that Rousseau addresses his eulogy in *A Discourse on Political Economy*:

> It is to law alone that men owe justice and liberty. It is this salutary organ of the will of all which establishes, in civil right, the natural equality between men. It is the celestial voice which dictates to each citizen the precepts of public reason, and teaches him to act according to the rules of his own judgment, and not to behave inconsistently with himself. It is with this voice alone that political rulers should speak when they command; for no sooner does one man, setting aside the law, claim to subject another to his private will, than he departs from the state of civil society, and confronts him face to face in the pure state of nature, in which obedience is prescribed solely by necessity (p. 240).

The commands of any ruler only have a valid claim to obedience in so far as they express the general will and interests of the whole community.

This brings us to the second point, how is the general will to be distinguished? In one sense of course it can be distinguished by its content 'for the rulers well know that the general will is always on the side which is most favourable to the public interest, that is to say, most equitable; so that it is needful only to act justly, to be certain of following the general will' (*Political Economy*, p. 242). It can also be arrived at by considering the source from which it comes – the whole body of the community. Here, however, major difficulties arise since there can be no guarantee that the expressed will of the majority, or even conceivably of the whole body, may not represent simply the accidental coalescence of particular selfish wills. To use Bosanquet's example,[2] the citizens of

---

1. Watkins, op. cit., p. 166.
2. Bernard Bosanquet, *The Philosophical Theory of the State*, 3rd edition, 1920, p. 107.

Athens in 482 B.C. might have decided in assembly to divide up amongst themselves the proceeds from the recently discovered rich silver beds, instead of allocating them for rebuilding the fleet; in which case they would almost certainly have been defeated by the Persians in the great sea battle of Salamis in 480 B.C.

Rousseau himself makes a clear distinction between the general will and the will of all which 'studies private interest indeed and is no more than the sum of individual desires', but he assumes that under conditions of free discussion, and in the absence of parties and factions, the differences between the various particular wills will cancel each other out, leaving the general will (*Social Contract*, Bk. II, Ch. 3, p. 72). Rousseau's formulation is not very clear here and at one point he talks of the general will as the sum of the differences, which as Professor Plamenatz points out would make the general will the sum of what was particular to each individual.[1] What Rousseau seems to mean is that the will actually expressed by an individual is compounded of two elements, a general element directed to the good of the community and a particular element directed to self-interest without regard to others. When the expressed wills are added together the particular elements cancel each other out, leaving the general element supreme. On this assumption it may be possible to ascertain what is the general will on any issue simply by counting votes. Ideally voting under optimum conditions will result in unanimity, but unanimity is only required for the creation of civil society not its day to day operation. Here majority decisions suffice, but only on the presumption 'that all the characteristics of the general will are still to be found in the majority; when these cease to be there, no matter what position men adopt, there is no longer any freedom' (*Social Contract*, Bk. IV, Ch. 2, p. 154). If this happens 'the meanest interest impudently flaunts the sacred name of the public good, then the general will is silenced: everyone, animated by secret motives, ceases to speak as a citizen any more than as if the state had never existed; and the people enacts in the guise of laws iniquitous decrees which have private interests as their only end' (p. 150). Since Rousseau accepts that a partial and particular vote may be given, not only by those who deliberately seek their own selfish interests, but by those who genuinely seek the common good, but are mistaken as to where it lies (p. 153); it is impossible for anyone to know in advance how he should vote or to be certain where the general interest resides, whether in the majority or in one of a number of minorities. Consequently one cannot determine what one's obligations are. The concept of the general will is one which, as Rousseau saw, cannot be tied to the mechanical device of majority decision making, except on the doubtful assumption that the majority always expresses the general will. Even in the ideal state envisaged by Rousseau in *The Social Contract*, it is difficult to see how one could ascribe infallibility on every issue which might arise to chance combinations of different votes. Yet if one once admits the possibility that on any one issue the minority rather than the majority may represent the general will, there is not only no way of ensuring that the general will shall prevail, but no way of even knowing what it is. If such a minority were to follow the advice given in Book. IV, Chapter 2, they would admit their error and conform to the majority view, without ever realizing that in so doing they were furthering the success of wrong policies.

What *The Social Contract* provides is an approach to politics which indicates the broad features one might expect to find in a free community, one in which a citizen could identify himself with the community because he himself played an active role in running it. It was this identification through active participation which provided for Rousseau the true basis for political allegiance. It was precisely because these features were so noticeably absent in the Europe of his day that Rousseau's works had such a revolutionary impact, in spite of his own distaste for violence. The Council of Geneva was not so far wrong when it decreed on 19 June 1762 that *The Social Contract* 'tends to the subversion of all Governments'.

READING

J. J. Rousseau, *A Discourse on Political Economy*.

J. Plamenatz, *Man and Society*, Vol. I, Ch. 10: Rousseau, section III, 'The General Will', pp. 391–418.

4. BENTHAM AND MILL

Although Bentham's objective in *A Fragment on Government* (1776) was to undermine the authority of the doctrines contained in William Blackstone's celebrated *Commentaries on the Laws of England* (1765–9), in the process he developed his own conceptions of the nature of law and obligation. The main burden of his attack is directed against the failure of Blackstone, and of the tradition which he represented, to comprehend the need to distinguish between the descriptive and prescriptive use of terms in legal theory. By transferring to law as it is the qualities which it ought to possess, laws made by fallible men are given a status and dignity which they do not warrant. By clothing all *de facto* laws with the authority of *de jure* status, unnecessary and harmful enactments are protected from scrutiny and reform. 'Thus much is certain', wrote Bentham,

> that a system that is never to be censured, will never be improved: that if nothing is ever to be found fault with, nothing will ever be mended: and that a resolution to justify every thing at any rate, and to disapprove of nothing, is a resolution which, pursued in future, must stand as an effectual bar to all the *additional* happiness we can ever hope for; pursued hitherto would have robbed us of that share of happiness which we enjoy already (*A Fragment on Government*, ed. W. Harrison, op. cit. p. 10).

Laws are not sacrosanct; they need to be subjected to the same scrutiny as all other man-made institutions and for Bentham that standard is the standard of utility. Utility, that is the tendency to produce happiness, is the prescriptive principle to which to refer 'a Law or institution in judging of its title to approbation or disapprobation' (p. 26, f. 1). If this principle were applied the statute book would be rid of all those laws which either serve no useful purpose or which actually possess disutility in that they produce more harm than good.

Bentham attempts to show how a purely expositional or descriptive science of jurisprudence might be built up from fundamental conceptions about men in society; conceptions which contain no built-in or hidden prescriptive elements and which are applicable to all human societies irrespective of their particular features. 'When a number of persons (whom we may style *subjects*) are supposed to be in the *habit* of paying *obedience* to a person, or an assemblage of persons, of a known and certain description (whom we may call *governor* or *governors*) such persons alto-gether (*subjects* and *governors*) are said to be in a state of *political* SOCIETY' (p. 38). When the habit of obedience is absent but there is a habit of conversing, we have a state of natural society. Since the habit of obedience is rarely completely absent, and never perfectly and absolutely present, the state of political society is a matter of degree Within this simple framework we can build up a pattern of descriptive. concepts and relationships. The laws of a political society are com-mands expressing the will of those who govern, commands which have as their object the performance of certain actions by subjects. The performance of these actions may be styled the duties of the subject. 'That is my *duty* to do, which I am liable to be *punished*, according to law, if I do not do' (p. 107). In this descriptive legal sense of duty (which Bentham calls political duty) one cannot talk of the duties of governors, except in the sense of their duties as individuals when not acting as members of the governing body; for if they are liable to punishment as a body according to law then they are not governors, in Bentham's view; since they do not in fact possess the characteristics embodied in the concept of governing. A governing body for Bentham possesses the political *right* to make men do those things which subjects are liable to do in accordance with the commands of the governors expressed as law. The 'political' (i.e. descriptive legal) rights of the subject cannot there-fore be rights against the governors, but only rights under the law against other subjects liable to punishment for non-fulfilment of legal duties. The legal rights with which Bentham deals here are positive rights which arise from the existence of a legal duty imposed by the governing body of the community.

Bentham also recognizes, as H. L. A. Hart points out,[1] the negative sense in which a legal right exists to do anything one is not expressly forbidden to do or specifically required to do: the right to act with the protection of the law where the law is silent. The only rights which men possess are legal rights, created or recognized by law. Such crea-tion or recognition necessarily involves the imposition of corresponding duties or obligations. 'Rights and obligations, though distinct and opposite in their nature, are simultaneous in their origin, and inseparable in their existence. In the nature of things, the law cannot grant a benefit to one without imposing, at the same time, some burden upon another'

1. H. L. A. Hart, 'Bentham: Lecture on a Master Mind', *Proceedings of the British Academy*, Vol. XLVIII, 1962, p. 313.

(*Theory of Legislation*, p. 93). While Bentham accepts the existence of
moral as well as legal duties, because it is possible to identify a rather
amorphous form of moral sanction, he does not allow for corresponding
moral rights. The only sense in which one can have a right or claim is
the legal sense. In particular Bentham strikes out at the notion of natural
rights, insisting that all that men naturally possess are faculties, not
rights. 'For *rights* are established to insure the exercise of means and
faculties. The right is the *guarantee*; the faculty is the thing guaranteed'
(ibid., p. 84). The only guarantees which Bentham will accept are legal
ones, because only legal guarantees are enforceable.

That is not to say that Bentham holds that only those rights which
are accorded by the law in any community at any point in time ought
to be accorded. As a law reformer Bentham was able to point to many
existing legal rights which ought to be restricted or abolished and others
which needed to be created or extended; but this process had nothing
in common with that of the advocates of self-evident, inalienable,
absolute principles of natural rights.

> There is no reasoning with fanatics, armed with *natural rights*, which
> each one understands as he pleases, and applies as he sees fit; of which
> nothing can be yielded, nor retrenched, which are inflexible, at the
> same time that they are unintelligible; which are consecrated as
> dogmas, from which it is a crime to vary. Instead of examining laws by
> their effects, instead of judging them as good or as bad, they consider
> them in relation to these pretended natural rights; that is to say, they
> substitute for the reasoning of experience the chimeras of their own
> imaginations (ibid., p. 85).

According to the principle of utility if it can be proved that the happiness
of the community will be increased to a greater extent by the conferment of legal rights than it is reduced by the corresponding imposition
of obligations, then such rights ought to be created. Whether any claim
ought to be taken up and made the basis for creating a legal right cannot
be decided in abstract, but only from a meticulous analysis of the effects
such an enactment would have in terms of the pains and pleasures it
would occasion for those affected.

The doctrine of natural rights is in Bentham's view not simply illogical
but highly dangerous. The natural rights' advocates proclaim

> 'Those laws must be obeyed which are accordant with nature; the
> others are null in fact; and instead of obeying them, they ought to be
> resisted. The moment natural rights are attacked every good citizen
> ought to rouse up in their defence. These rights evident in themselves,
> do not need to be proved, it is sufficient to declare them. How prove

what is evident already? To doubt implies a want of sense, or a fault of intellect' (p. 85).

The dangers to society inherent in the contemporary doctrine of natural rights were also seen by Bentham as inherent in the medieval doctrine of natural law, with which indeed it was closely tied. Bentham argues that when Blackstone declared that '"if a human law commands a thing forbidden by the natural or divine law, we are bound to transgress that human law"' (pp. 85–6), he is compromising the very authority of government which it was his avowed purpose to protect. 'Is there,' retorts Bentham, 'a single state which can maintain itself a day, if each individual holds himself bound in conscience to resist the laws, whenever they are not conformed to his particular ideas of natural or Divine Law?' (p. 86). Equally untenable as a basis for determining when men might justifiably disobey the government are theories of social contract, which hold that there exists an express or tacit compact between ruler and subjects whereby the latter promise general obedience on condition that the former rule in accordance with the established laws or other agreed terms; such terms being broken the subjects are absolved from their obligation of obedience. Bentham counters by arguing that promises and covenants have no overriding claim to compliance irrespective of their content and purpose.

> Suppose the King to promise that he would govern his subjects *not* according to Law; *not* in the view to promote their happiness: – would this be binding upon *him*? Suppose the people to promise they would obey him *at all events*, let him govern as he will; let him govern to their destruction. Would this be binding upon *them*? Suppose the constant and universal effect of an observance of promises were to produce *mischief*, would it *then* be men's *duty*[1] to observe them? Would it *then* be *right* to make Laws, and apply punishments to *oblige* men to observe them? (*A Fragment on Government*, pp. 55–6).

The principle of utility alone provides the justification both for the intrinsic obligation to keep promises and obey laws and for holding some promises and laws to be invalid.

Bentham's answer to the problem of political obligation is disarmingly simple.

> It is *then*, we may say, and not till then, allowable to, if not incumbent on, every man, as well as on the score of *duty* as of *interest*, to enter

---

1. Bentham is here using the term *duty* in a moral not a legal sense, for legal duties are not affected by the content or purpose of the law but turn solely on liability to punishment for non-compliance.

into measures of resistance; when, according to the best calculations
he is able to make, *the probable mischiefs of resistance* (speaking with
respect to the community in general) *appear less to him than the probable
mischiefs of submission*. This then is to him, that is to each man in
particular, *the juncture for resistance* (p. 93).

While an individual may embark on conscious and forcible disobedience
of the law if he is personally convinced that such disobedience will cause
less harm than good to the community (e.g. by drawing public attention
to the aims and consequences of the law in question), Bentham is not
prepared to concede a right of general revolt to any group of 'malcon-
tents' who have convinced themselves that a revolution will be socially
beneficial. While it suffices for an individual act of resistance that a
person has, to the best of his abilities, weighed up the probable consequences of his action, where the act of self-conviction provides the
'juncture' or sure indication that the time has come to resist; in the case
of groups of revolutionaries Bentham would appear to require some
objective indication, some 'sign' or '*common* signal alike conspicuous
and perceptible to all' (pp. 93–4) of the 'juncture'. 'Unless such a sign
then, which I think impossible, can be shewn, the *field*, if one may say
so, of the supreme governor's authority, though not infinite, must un-
avoidably, I think, *unless where limited by express convention*,[1] be allowed
to be *indefinite*' (p. 94). The precise meaning of this passage is far from
clear. Bentham seems to be arguing that unless there exists an objective
sign to show what constitutes a 'juncture' for resistance the government
in any state will have, and will be accepted by the mass of the people as
having, unlimited authority to deal with the revolutionaries. In such
circumstances revolutionary action would not be justifiable on utilitarian
grounds because it would have little or no chance of success. If revolutionary action is doomed to failure protestations about its beneficial
results are irrelevant, and if it succeeds in spite of the bitter opposition
of government and people the results will not be beneficial.

Bentham proceeds to set out for his readers the common signal of
resistance which 'we despaired of finding' (p. 99). The argument is
again not easy to follow. Bentham points out that states exist which
do not possess the full powers of government, having submitted themselves for certain specified purposes to another body, and argues from
this that such a limitation of power may equally take place within a
state with regard to the governing body. For Bentham it is the habit

---

1. By 'convention' Bentham means a constitutional rule embodied in law or
   formal agreement between contracting parties.

and disposition to obedience which establishes the degree of political power existing in any society. Consequently the habit may be present for certain kinds or degrees of governmental acts and not for others. What we may then have is a convention or agreement defining the limits within which the government may act and expect to be obeyed. Bentham proceeds to consider what happens if the convention is flaunted.

> A certain act is in the instrument of convention specified, with respect to which the government is therein precluded from issuing a law to a certain effect: whether to the effect of commanding the act, of permitting it, or of forbidding it. A law is issued to that effect notwithstanding. The issuing then of such a law (the sense of it, and likewise the sense of that part of the convention which provides against it being supposed clear) is a fact notorious and visible to all: in the issuing then of such a law we have a fact which is *capable* of being taken for that common signal we have been speaking of. These bounds the supreme body in question has marked out to its authority: of such a demarcation then what is the effect? either none at all, or this: that the disposition to obedience confines itself within these bounds. Beyond them the disposition is stopped from extending: beyond them the subject is no more prepared to obey the governing body of his own state, than that of any other (*A Fragment on Government*, p. 99).

It appears that it is not so much the fact that a law has been issued contrary to an established convention restricting the powers of the governors, which constitutes the justification for resistance, but the expectation that such a command will not be obeyed by subjects whose habit of and disposition to obedience is expressed in terms of the convention. If no convention of limitation exists then there can be no common signal for resistance. Resistance can be considered only in those states which have established recognized limitations on the powers of government and only in defence of those limitations against encroachment. The principle of utility should be applied to determine whether to resort to resistance 'according as it should appear to them, worth their while – according to what should appear to them the importance of the matter in dispute – according to what should appear to them the probability or improbability of success – *according*, in short, *as the mischiefs of submission, should appear to bear a less, or a greater ratio to the mischief of resistance*' (pp. 101–2).

  Bentham's discussion of political obligation brings out the limitations of his concept of duty, viz. that men have a legal or moral duty to do those acts for which they are liable to incur the sanctions of legal punishment or moral punishment (popular disapproval) in the event of non-fulfilment. In this sense resistance to government can only be *'commendable;* or in other words, reconcilable to just notions' (p. 93), if it not merely meets with public approval; but if failure to resist would give rise to strong public disapproval. Not only is such a situation very unlikely to occur in any state but especially in a despotic one where public disapproval may not express itself. Bentham's conception fails because it equates duty with public approval, an equation not required by utilitarian theory. It is not the descriptive sense of moral duty tied to the sanction of popular opinion which is needed to establish the justness or commendability of acts of disobedience; but the prescriptive sense of moral duty as the obligation which men have to bring about the greatest good of all the members of the community.

When John Stuart Mill comes to discuss the connection between justice and utility in *Utilitarianism* he seeks to clarify and modify Bentham's teaching on rights and duties. Instead of defining moral duty and obligation descriptively in terms of liability to punishment, Mill defines it prescriptively in terms of deserving punishment.

> It is a part of the notion of Duty in every one of its forms, that a person may rightfully be compelled to fulfil it. Duty is a thing which may be *exacted* from a person, as one exacts a debt. Unless we think that it may be exacted from him, we do not call it his duty. Reasons of prudence, or the interest of other people, may militate against actually exacting it; but the person himself, it is clearly understood, would not be entitled to complain. There are other things, on the contrary, which we wish that people should do, which we like or admire them for doing, perhaps like or despise them for not doing, but yet admit that they are not bound to do; it is not a case of moral obligation, we do not blame them, that is, we do not think that they are proper objects of punishment.

We call any conduct wrong, 'according as we think that the person ought, or ought not, to be punished for it; and we say, it would be right to do so and so, or merely that it would be desirable or laudable, according as we would wish to see the person whom it concerns, compelled, or only persuaded and exhorted, to act in that manner' (*Utilitarianism*, p. 45). Duties themselves may be divided into duties of perfect obligation, where a 'correlative *right* resides in some person or persons' that the act should be performed for them, and duties of imperfect obligation, where 'the particular occasions of performing it are left to our choice; as in the case of charity or beneficence, which we are indeed bound to practise, but not towards any definite person, nor at any prescribed time' and where consequently no correlative right arises (p. 46).

Bentham, as we have seen, associates punishment with the purely descriptive notion of moral duty – you *will* suffer the sanction of popular disapproval in one or other of its various forms if you commit certain kinds of action: but whether such punishment is merited or not is a quite different kind of question to be decided by reference to utility as a prescriptive principle. Mill, on the other hand, used 'merited punishment' as his criterion for a purely prescriptive concept of moral duty; but it is questionable whether it can satisfactorily be applied to duties of imperfect obligation. In what sense can one say, or indeed does it make sense to say, that a person ought to be compelled to be generous or ought to be punished for not being generous? Quite apart from any practical difficulties the notions of compulsion and generosity are incompatible. The defect in Mill's approach would appear to lie, not with his choice of generosity as an example of a duty of imperfect obligation, but with his associating the idea of duty with that of exacting performance under threat of punishment.

The duties of perfect obligation are seen by Mill to coincide with the requirements of Justice. 'Justice implies something which it is not only right to do, and wrong not to do, but which some individual person can claim from us as a moral right' (p. 46). Unlike Bentham, Mill accepts that there are rights other than legal rights – claims which men have on society which may not be accorded or protected by law. These Mill terms moral rights. 'When we call anything a person's right, we mean that he has a valid claim on society to protect him in the possession of it, either by the force of law, or by that of education and opinion. If he has what we consider a sufficient claim, on whatever account, to have something guaranteed to him by society, we say that he has a right to it. If we desire to prove that anything does not belong to him by right, we think this done as soon as it is admitted that society ought not to take measures for securing it to him, but should leave him to chance, or to his own exertions' (pp. 49–50). Moral rights derive from and express the indispensable need which men have for security, on which all else in life depends. 'Our notion, therefore, of the claim we have on our fellow creatures to join in making safe for us the very groundwork of our existence, gathers feelings around it so much more intense than those concerned in any of the more common cases of utility, that the difference or degree (as is often the case in psychology) becomes a real difference in kind. The claim assumes that character of absoluteness, that apparent infinity, and incommensurability with all the considerations, which constitute the distinction between the feeling of right and wrong and that of ordinary expediency and inexpediency' (pp. 50–1). Moral rules of this kind are binding in a different and more fundamental way than mere maxims or precepts of prudence, since conformity with the former is a condition of human existence.

> Justice remains the appropriate name for certain social utilities which are vastly more important, and therefore more absolute and imperative, than any others are as a class (though not more so than others may be in particular cases); and which, therefore, ought to be, as well as naturally are, guarded by a sentiment not only different in degree, but also in kind; distinguished from the milder feeling which attaches to the mere idea of promoting human pleasure or convenience, at once by the more definite nature of its commands, and by the sterner character of its sanctions (p. 60).

According to Mill questions of right or wrong have first to be tackled by reference to the secondary principles exhibited in the specific duties and rights of justice. It is only in cases of actual conflict between specific moral rights or duties that the ultimate principle of the greatest happiness needs to be or should be appealed to.[1]

READING

J. Bentham, *A Fragment on Government*, Preface, Chs. I, IV and V.

J. S. Mill, *Utilitarianism*, Ch. V.

D. J. Manning, *The Mind of Jeremy Bentham*, Chs. IX–XIII.

5. HEGEL

The full title of Hegel's *Philosophy of Right – Natural Law and Political Science in Outline: Elements of the Philosophy of Right* – indicates both the close connection which Hegel saw between right and law, and the distinction which he made between natural law and positive law. Natural

---

1. For a brief but stimulating discussion of the relationship between ultimate and secondary principles in Mill, see *Theories of Ethics*, edited by Philippa Foot, 1967, 'The Interpretation of the Moral Philosophy of J. S. Mill' by J. O. Urmson and 'Interpretation of Mill's Utilitarianism' by J. J. D. Mabbott. (Also in *Mill: A Collection of Critical Essays*, ed. J. B. Schneewind.)

law for Hegel was not of course the natural law of the medieval school-men – the fundamental unchanging principles of human behaviour vouchsafed to all men through God's gift of reason, valid in all places and at all times. Hegel's philosophy is a philosophy of development and evolution towards an ultimate ideal, an ideal to be realized on earth not in heaven. When men attain overall self-consciousness law in the accepted sense, as the commands of an external authority, will have no place for men will fully identify themselves with a world they comprehend. But, just because positive law developed out of custom and will disappear when the absolute idea is realized, it follows that the principles of natural or rational law will vary according to the stage of development which mankind has reached. The role of the philosophy of law is to discern what is the underlying purpose of the concept of law and to determine how this purpose may best be realized or posited in the particular conditions of the time. It is not possible to do this simply by reference to the principle of consistency. 'A particular law may be shown to be wholly grounded in and consistent with the circumstances and with existing legally established institutions, and yet be wrong and irrational in its essential character' (*Philosophy of Right*, p. 17). In consequence men may be forced to be illogical and inconsistent in order to behave rationally, as did the Roman jurists and praetors who were forced to devise empty verbal distinctions and resort to foolish subter-fuges in order to evade the consequences of unjust and irrational laws.

Hegel criticizes the historical school of jurists led by Savigny, who argued that the laws and institutions of a people were justifiable simply and solely in historical terms – in so far as they satisfied the needs of the community at the time. Hegel does not of course deny the impor-tance of historical understanding for determining the justifiability of any particular laws or institutions: what he denies is that historical evidence alone provides such a justification. 'Understanding,' however, 'has nothing whatever to do with the satisfaction of the demands of reason or with philosophical science' (ibid., p. 20). The purpose served by laws and institutions is what is crucial here, not the 'mere' historical facts. Moreover Hegel points out that the logical corollary of the historical approach is that since institutions are justified in terms of the conditions which brought them about, the passing away of these conditions leaves them without justification. The laws and institutions of the past cannot for Hegel be justified today in terms of the validity of their origin. Con-sequently Hegel's fundamental approach to law has far more in common with that of Bentham than of Burke. Burke's proud enunciations of the need to preserve the values of prescription and tradition against the narrow claims of reason finds no more support in Hegel than in Bentham. Both declaim rational theories of politics, although these differ sharply in their content. Hegel, like Bentham, supports the cause of the French Revolution in its opening phase, on the very grounds which Burke uses to attack it – its denial of the validity of existing institutions. In 1817 Hegel wrote 'One must regard the start of the French Revolution as the struggle of rational constitutional law against the mass of positive law and privileges by which it had been stifled' (*Proceedings of the Estates Assembly in Wurtemberg* in *Political Writings*, p. 282). Fourteen years later he was to make essentially the same point with regard to England. 'The reason why England,' he wrote, 'is so remarkably behind the other civilized states of Europe in institutions derived from true rights is simply that there the governing power lies in the hands of those possessed of so many privileges which contradict a rational constitutional law and true legislation' (*The English Reform Bill* in ibid., p. 300).

In the *Phenomenology* Hegel makes more explicit the philosophical relationship between reason and law. The reason of the self-conscious conscientious person discloses the content of immediate ethical laws, or 'commands' as Hegel terms them. 'These laws or spheres of the substance of ethical life are directly recognized and acknowledged. We cannot ask for their origin and justification, nor is there something else to search for as their warrant' (p. 441). Examples of such 'commands' are 'every one ought to tell the truth' or 'love thy neighbour as thyself'. In themselves, however, they lack content in that they only tell us *in abstraction* how we ought to act, not how to act or even whether we are capable of acting in any particular situation. I can tell the truth only if I know what the truth is; I can love my neighbour only if I know what will bring him good. Ethical laws or commands need to be 'determined', i.e. formulated as positive laws of the state, before they can provide us with a clear guide to action. But Hegel is at pains to stress that positive laws must conform to ethical principles and that they do not acquire this simply because they proceed from some particular source.

> The law as determinate has an accidental content: this means here that it is a law made by a particular individual conscious of an arbitrary content. To legislate immediately in that way is thus tyrannical insolence and wickedness, which makes caprice into a law, and morality into obedience to such caprice – obedience to laws which are *merely* laws and not at the same time commands (p. 450).

What remains unclear, however, is *who* is to determine whether any particular law conforms to the requirements of the laws of ethics and how the determination is to be made. In the *Phenomenology* Hegel characterizes 'the spiritual reality' as implicitly existing in the shape of eternal law grounded not in the will of a given individual but 'in the pure and absolute will of all', which has immediate validity in the world. 'Since, however, this existing law is absolutely valid, the obedience given by self-consciousness is not service rendered to a master, whose orders are mere caprice and in which it does not recognize its own nature. On the contrary, the laws are thoughts of its own absolute consciousness, thoughts which are its own immediate possession' (p. 451).

Hegel distinguishes two forms which the concept of law assumes in the outside world – divine law and human law. By divine law in this context Hegel means not the law of God but the principles which underlie family life. The family for Hegel is the area of 'immediate ethical existence' for it creates a natural network of human relations which sustains all its members, but above all the female members whose roles are confined within it. The male members are forced to move into the wider social world in order to sustain and support the family and there they become subject to human law. Just as family life provides a higher and wider framework for existence than the individual can find or provide for himself in isolation, when acting in obedience to what Hegel terms 'the law of the heart'; so the community takes the individual beyond the ethical limits which the family necessarily prescribes. Human law expresses universality in that it 'is the law known to everybody, familiar and recognized, and is the everyday Customary Convention'. It is particularized in the form of laws promulgated by a Government. 'Its true and complete nature is seen in its authoritative validity openly and unmistakably manifested, an existence which takes the form of unconstrained independent objective fact, and is immediately apprehended with conscious certainty in this form' (p. 467).

Thus for Hegel positive law can only fulfil its role if it is accepted by members of the community who identify their purposes with its own. If this identification is not realized, however, it does not follow that the fault lies in the law: indeed, in Hegel's view it is much more likely to be the fault of the individual pitting his own personal interest and narrow view against that of the community, whose overriding purpose he has failed or refused to recognize.

The accepted and established laws are defended against the law of a single individual because they are not empty necessity, unconscious and dead, but are spiritual substance and universality, in which those in whom this spiritual substance is realized live as individuals, and are conscious of their own selves. Hence, even when they complain of this ordinance, as if it went contrary to their own inmost law, and maintain in opposition to it the claims of the 'heart', in point of fact they inwardly cling to it as being their essential nature; and if they are deprived of this ordinance, or put themselves out of range of its influence, they lose everything. Since, then, it is precisely in this that the reality and power of public ordinance consist, the latter appears as the essence, self-identical and everywhere alive, and individuality appears as its form (pp. 398–9).

It is the purpose of education to make men ethical, to assist them to pass from the realms of instinctive behaviour to become self-conscious crea- tures aware of their role in the community. 'The final purpose of education therefore' writes Hegel, in *Philosophy of Right*, (p. 125), 'is liberation and the struggle for a higher liberation still; education is the absolute transition from an ethical substantiality which is immediate and natural to the one which is intellectual and so both infinitely sub- jective and lofty enough to have attained universality of form. In the individual subject, this liberation is the hard struggle against pure subjectivity of demeanour, against the immediacy of desire, against the empty subjectivity of feeling and the caprice of inclination.' If the state fails to see that such an education is provided for its citizens, then it is likely to find that they fail to take the positive attitude to the com- munity's laws which is required if the laws are to fulfil their proper role, even where the content of the laws expresses the needs and purposes of the community.

Philosophy of Right, surprisingly, tells us very little about the char- acter which law as right may be expected to exhibit when it is posited as positive law. To be binding, Hegel tells us, laws must be universally known.

> To hang the laws so high that no citizen could read them (as Dionysius the Tyrant did) is injustice of one and the same kind as to bury them in row upon row of learned tomes, collections of dissenting judgments and opinions, records of customs etc., and in a dead language too, so that knowledge of the law of the land is accessible only to those who have made it their professional study (p. 138).

It is for this reason that Hegel calls for the compilation of a public legal code of simple general principles to provide the basis for adjudication on particular disputes in public courts of justice. Hegel recognizes that in a criminal case a court is unable, in the absence of a confession, to 'prove' guilt or innocence, since the basis of knowledge and truth here is simply 'a given sensuous intuition and subjective sense-certainty' on the part of those responsible for trying the case. Hegel seeks to justify the 'formal illogicality' of the process by which the truth is established in a court by pointing out that a court cannot fulfil its necessary rational role of administering justice unless it ascertains the facts. This requirement 'properly qualifies a court for this task and so gives it an exclusive inherent right to perform it and lays on it the necessity of performing it' (p. 144).

The punishment of the criminal himself is justified by Hegel in retributive terms. In so far as a criminal act is one carried out by a person who knows he is doing wrong, who knows he is deliberately pitting his will against a universal right embodied in a particular person or group, the act itself is recognized as criminal and therefore meriting punishment. The criminal has to be treated as a rational human being, who by willing an act known to be wrong has willed his own punishment, since punishment is a necessary corollary of crime. Punishment is his due and his right in the sense that, as a responsible being, his act of defiance is an act which recognizes the validity of the right infringed.

> The injury [the penalty] which falls on the criminal is not merely *implicitly* just – as just, it is *eo ipso* his implicit will, an embodiment of his freedom, his right; on the contrary it is also a right *established* within the criminal himself, i.e. in his own objectively embodied will, in his action. The reason for this is that his action is the action of a rational being and this implies that it is something universal and that by doing it the criminal has laid down a law which he has explicitly recognized in his action and under which in consequence he should be brought as under his right (p. 70).

The conceptions embodied in preventive, deterrent and reformative, theories of punishment all make the mistake of assuming that punishment as punishment is evil and therefore needs to be justified. The considerations inherent in such theories are only capable of being made use of, especially with reference to methods of punishment, if they 'presuppose as their foundation the fact that punishment is inherently and actually just' (p. 70). They are not, however, capable of dealing with the amount of punishment to be imposed, which must be decided by reference to retributive principles. This does not mean punishing the criminal with the same injury he himself inflicted, but with a punishment of comparable 'value'; a value which can be approximately ascertained if we consider both the crime and the punishment 'in respect of their universal property of being injuries' (p. 72).

The authority of the law over all members of the community, criminals and non-criminals, officials and ordinary citizens, is an expression of its sovereignty and 'depends on the fact that the particular functions and powers of the state are not self-subsistent or firmly grounded either on their own account or in the particular will of the individual functionaries, but have their roots ultimately in the unity of the state as their single self' (pp. 179–80). In contrast to feudal society where the state was an aggregate of independent Corporations and societies, the modern constitutional state is an organism exercising sovereignty over its constituent parts. These cease to be self-subsistent in their aims and modes of working, partly by 'unconscious necessity' and partly by the influence of the public authority, and they come to be dependent on and determined by the aims and purposes of the community as a whole. Individuals and social institutions alike are required to serve the general welfare of the state. 'The welfare of the state has claims to recognition totally different from those of the welfare of individuals' (p. 215). In consequence if the state feels its interests threatened it has the right to require that the rights and interests of individuals be put aside. Individuals have a duty to maintain the independence and sovereignty of the state 'at the risk and the sacrifice of property and life, as well as of opinion and everything else comprised in the compass of life' (p. 209).

Personal sacrifice to maintain the independent existence of the community is for Hegel not simply the supreme duty of every citizen but his most fundamental right and highest dignity. He categorically rejects the notion that the state simply exists to secure individual life and property: on the contrary the individual must pass to a higher plane of existence than that expressed in terms of concern for his own skin and its trappings. War has for Hegel an ethical value, for by its agency 'the ethical health of peoples is preserved in their indifference to the stabilization of finite institutions; just as the blowing of the winds preserves the sea from the foulness that would be the result of a prolonged calm, so also corruption in nations would be the product of prolonged, let alone "perpetual" peace' (p. 210). That is not to say, however, as has been suggested, that Hegel glorifies war or regards it as good in itself. War for Hegel is simply the inevitable outcome of a situation where conflicts between states as autonomous units cannot be harmoniously settled by negotiation. A state is only justified, therefore, in embarking on war if it can show that its own particular interests and welfare are at stake. Considered in the context of World History, however, Hegel claims to divine an objective justification in universal terms of the acts of war undertaken by particular states in furtherance of their particular ends.

In these terms history ceases to appear as 'the slaughter-bench at which the happiness of peoples, the wisdom of States, and the virtue of individuals have been victimized' (*Philosophy of History*, p. 22). The 'manifestations of vitality on the part of individuals and peoples, in which they seek to satisfy their own purposes, are, at the same time the means and instruments of a higher and broader purpose of which they know nothing'. With bold confidence Hegel declaims: 'Reason governs the world, and has consequently governed its history' (p. 26). Particular states and peoples are destined at different stages in world history to realize some new endeavour or purpose necessary for the advancement of mankind towards its goal, the Absolute Idea. In *Philosophy of History* Hegel speaks of the actions of such states and people as moral. In *Philosophy of Right* he goes further and declares that anything a state does to further its own objects, where these coincide with the grand purpose of realizing the Absolute Idea, is justified.

> The nation to which is ascribed a moment of the Idea in the form of a natural principle is entrusted with giving complete effect to it in the advance of the self-developing self-consciousness of the world-mind.[1] This nation is dominant in world history during this one epoch, and it is only once that it can make its hour strike. In contrast with this its absolute right of being the vehicle of this present stage in the world mind's development, the minds of other nations are without rights, and they, along with those whose hour has struck already, count no longer in world history (*Philosophy of Right*, pp. 217–18).

In conformity with this appraisal one might expect Hegel to make the furtherance of this great universal enterprise the criterion for the determination of the issue of political obligation. For surely if my state is hindering the realization of the Idea by its opposition to the nation which is its present vehicle, I ought to oppose my will to that of my own state and identify myself with the will of its adversary in order that the universal design at this stage may be achieved? Hegel draws no such conclusion. On the contrary he would almost certainly have argued that

---

1. The world-mind for Hegel is the universal manifested in the history of the world, the idea made actual at a particular period in time as a stage in the development towards its final realization as the Absolute Idea. It is not conceived as a separate physical entity, as a thinking organism or group-mind.

it can never be a man's duty to do anything which would assist his country's enemies, even if those enemies have historical right on their side. Such right could never require, or be furthered by, the acceptance of assistance from those who betray their own land and people.

As far as obedience to the laws of one's own state is concerned Hegel's position is unclear. He preaches general obedience to the state, an obedience which is subject to fewer and fewer exceptions as one moves nearer to the ideal state which fulfils in entirety the state's inherent spirit and purposes. If, however, the state completely fails to realize its purposes in the world, if its institutions have become outdated, restrictive and oppressive then Hegel sees the true Spirit of the state manifesting itself in resistance to established authority. Writing of France before 1789 Hegel declared,

> The political condition of France at that time presents nothing but a confused mass of privileges altogether contravening Thought and Reason – an utterly irrational state of things, and one with which the greatest corruption of morals, of Spirit was associated – an empire characterized by Destitution of Right, and which, when its real state begins to be recognized, becomes shameless destitution of Right. The fearfully heavy burdens that pressed upon the people . . . gave the first impulse to discontent. The new Spirit began to agitate men's minds: oppression drove men to investigation. It was perceived that the sums extorted from the people were not expended in furthering the objects of the State, but were lavished in the most unreasonable fashion. The entire political system appeared one mass of injustice. The change was necessarily violent, because the work of transformation was not undertaken by the government. . . . The conception, the idea of Right asserted its authority *all at once*, and the old framework of injustice could offer no resistance to its onslaught (*Philosophy of History*, pp. 465–6).

Thus it would appear that where the established government fails to carry out the fundamental purposes of the state and fails to carry out essential basic reconstruction of its institutions in accordance with the dictates of reason, then the people are justified in taking matters into their own hands and effecting a revolution. Yet two pages further on Hegel writes of 'the supreme obligation of individuals to subject their particular wills' to the laws and constitution of the state 'as in principle fixed and immutable' and of the need for citizens to subordinate their opinions respecting law, constitution and government to the interest of the state 'and to insist upon them no farther than that interest will allow' (p. 468). These two statements can perhaps be reconciled in the distinction which Hegel draws between the state and its organs and officials, between the idea of the state and its actuality, between the political state of governmental institutions and the state as the totality of the life of the members of the community. The difficulty lies not so much in seeing that such distinctions could in theory substantiate different and non-contradictory attitudes to the problem of political obedience, but how it could be substantiated that one applied rather than the other in any particular case.

READING

Hegel, *Philosophy of Right*, pp. 134–44 and 208–23.

Hegel, *Phenomenology of Mind*, Sections V C(b), 'Reason as Lawgiver', and V C(c), 'Reason as Test of Laws', pp. 439–53.

6. MARX AND ENGELS

The state for Marx and Engels is the product of society at a certain stage of development; characterized on the one hand by the emergence of classes with conflicting interests and on the other by the institution of a public power separated from the mass of the people but maintained by them. This power, apparently standing above society and its antagonisms, 'is without exception the state of the ruling class, and in all cases continues to be essentially a machine for holding down the oppressed, exploited class'.[1] The state does not simply perform the negative role of maintaining order, i.e. the existing order, but it positively asserts itself by the promulgation of laws. Both will and force are essential ingredients of the modern state. 'The state does not rest on a dominating will, but the State which arises out of the material mode of life of individuals has also the form of a dominating will.'[2] The dominating will of the state expresses neither the immediate will of the

1. F. Engels, *The Origin of the Family, Private Property and the State*, 1884, London, 1942, p. 201.
2. K. Marx and F. Engels, *The German Ideology* (written 1845–6), quoted in *Karl Marx: Selected Writings in Sociology and Social Philosophy*, edited by T. B. Bottomore and Maximilien Rubel, Pelican Books, 1963, p. 232.

sovereign (as with Hobbes) nor the reality of the moral idea (as with Hegel). Since law is made by individuals it will bear the marks of their will; but the general content of the law is determined by the economic situation of the class such individuals represent and this exists quite independently of the will of the individuals concerned. On the other hand law must not only embody the fundamental interests of the ruling class it must assume a universal form which can claim validity and obedience as the embodiment of right and justice. In consequence the laws of any particular state will not assume the simple form of instruments of class oppression. Engels wrote,

> In a modern state law must not only correspond to the general economic condition and be its expression, but must also be an *internally coherent* expression which does not, owing to inner contradictions, reduce itself to nought. And in order to achieve this the faithful reflection of economic conditions suffers increasingly. All the more so the more rarely it happens that a code of law is the blunt, unmitigated, unadulterated expression of the domination of a class – this in itself would offend the 'conception of right'.[1]

In a bourgeois state the laws can express only in an adulterated form the class interests of the bourgeoisie, because of the need 'to do away with the contradictions arising from the direct translation of economic relations into legal principles, and to establish a harmonious system of law' (p. 443). The influence and compulsion of further economic development creates further contradictions including those arising from the growing power of the proletariat.

The attitude of a ruling class towards the law and the constitution is ambivalent. Accepting as it does its natural right to rule and the superiority of its own form of rule, it glorifies the acts of revolution which brought it to power. At the same time the ruling class refuses to accept the right of others to take similar action to replace it. Every successful revolution is for its makers the last revolution, whose settlement should be accepted for all time. Consequently the revolutionaries of yesterday are the constitutionalists of today. Engels made this point very forcibly to Bebel, one of the leaders of the German Social Democratic Party, in 1884 following the successes of the Party at the Reichstag polls, in spite of Bismarck's Socialist Law of 1878 banning workers' organizations, publications and meetings. 'Throughout the whole of Europe,' he wrote,

1. Letter from Engels to Conrad Schmidt, 27 October, 1890, in Feuer, op. cit., pp. 442–3.

the existing political situation is the product of revolutions. The legal basis, historic right, legitimacy, have been everywhere riddled through and through a thousand times or entirely overthrown. But it is in the nature of all parties or classes which have come to power through revolution, to demand that the new basis of right created by the revolution should also be unconditionally recognized and regarded as holy. The right to revolution *did* exist – otherwise the present rulers would not be rightful – but from now onwards it is to exist no more.[1]

Engels argues that it ill-becomes those who created the German Empire by the overthrow of the German Confederation and by civil war to condemn others as revolutionaries. The parties of Germany are all parties which have either participated in revolutions or which are prepared to do so under certain conditions: the Liberals participated in the March 1848 revolution which the Conservatives helped to overthrow in November, while the Catholic Centre Party recognized the Church as the highest power above the state. 'And these,' he declared,

> are the parties which demand from us that *we, we alone of them all*, should declare that in no circumstances will we resort to force and that we will submit to every oppression, to every act of violence, not only as soon as it is merely formally legal – legal according to the judgment of our adversaries – but also when it is directly illegal. Indeed, no party has renounced the right to armed resistance, *in certain circumstances*, without lying. None has ever been able to relinquish this ultimate right (*Selected Correspondence*, p. 429).

For Marx and Engels the question of the method to be used for the realization of a socialist society was solely one of efficacy in the conditions ruling at the time. Engels wrote in 1889: 'Any means leading to the goal is suitable for me as a revolutionary – both the most violent and that which seems the most peaceful'.[2] The proletarian revolution which Marx and Engels sought was not a political overthrow of established governments in capitalist societies but the economic and social transformation of bourgeois society. The social transformation *was* the revolution – that transformation might come about in some countries by political revolution, in others by peaceful means. The need to distinguish clearly between social and political revolutions and to see that the second must be subordinated to and derived from the first was emphasized by Marx in his very early writings. In an article written in

1. Engels to Bebel, 18 November 1884, in *K. Marx and F. Engels. Selected Correspondence 1846–1895*, p. 427.
2. Engels to G. Trier, 18 December 1889, in *K. Marx, F. Engels and V. I. Lenin on Scientific Communism*, Moscow, 1967, p. 199.

1844, following the uprising of the Silesian weavers, Marx contrasts the social understanding of the former that private property is its enemy with the political understanding of those who see 'the source of bad social conditions in *will* and all the means of improvement in *force* and the *overthrow* of a particular form of State'.[1] The social aspect of a revolution expresses the real universal needs of men since 'it is a human protest against an inhuman life', a protest against exclusion from society; whereas the political aspect of revolution is simply the attempt of one group to end their exclusion from political life and power. 'Its standpoint is that of the State, an *abstract* whole, which *only* exists by virtue of its separation from real life.' A political revolution organizes 'in accordance with this *narrow* and *discordant* outlook, a ruling group in society at the expense of society' (p. 242). Three years later Marx hammered the lesson home. 'If the proletariat destroys the political rule of the bourgeoisie, that will only be a temporary victory', so long as 'the material conditions are not yet created which make necessary the abolition of the bourgeois mode of production and thus the definite overthrow of bourgeois political rule'.[2]

The crucial points to be determined, therefore, were: when had the material conditions been created which made possible a proletarian social revolution and what were the tactics which the proletariat ought to pursue in the interim? In 1848 when Europe was convulsed with a wave of revolutions, sparked off by the February Revolution in Paris where the armed workers proclaimed a 'social' republic, Marx and Engels concluded that the great decisive struggle had broken out. This struggle, in their view, 'would have to be fought out in a single, long and changeful period of revolution', which 'could only end with the final victory of the proletariat'.[3] In his address to the Communist League in 1850 Marx called on the proletariat to organize itself in an independent Worker's Party, with both secret and open sections. Such a party, while it should be prepared to collaborate with the democratic petty bourgeoisie in effecting a democratic bourgeois revolution, would aim 'to make the revolution permanent, until all more or less possessing

1. 'Critical Notes on "The King of Prussia and Social Reform"', published in *Vorwärts* (Paris). Extract in Bottomore and Rubel, op. cit., p. 241.
2. Article in *Deutscher-Brüsseler Zeitung*, Oct./Nov. 1847, extract in Bottomore and Rubel, op. cit., p. 244.
3. F. Engels: Introduction (1895), to *The Class Struggles in France 1848-50* by K. Marx (published in *Neue Rheinische Zeitung*, 1850-2); Introduction reprinted in Engels, *Selected Writings*, p. 282.

classes have been displaced from domination, until the proletariat has conquered state power' – and 'at least the decisive productive forces are concentrated in the hands of the proletarians'.[1] In furtherance of this aim the proletariat is called on to arm itself and establish its own revolutionary workers' government alongside the new official government. These organs of workers' power would put forward their own independent demands against the government with the object of undermining its authority. The more concessions that are granted by the bourgeois government, the more extensive and unacceptable must be the demands made upon it. 'If the democrats propose proportional taxes, the workers must demand progressive taxes; if the democrats themselves put forward a moderate progressive tax, the workers must insist on a tax with rates which rise so steeply that large-scale capital is ruined by it; if the democrats demand the regulation of state debts, the workers demand state bankruptcy' (*Address to the Communist League*, p. 168).

By the autumn of 1850 the perspective had completely changed – the Right triumphed in France over the democratic centre and universal suffrage had been abolished. Marx now spoke in terms of the workers having to endure '15, 20, 50 years of civil war in order to change the circumstances, in order to make yourselves fit for power'.[2] Marx had not been advocating proletarian revolutions in 1848, but he had conceived the prospect that a wave of successful bourgeois revolutions in Europe would create conditions conducive to the early triumph of the proletariat. *The Communist Manifesto* had proclaimed that 'the bourgeois revolution in Germany will be but the prelude to an immediately following proletarian revolution'.[3] Not only was this perspective changed by the defeat of bourgeois revolutions, but it was followed by the continued growth of the capitalist economy. In 1895 Engels openly

---

1. K. Marx, *Address to the Communist League*, adopted by the Central Council of the League in March 1850. *Karl Marx Selected Works*, Vol. II, p. 161. In *The Class Struggles in France 1848–1850*, Marx wrote (1850) that 'revolutionary socialism', 'communism' is *'the declaration of the permanence of the revolution, the class dictatorship* of the proletariat as the inevitable transit point to the *abolition of class differences generally*, to the abolition of all the productive relations on which they rest, to the abolition of all the social relations that correspond to these relations of production, to the revolutionizing of all the ideas that result from these social connections' (ibid., p. 289).
2. Quoted and translated in Shlomo Avineri, *The Social and Political Thought of Karl Marx*, 1968, p. 195, from *Marx-Engels Werke* VIII, pp. 598–601, East Berlin, 1956– .
3. Feuer, op. cit., p. 82.

admitted that Marx and he had been wrong in their assessment in 1848, since 'the state of economic development on the continent at that time was not, by a long way, ripe for the removal of capitalist production' which 'still had great capacity for expansion'.[1]

At various times during his life Marx's revolutionary optimism returned. He had hopes of revolutionary repercussions in Britain and Russia from the impact of the Crimean War, of a German revolution in 1862–3, of the Polish insurrection of 1863 opening up 'an era of revolution', of a revolutionary upsurge emanating from Spain in 1868 and finally of revolution spreading from the east in 1877 after initial Russian defeats in the Russo-Turkish War. In none of these instances, however, did Marx and Engels become involved in direct agitational activity as they had been in 1848.

In September 1870, immediately following on the proclamation of a Republic in France, after the Prussian victory at Sedan, the General Council of the International Working Men's Association issued an address written by Marx warning the French workers that 'Any attempt at upsetting the new government in the present crisis when the enemy is almost knocking at the doors of Paris, would be a desperate folly'.[2] Marx and Engels' opposition to a rising at the time was not based, however, on the view that the economic conditions were still not ripe for the removal of capitalist production (although this is strongly implied by Engels in 1895).[3] On the contrary their objection was to a premature uprising under conditions which would inevitably lead to defeat. In particular they were concerned to ensure that no uprising took place before peace had been concluded between France and Prussia. Engels wrote 'It would be appalling if as their last act of war the German armies had to fight out a battle with the Parisian workers at the barricades. It would throw us back fifty years.'[4] When, however, the workers of Paris took matters into their own hands and set up the Paris Commune in

1. F. Engels, Introduction to *The Class Struggles in France 1848–1850* (Marx), 1895, in *Engels: Selected Writings*, p. 285.
2. K. Marx, 'Second Address of the General Council of the International Working Men's Association', 9 September 1870. *Karl Marx Selected Works*, Vol. II, p. 473.
3. Engels wrote in Introduction to *The Class Struggles in France 1848–1850* (Marx) of the Paris Commune of 1871, 'And once again twenty years after the time described in this work of ours (i.e. *The Class Struggles in France 1848–1850*), it was proved how impossible, even then, was this rule of the working class'. *Engels: Selected Writings*, p. 287.
4. Engels to Marx, 12 September 1870. *Selected Correspondence*, p. 305.

March 1871, Marx gave its members his support and the benefit of his advice.[1] He remained convinced, however, that the Commune was bound to fail,[2] and his brilliant defence of it was not published until after the Commune's bloody suppression in May 1871. The significance of the Paris Commune for Marx and Engels did not lie in any demonstration of the conditions for a successful proletarian revolution, but in the proof that 'the working class cannot simply lay hold of the ready-made state machinery and wield it for its own purposes'.[3] The Commune was for Marx 'the political form at last discovered under which to work out the economic emancipation of labour',[4] for Engels it was 'the Dictatorship of the Proletariat'.[5] Marx's considered view of the Commune is made clear in a letter written in 1881.

> One thing you can at any rate be sure of: a socialist government does not come into power in a country unless conditions are so developed that it can above all take the necessary measures for intimidating the mass of the bourgeoisie sufficiently to gain time – the first *desideratum* [requisite] – for lasting action. Perhaps you will point to the Paris Commune; but apart from the fact that this was merely the rising of a town under exceptional conditions, the majority of the Commune was in no sense socialist, nor could it be. With a small amount of sound common sense, however, they could have reached a compromise with Versailles useful to the whole mass of the people – the only thing that could be reached at the time.[6]

In *The Communist Manifesto* Marx and Engels had proclaimed that 'the first step in the revolution of the working class is to raise the prole-

1. See letter from Marx to Beesly, 12 June 1871, in which Marx gives details of his communications with the Commune in which, among other things, he advised them, without success, to fortify the northern side of the heights of Montmartre where the Prussians were, ibid., pp. 313–15.
2. See letter to Kugelmann, 17 April 1871, ibid., pp. 310–11. The whole question of Marx's relation to the Paris Commune is discussed in H. Collins and C. Abramsky, *Karl Marx and the British Labour Movement: Years of the First International*, 1965, Chs. XI and XII.
3. Preface to the German Edition of *The Communist Manifesto*, 1872, *Karl Marx Selected Works*, Vol. I, p. 190. Marx had in 1852 spoken in terms of the need to smash the state machine, *18th Brumaire*, in ibid., Vol. II, p. 413.
4. K. Marx, *The Civil War in France*, in Feuer, op. cit., p. 409.
5. Engels, Introduction to *The Civil War in France*, in *Engels: Selected Writings*, p. 310. The form of dictatorship of the proletariat is discussed in Chapter 6, section vi, below.
6. Marx to Domela Nieuwenhuis, 22 February 1881, in ibid., pp. 386–7. The reference to Versailles is to the seat of the Thiers Government and the National Assembly at the time.

tariat to the position of ruling class, to win the battle of democracy'.[1]
By this Marx and Engels meant not simply campaigning for universal
suffrage, but fighting for it as part of a programme of demands designed
to radically alter the balance of class forces in society and to improve
the position of the exploited. The demands of the Communist party of
Germany, issued a few weeks after *The Manifesto*, included a call for
universal suffrage alongside the universal arming of the people, universal
free elementary education, nationalization of large estates and mines
and transport, steeply graded progressive income tax, and a state-
guaranteed living for the workers.[2] What was important for Marx and
Engels was the use to which the franchise would be put by the workers:
it was not an end in itself. Marx had declared in 1852, 'Universal
Suffrage is the equivalent of political power for the working class of
England', but this was because in England the proletariat, as the
majority of the population, had 'in a long, underground civil war' gained
'a clear consciousness of its position as a class'. He concluded, 'The
carrying of universal suffrage in England would, therefore, be a far more
socialistic measure than anything which has been honoured with that
name on the continent'.[3] Forty years later Engels argued that universal
suffrage had fallen into disrepute in France because it had become an
instrument of Bonapartist rule; in Spain and Latin America it was
regarded as a snare to be avoided; and in Switzerland it had not proved
advantageous to the workers' party. The German workers on the other
hand had used the franchise in a new way – 'they have transformed it
from a means of deception, which it was heretofore, into an instrument
of emancipation'.[4]

The success of the German Social Democratic party in getting an
increasing share of the popular vote at the Reichstag elections (two
million votes, over a quarter of the total), showed that in Germany at
least the immediate task of the workers was to concentrate on keeping

1. Feuer, op. cit., p. 69.
2. F. Engels, *History of the Communist League* in *Karl Marx Selected Works*,
   Vol. II, pp. 17–18.
3. K. Marx, 'The Chartists', *The New York Daily Tribune*, 25 August 1852,
   quoted in S. Avineri, op. cit., p. 214. Contrast this statement with his contemptuous characterization of the function of universal suffrage in 1871 as
   'deciding once in three or six years which member of the ruling class was to
   misrepresent the people in Parliament' (*The Civil War in France*, in Selected
   Works Vol. II, p. 500).
4. F. Engels, Introduction to *The Class Struggles in France*, *Engels: Selected
   Writings*, p. 289.

the vote growing until it became the decisive power in the land. It was above all essential in Engels's view that the German workers should not be provoked into illegal conspiracies and street fighting which could only delay the success of the workers' cause and result in heavy loss of life. The conditions for street fighting had changed markedly since 1848 to the advantage of the military and this meant that the class struggle had now to be waged under different conditions. 'The time of surprise attacks, of revolutions carried through by small conscious minorities at the head of unconscious masses, is past. Where it is a question of a complete transformation of the social organization, the masses themselves must also be in it, must themselves already have grasped what is at stake, what they are going in for with body and soul' (p. 294). This did not mean that the workers renounced their right to revolution or the right to use force. On the contrary it was likely that the workers in Germany would find it necessary to use force against an attempted *coup d'état* or breach of the constitution by 'the forces of law and order' aimed at frustrating the legal rise to power of the workers' party. Engels in 1895 was not taking up any different a position from that which he and Marx had maintained in 1879 against the right-wing of the German Social Democratic Party who would '*forbid* themselves to take advantage at any future time of a tremendous external event, a sudden revolutionary upsurge arising from it, or even a *victory* of the people gained in a conflict arising from it'.[1]

The principle of democracy was for Marx and Engels subordinate to the principle of working-class power. In 1852 Marx had written of France 'Universal suffrage had achieved its mission. The majority of the people had passed through the school of development, which is all that universal suffrage can serve for in a revolutionary situation. It had to be set aside by a revolution or by reaction'.[2] The key point for Marx and Engels was the nature of the revolutionary situation that developed. Revolutionary opportunities must not be subordinated to considerations of formal democratic procedures. In 1884 Engels insisted that the Social Democrats could not expect in the moment of crisis to have a majority of the electorate behind them. They would have to face '*the whole collective reaction which will group itself around pure democracy*'.[3] The con-

---

1. Draft letter from Marx and Engels to Bebel, Liebknecht, Bracke and others, September 1879, in *Selected Correspondence*, p. 372.
2. Marx, *The Class Struggles in France 1848–1850* in *Karl Marx: Selected Works*, Vol. II, p. 301.
3. Engels to Bebel, 11 December 1884. *Selected Correspondence*, p. 434.

ception of democracy alters with every *demos*, each class needs its own forms of democracy for its own purposes: 'the proletariat too requires democratic *forms* for the seizure of political power, but, like all political forms, these serve it as means'.[1] To make democracy an end instead of a means would result in subordinating the interests of the workers in Germany to those of the peasants and petty bourgeois.

Finally it is necessary to distinguish between the means which would be required for the gaining of political power and those required for bringing about the transformation of bourgeois society. While Marx accepted that at different periods it might be possible to achieve power by peaceful and constitutional means (in 1872 he mentions America, England and Holland)[2] there is no evidence to suggest he envisaged a peaceful transformation of capitalist society. Engels tells us that even in England Marx did not expect the English ruling classes to submit without a 'pro-slavery' rebellion against the realization of the social revolution by peaceful and legal means.[3] It was left to Engels in 1891 to hold out the possibility of a peaceful and legal *social* revolution. 'It may be assumed,' he wrote,

> that the old society could grow peacefully into a new in countries where popular representation holds all power in its own hands and where it can constitutionally do whatever it likes as long as it has the majority of the people behind it: in democratic republics such as France and America, and in monarchies such as Britain . . ., [but not in Germany] where the government is almost all-powerful and where the Reichstag and all other representative bodies have no real power.[4]

What may be noted in all their discussions and writings about the overthrow of capitalism is that neither Marx nor Engels were able to use Marx's laws of development of capitalist society to predict where and when the power of the bourgeoisie would be successfully overthrown by the proletariat, or to show that the actual development of capitalism in any country was actually following the path to destruction laid down for it. The prophetic words of *Capital* remain unfulfilled.

1. Engels to Bernstein, 24 March 1884, in ibid., p. 435.
2. Speech at Hague Congress of the Working Men's International Association, 18 September 1872, in *Marx; Engels; Lenin: On Scientific Communism*, p. 201.
3. Engels: Preface to the English edition of K. Marx, *Capital*, Vol. I (1886), in ibid., p. 200.
4. Engels's criticism of the draft of the new programme of the German Social Democratic party, sent to Kautsky on 29 June 1891, in ibid., pp. 199–200.

While there is thus a progressive diminution in the number of the capitalist magnates . . ., there occurs a corresponding increase in the mass of
poverty, oppression, enslavement, degeneration, and exploitation; but
at same time there is a steady intensification of the wrath of the
working class – a class which grows ever more numerous, and is dis-
ciplined, unified and organized by the very mechanism of the capitalist
method of production. Capitalist monopoly becomes a fetter upon the
method of production which has flourished with it and under it. The
centralization of the means of production and the socialization of labour
reach a point where they prove incompatible with their capitalist husk.
This bursts asunder. The knell of capitalist private property sounds.
The expropriators are expropriated.[1]

READING

K. Marx, Excerpts from *The Class Struggles in France 1848–1850; The Eighteenth
Brumaire of Louis Bonaparte; The Civil War in France;* in *Marx and Engels
Basic Writings in Politics and Philosophy,* edited by Lewis S. Feuer.

F. Engels, Introduction to *The Class Struggles in France* in *Engels: Selected
Writings,* edited by W. O. Henderson.

S. Avineri, *The Social and Political Thought of Karl Marx,* Chs. 6–8.

1. K. Marx, *Capital,* Vol. I, 1867, translated by Eden and Cedar Paul 1930,
p. 847.

CHAPTER 4

Liberty and Tyranny

1. HOBBES

Many of the difficulties in understanding Hobbes's views on liberty, and some of the differences in their interpretation, stem from his failure to distinguish between the various senses in which he uses the term. Professor Wernham has identified four separate meanings which Hobbes attaches to the concept of freedom or liberty.[1] In the first place a man may be free in that he is able to make a choice between alternative courses of action. This freedom of choice in relation to any problem or situation ends as soon as he has determined how to act. It is this kind of freedom which Hobbes has in mind when he writes of a man who throws his goods into the sea for fear that the ship might sink as 'one that *was* free' (my italics), for he might have willed to do otherwise. In this sense every man is always free in his deliberations no matter what external pressures or restraints he is subjected to. Indeed the imposition of a pressure felt as external and alien, may create the necessity of choice – forcing men to be free in a quite different sense to that defended by Rousseau.[2]

Secondly Hobbes speaks of a man being free when he is not subject to any obligations. Obligations may arise from God, from natural law and from the sovereign power established under the covenant or contract.[3] Where all three are silent men are free from any spiritual, natural or legal requirement to act or to refrain from action. Of course the absence of a duty barrier across a path of action does not mean that I will follow that path or even consider doing so. Moreover should I freely choose to go ahead I may be debarred from proceeding by external obstacles. On the other hand the existence of an obligation still

---

1. Professor A. J. Wernham, 'Liberty and Obligation in Hobbes', in *Hobbes Studies*, edited by K. C. Brown, Oxford, 1965.
2. See section 3 below, p. 154.
3. See Chapter 2, section 1 above, for a discussion of the extent and form of the obligations which in Hobbes's view are imposed by religion and natural law.

leaves me free to decide whether or not I will fulfil it. Hobbes points out that 'generally all actions which men doe in Commonwealths, for *feare* of the law are actions, which the doers have *liberty* to omit' (*Leviathan*, p. 111).

The third way in which Hobbes uses the term freedom is to indicate the absence of compulsion and is to be found whenever a man acts from motives other than from fear or terror. Not only those who are not subject to force are free in this sense, but all those subject to it who refuse to submit or are able to escape from its consequences. For Hobbes a man remains free as long as he acts in accordance with his will; he may be kept in chains but he is inwardly free as long as he does not himself will his imprisonment. He who resists the will of others shows by his resistance that he is a free man. No man can be compelled to be unfree if he is willing to take the necessary risks and suffer the necessary consequences.

Lastly, Hobbes takes liberty to mean the absence of external impediments or obstacles to a man's will. 'A FREE-MAN, *is he, that in those things, which by his strength and wit he is able to do, is not hindered to do what he has a will to do*' (p. 110). A man who exercises his freedom of choice to do something within his capabilities is then free to give effect to his choice in so far as there are no external hindrances which prevent him. But Hobbes insists that though impediments may often take away part of a man's power to do what he wants they 'cannot hinder him from using the power left him, according as his judgment, and reason shall dictate to him' (p. 66). The existence of an obstacle to the realization of his will does not obliterate or nullify the will, rather it requires the agent to make another free choice and decide whether and how to proceed in the new conditions then prevailing.

In the state of nature Hobbes tells us that each man has the liberty 'to use his own power, as he will himselfe, for the preservation of his own Nature; that is to say, of his own Life; and consequently of doing any thing, which in his own Judgment and Reason, hee shall conceive to be the aptest means thereunto' (p. 66). He has freedom of choice and has no obligations to his fellow men, other than those contained in the general precepts of prudence deducible by Reason, which he terms the Laws of Nature. These require him to do nothing which is destructive of his life and subject to this to 'be contented with so much liberty against other men, as he would allow other men against himselfe' (p. 67). A man's obligation to others under natural law does not restrict his liberty to attack and kill them if in his view they constitute a danger to his own life. As the state of nature for Hobbes is one of continuous war 'of every man against man', each man will find himself driven to attack others as potential aggressors against himself. The very existence of other creatures is seen by Hobbes's natural man as an obstacle to the realization of his most fundamental and natural objective, to stay alive. Effective freedom of action is thus strictly limited in the state of nature and the limitation springs from the very absence of defined obligations backed up by sanctions. Without security and order there can be no possibility of rational choice, no chance of pursuing worthwhile goals with any expectation of success. Both negative freedom (the absence of restraint) and positive freedom (self-mastery) are impossible in any meaningful sense as long as I am at the mercy of the unrestrained licence of wilful, frightened men.

It is just these conditions of order and security which are provided by the 'lawes' of a Commonwealth armed with a sword powerful enough to enforce its commands. In place of natural liberty is substituted the liberty of subjects which 'lyeth – only in those things, which in regulating their actions, the Sovereign hath prætermitted' (i.e. omitted to mention) (p. 112). In the state of nature each man was theoretically entitled to do anything he thought necessary to protect his life and secure his interests; but in practice he was thwarted and threatened at every turn. In civil society he is restricted to acting in accordance with the law, but in these actions he has the full protection of the sovereign power. His obligations to natural law are overlaid by his obligations to the positive law of the sovereign. Natural law precepts *still* apply where the law is silent and may indeed be held to be binding much more strictly, in that the existence of an ordered society makes it possible to carry out these precepts without danger to oneself. Fear of all men is replaced by fear of the sovereign; fear of the unknown and unknowable dangers of the state of war by fear of known rules and punishments. Provided the subject keeps within the law he can hope to realize his will and purposes and can plan his life and make his choices on this assumption. Awe of Leviathan's sword will frighten would-be law breakers into choosing the path of conformity and will thus remove the greatest obstacle to peace, itself the necessary condition of freedom.

The authority of the sovereign over his subjects is limited only by the nature of the end for which the Commonwealth is established, 'the Peace of the Subjects within themselves, and their Defence against a common Enemy' (p. 114). It follows that a ruler must be in a position to provide the order and protection which is the purpose of his office. 'The Obligation of Subjects to the Soveraign, is understood to last as long, and no longer, than the power lasteth, by which he is able to protect them' (p. 116). If the Sovereign power collapses, or is usurped or conquered, all allegiance ceases. For Hobbes there can be no *de jure* authority without the *de facto* power. One can see the cold logic of this argument, though it clearly leaves the follower of Hobbes in a difficult position while the outcome of a rebellion is still unresolved. More difficult to follow is Hobbes's assertion that men both singly and collectively, innocent or guilty, have the liberty to defend their lives even against the sovereign if the alternative is death. Hobbes appears to mean something more than that a subject always has the free choice of either submitting to authority or resisting it, or that he can only maintain himself as a free man by resisting compulsion; though both these elements seem to be present. Hobbes's starting point is that every man has a natural right or liberty 'to use his own power, as he will himselfe, for the preservation of his own Nature' and is forbidden from doing anything which is destructive of his life. When Hobbes speaks of man's 'liberty' to preserve himself he is referring to an obligation which arises out of man's very nature, a matter of necessity rather than of duty. It follows therefore that a man cannot be construed as having contracted on entering civil society to kill or injure himself or to put his life in jeopardy. But whereas a man may always refuse to injure himself he may only refuse to risk his life in fighting others if the community is not thereby endangered for 'when the Defence of the Common-wealth requireth at once the help of all that are able to bear Arms, every one is obliged' (p. 115).

Hobbes proceeds to argue that men who are wanted by the sovereign for crimes committed have the liberty to join together and take up arms against the ruler in just defence of their lives. It is essential to realize that there is no question here of the sovereign acting unjustly in putting the rebels to the sword. Indeed Hobbes insists that their offence is so serious that 'vengeance is lawfully extended ... to the third and fourth generation' (p. 169). Hobbes recognizes, however, that rebels are justi-fied in their own eyes and in terms of the natural liberty of self-preserva-tion in acting to defend themselves against their lawful Sovereign. For his part the Sovereign is not only justified but required to exterminate the rebels; both because they have broken his laws and because their existence constitutes a threat to the community.

The weakness of Hobbes's argument lies in his assertion that rebels can never have a better case for rebellion than the ruler has for its repression. In Hobbes's view, therefore, no man can ever have grounds 'to resist the Sword of the Common-wealth, in defence of another man' (p. 115). Hobbes rests his case on the assumption that the inevitable consequence of rebellion and disobedience is the 'perpetuall warre of every man against his neighbour' (p. 109), and this must necessarily always be far worse than the 'inconveniences' of being subject to 'the luste and other irregular passions' of the sovereign. But once it is seen that the consequences of revolt are not a return to the state of nature and the condition of permanent or perpetual war, but another form of Commonwealth or another Sovereign, then it may be argued that the peace and security of subjects may be better served by revolt than by submission. It is just this alternative which John Locke considers in his *Second Treatise of Government*.

READING

Thomas Hobbes, *Leviathan*, Ch. XXI.

K. Brown (ed.) *Hobbes Studies*: J. R. Pennock, 'Hobbes's Confusing "clarity" – the Case of "Liberty"'; A. G. Wernham, 'Liberty and Obligation in Hobbes'.

2. LOCKE

Liberty for Locke is not simply a matter of doing what you like, but of being free to do what you ought to do. The absence of restrictions and interferences is a necessary but not a sufficient condition of liberty which requires positive adherence to the principles of natural law. If one considers natural man, i.e. man outside civil society, one finds him in 'a State of Perfect Freedom', but such a state is 'not a State of Licence' for

> The *State of Nature* has a Law of Nature to govern it, which obliges every one: And Reason, which is that Law, teaches all Mankind, who will but consult it, that being all equal and independent, no one ought to harm another in his Life, Health, Liberty, or Possessions. . . . Every one as he is *bound to preserve himself*, and not to quit his Station wilfully; so by the like reason when his own Preservation comes not in

competition, ought he, as much as he can, *to preserve the rest of Mankind*, and may not unless it be to do Justice on an Offender, take away, or impair the life, or what tends to the Preservation of the Life, the Liberty, Health, Limb or Goods of another (II, s. 6).

Clearly a man is able to choose to disobey or ignore the laws of nature but by so doing he 'declares himself to quit the Principles of Human Nature, and to be a noxious Creature' and may be rightfully punished by any man (II, s. 10). It is because man has reason that he has 'the Liberty to dispose of his Actions and Possessions according to his own Will' (II, s. 59), but as reason is the gift of God he is under an obligation to the Law of Nature which right reason discloses to him. 'The *Freedom* then of Man and Liberty of acting according to his own Will, is *grounded* on his having *Reason*, which is able to instruct him in that Law he is to govern himself by, and make him know how far he is left to the freedom of his own will' (II, s. 63). Positive freedom conceived in terms of acting as one wills has to be restricted by the laws of reason if men are not to degenerate into brutes. True freedom can exist only where men have the opportunity, the capacity and the will to live in accordance with rationally determined postulates of natural law. Not all men, however, fulfil these conditions and in so far as such men, whether from ignorance or personal bias, advance their own interests at the expense of others, they prevent others from achieving the true freedom of which they are capable. Though the latter have the natural right to restrain and punish those who transgress the Natural Law, there is no guarantee that they will succeed in doing so. It is 'the corruption and vitiousness of degenerate Men' (II, s. 128) that forces virtuous men to quit the natural condition where the licence of the stupid and base endangers the liberty of the rational and just.

Men enter civil society in order to attain a greater degree of effective freedom than is available to them outside it. It necessarily follows from this that one cannot accept a form of government within society which produces less freedom than would be available in the natural state with all its inconveniences. Absolute monarchy claiming divine authority for the exercise of unlimited arbitrary power over its subjects is not for Locke a form of civil government, but slavery.

> *Freedom of Men under* Government, is, to have a standing Rule to live by, common to every one of that Society, and made by the Legislative Power erected in it; A Liberty to follow my own Will in all things, where the Rule prescribes not; and not to be subject to the inconstant uncertain, unknown, Arbitrary Will of another Man. As *Freedom*

of *Nature* is to be under no other restraint but the Law of Nature
(II, s. 22).

Absolute monarchy is indefensible:

> As if when Men quitting the State of Nature entered into Society, they
> agreed that all of them but one, should be under the restraint of Laws,
> but that he should still retain all the Liberty of the State of Nature,
> increased with Power, and made licentious by Impunity. This is to
> think that Men are so foolish that they take care to avoid what Mis-
> chiefs may be done them by *Pole-Cats* or *Foxes*, but are content, nay
> think it Safety, to be devoured by *Lions* (II, s. 93).

Absolute power is the antithesis of freedom for its puts one man into
the power of another. It is forbidden by natural law as a threat to my
very existence,

> for no body can desire *to have me in his Absolute Power*, unless it be to
> compel me by force to that, which is against the Right of my Free-
> dom, i.e. to make me a Slave. To be free from such force is the only
> security of my Preservation: and reason bids me look on him, as an
> Enemy to my Preservation, who would take away that *Freedom*, which
> is the Fence to it: so that he who makes an *attempt to enslave* me,
> thereby puts himself into a State of War with me (II, s. 17).

Though men who enter society give up their claim to determine when
their rights, liberties or property have been infringed and to punish the
culprits, the rights themselves remain except that they are now protected
by law. The law appears to Locke, not as a restriction on men's rights,
but as a guarantor of them.

> For *Law* in its true Notion, is not so much the Limitation as *the direc-
> tion of a free and intelligent Agent* to his proper Interest, and prescribes
> no farther than it is for the general Good of those under that Law. . . .
> *the end of Law* is not to abolish or restrain, but *to preserve and enlarge
> Freedom*: For in all the states of created beings capable of Laws, *where
> there is no Law, there is no Freedom*. For *Liberty* is to be free from
> restraint and violence from others which cannot be, where there is no
> Law: But Freedom is not, as we are told, *A Liberty for every Man to do
> what he lists* . . . But a *Liberty* to dispose, and order, as he lists, his
> Person, Actions, Possessions, and his whole Property, within the Allow-
> ance of those Laws under which he is; and therein not to be subject to
> the arbitrary Will of another, but freely follow his own (II, s. 57).

The wording of this passage is worth comparing with Rousseau's views
discussed below (pp. 153–4), for Rousseau also conceives the purpose of
law to be 'the direction of a free and intelligent Agent to his proper
Interest'. But whereas Rousseau insists that a man's 'proper Interest'

is the same as the general good of the community and is actually willed by all men in their higher selves, Locke conceives the general good as the justification for imposing limits on what a man may do, so that a man may be better able 'to dispose and order as he lists'. The emphasis with Locke is on individuals asserting their own wills under the protection of the law, not on conformity to the general will of the community. The public good is 'the good of every particular Member of that Society' (I, s. 92), not the good of the community considered as a unity.

While Locke is primarily concerned to emphasize the need for 'establish'd, standing Laws, promulgated and known to the People', applied by *'indifferent* and upright *Judges'* as essential institutional barriers against arbitrary rule, he does not fail to see the importance of the ends which such institutions serve. He insists that 'all this to be directed to no other *end,* but the *Peace, Safety* and *publick good* of the People'. The restrictions imposed by a political society need to be justified in terms of what a rational free man could be persuaded to forego of his natural rights for the general advantage. 'The power of the Society, or *Legislative* constituted by them *can never be suppos'd to extend farther than the common good'* (II, s. 131).

The difficulty which arises, however, is how one is to determine when the plea of the common good is being legitimately made, for who is to judge in any particular instance? Locke was convinced that the creation of civil society rested on the individual renouncing his right to determine where his rights lay under natural law; but he was equally convinced of the dangers of oppression in civil society. Though he believed that the establishment of constitutional government, and in particular of a representative legislature, was the main protection needed against arbitrary interference, he did not deny men the right to take action against a constitutional government which failed to fulfil its obligations either by exceeding its authority or by infringing the basic rights of the subject. Locke accords to every private individual the right to defend his rights and liberties from unlawful invasion by the government, as determined by reference to the provisions of the law and the constitution; while accepting both that individual disobedience is unlikely to be of much avail against a government and that individuals who are judges in their own disputes are liable to be partial. He therefore makes provision for the people as a whole to judge between a ruler and a subject on matters of major concern. 'If a Controversie arise betwixt a Prince and some of the People, in a matter where the Law is silent, or doubtful, and the thing be of great Consequence, I should think the proper *Umpire*, in such a Case, should be the Body of the *People*' (II, s. 242), who have the right to remove the Prince if they determine he has abused the trust reposed in him. The right of appeal which an aggrieved person has to his fellows does not in Locke's opinion constitute a danger to a well run state. Individual acts of injustice are unlikely to move the people to resistance unless 'they have a perswasion, grounded upon manifest evidence, that designs are carrying on against their Liberties,' and that all are threatened by the evil intentions of their ruler (II, s. 230). A readiness in the last resort to resist unlawful authority is both right and necessary if men's liberties are to be protected.

In Locke's view men are born free, that is they are born with a capacity to determine their own actions in accordance with the dictates of Reason. Because children are incapable of exercising the freedom they are born to, they are subject to the will and commands of their parents; who must exercise their control so that the children prove capable of attaining the state of freedom when they become of age. 'To inform the Mind, and govern the Actions of their yet ignorant Nonage, till Reason shall take its place, and ease them of that Trouble, is what the Children want, and the Parents are bound to' (II, s. 58). When he reaches maturity the son is at liberty to decide for himself whether to accept the rights and obligations of the society in which he was born. If he disclaims his father's government he forfeits any claims he may have to his father's possessions (II, s. 117). The rational individual has the responsibility and the right to determine for himself his own way of life, but once the decision is taken he is bound by the consequences for life.

READING

John Locke, *Second Treatise of Government*, Chs. I, VI and IX.

J. W. Gough, *John Locke's Political Philosophy*, 1950, Ch. II, 'The Rights of the Individual'.

John W. Yolton (ed.), *John Locke: Problems and Perspectives*, Raymond Polin, 'Locke's Conception of Freedom'.

3. ROUSSEAU

Rousseau is not concerned with the philosophical meaning of the term liberty, but with what it means to *be* free. His approach to liberty was that of a man who had suffered deeply from the scorns and restraints of a non-permissive society and from the inward bruising of a torn and searching conscience. Rousseau was at odds with himself and with the world at large and in his own wretchedness he saw mirrored the fate of all mankind. He sought in his writings for the path which men might follow from servitude to freedom, where each might become the noble being he sees and laments in his cups. Living in the midst of a corrupt society Rousseau was concerned to explain how man came to this miserable state. He attempted to do so by the use of hypotheses aimed at reconstructing the conditions which men might have lived in and the influences they might have been subject to in the state of nature before the emergence of organized society.

Uncivilized man, as portrayed by Rousseau in *A Discourse on the Origin of Inequality*, is a remote and unfamiliar figure

> wandering up and down the forests, without industry, without speech, and without home, an equal stranger to war and to all ties, neither standing in need of his fellow creatures nor having any desire to hurt them . . . being self-sufficient and subject to so few passions he could have no feelings or knowledge but such as benefitted his situation (p. 188).

Such a man was wild, rather than wicked, amoral rather than immoral, differing from other wild creatures in that whereas they reacted instinctively to their environment he had the capacity to act freely and to reject Nature's commands. This natural liberty, in which every man had to choose for himself what was necessary to meet his simple immediate needs and purposes, was gradually destroyed. It was eroded because man was blessed and cursed with the faculty of self-improvement which 'successively producing in different ages his discoveries and his errors, his vices and his virtues, makes him at length a tyrant both over himself and over nature' (p. 171). The desire for self-improvement leads man to give up the life of a wandering hunter and to set up the first society, the family, 'the more united because liberty and reciprocal attachment were the only bonds of its union' (p. 196). But along with the creation of the family we have the institution of private property, the disappearance of natural equality and the emergence of organized civil society with its laws and institutions. Bitterly Rousseau draws together the threads of his argument

> Such was, or may well have been, the origin of society and law, which bound new fetters on the poor, and gave new powers to the rich; which irretrievably destroyed natural liberty, eternally fixed the law of property and inequality, converted clever usurpation into unalterable right, and, for the advantage of a few ambitious individuals, subjected all mankind to perpetual labour, slavery and wretchedness (p. 205).

What a contrast is to be found between the savage and the civilized man, between natural man subject to no one, free to live and free from work, and artificial man who must for ever toil and drudge in the service of the rich and powerful. Civilized man has sunk so low that, 'proud of his slavery, he speaks with disdain of those who have not the honour of slaving'. It is this willing submission to alien authority, this 'praise of the tranquillity they enjoy in their chains' (p. 209) that Rousseau so depises in modern man, trained and conditioned to obey his masters and desirous of enslaving others. Such a creature may lick with gratitude the jackboots of his oppressors but he cannot be held to have any obligation to them. 'To renounce freedom is to renounce one's humanity, one's rights as a man and equally one's duties' (*The Social Contract*, Bk. I, Ch. 4, p. 55).

But Rousseau is not a philosopher of despair. Man is not born for slavery. He was tricked into assenting to the establishment of institutions of oppression when his aim had been the creation of means to protect his liberty from the encroachments of his oppressors. Moreover not all men succumbed, some succeeded in creating free societies, as in ancient Sparta or contemporary Geneva, societies of citizens not of mere subjects and their example can be followed by others. In *The Social Contract* Rousseau sets out to show how this can be done, how natural freedom can be transformed into civil freedom and men liberated from the bondage of the servile societies he saw around him. His purpose was not to legitimize existing societies but to show what changes had to be made before such societies might be made legitimate. 'How to find a form of association which will defend the person and goods of each member with the collective force of all, and under which each individual, while uniting himself with the others, obeys no one but himself, and remains as free as before' (Bk. I, Ch. 6, p. 60).

The freedom Rousseau seeks for in society is the negative freedom which primitive man enjoys in the state of nature where no one is subject to the will of another. The freedom he provides is the positive moral freedom for men to realize their true selves in the service of the community at the expense of negative freedom. The key to the transformation is to be found in Rousseau's conception of the nature of man. Man in the natural state exhibits two basic qualities – the desire of self-preservation and the disposition of compassion which Rousseau describes as 'an innate repugnance at seeing a fellow-creature suffer' (*The Origin of Inequality*, p. 182). In natural man these two qualities are in a rough and ready harmony with one another, causing neither travail to himself nor injury to others. But society transforms man's desire for self-preservation into egoism and the drive for self-advancement at the expense of others. Compassion then has to play a different role and 'by moderating the violence of love of self in each individual, contributes to the preservation of the whole species' (p. 184). Thus in society the two great motivating forces of man's inner being assume the forms of a particular egoistic will and a general unselfish will, in continuous battle with one another for possession of each man's soul. It is to the triumph in society of the particular will to self-advancement at the expense of the general will to service, that Rousseau ascribes the depravity of man's condition. The remedy is to break the hold of selfishness and to make the will to service the dominant motivating force in the hearts of men and in society. In so far as this is effected, men will be liberated from their social chains and attain positive freedom.

The freedom which man can aspire to in society is not the natural freedom to do what he wills, but the civil freedom of living under laws which he has himself made, instead of being subject to the arbitrary will of another man; and the moral freedom of living in accordance with his higher social self, instead of his narrow egoistical self. Civil freedom is for Rousseau the supreme value and he is prepared to sacrifice all else to it. He accepts that there 'are some situations so unfortunate that one can preserve one's freedom only at the expense of the freedom of someone else; and the citizen can be perfectly free only if the slave is absolutely a slave', but he insists 'you peoples of the modern world, you have no slaves, but you are slaves yourselves; you pay for their liberty with your own' (*The Social Contract*, Bk. III, Ch. 15, p. 143).[1] But while

1. On the other hand in his *Lettres écrites de la montagne*, written two years later, in 1764, he returns to the notion of negative liberty, but in a social form which specifically precludes liberty at the expense of others. 'Liberty consists less in doing one's own will than in not being subject to that of another; it consists further in not subjecting the will of others to our own.' (Quoted and translated by M. Cranston in his introduction to Rousseau: *The Social Contract*, p. 32.)

it is a necessary condition of civil freedom that men should only obey laws they have helped to frame, it is not a sufficient condition. To be sufficient, laws so made must be laws which truly reflect and express the general will of the community.[1] Where the general will no longer resides in the majority civil liberty is no longer possible. Where the laws of the state do express the general will, however, they give effect to what every man truly desires, for the general will is the common moral will of all men. It follows that if a man refuses to comply with such laws he is acting in opposition not just to his own interests but to what he truly wills. In forcing him to conform, the community not only protects his interests along with those of his fellows, but it literally forces him to be free. The general will of the whole community comes to the aid of those in whom the general will is no longer the conscious dominant will, guiding their actions and their thoughts. But although a man may be forced to be free in the civil sense of being made to fulfil the functions and requirements of a citizen of a self-governing community he cannot be morally free unless and until he *consciously* wills the common good. To be morally free a man must liberate himself from his own appetites and identify himself with the community of which he forms a part – then only does he become 'the master of himself'. A man may aspire to moral freedom even in a corrupt state where under the name of law there is everywhere 'the rule of self-interest and human passion'. The wise man in such conditions finds freedom by obeying the eternal laws of nature and of order 'written in the depths of his heart by conscience and reason' (*Émile*, p. 437).

Just as Christians argue that a man attains religious freedom by serving God, so Rousseau argues that man attains moral freedom by serving society. In neither case is it accepted that such service destroys man's individuality; on the contrary it is contended that meaningful individuality is only possible if one is not enslaved by sordid passions, prejudices and appetites. Each man, for Rousseau, must find his own particular way of serving the community and in *Émile* he sets out his ideas as to how education can be used to bring out and develop the latent capacities of the child. Émile is to be 'trained from the outset to be as self-reliant as possible' (p. 83) and 'to develop his own tastes, his own talents, to take the first step towards the object which appeals to his individuality' (p. 155). Individuality of course must not be allowed to take anti-social forms. In *A Discourse on Political Economy*,

1. See Chapter III, section 3, pp. 111–13 above for a discussion of the distinction between the general will and the will of all.

Rousseau makes a strong plea that education should not be left to the prejudices of parents, but should be controlled by the state. 'If children are brought up in common in the bosom of equality: if they are imbued with the laws of the State and the precepts of the general will ... we cannot doubt that they will learn to cherish one another mutually as brothers, to will nothing contrary to the will of society' (p. 252).

The education of its future citizens was for Rousseau the most important business of the state for it involved nothing less than 'learning to deserve to live' as members of the community, consciously expressing the general will. In *The Social Contract*, Rousseau goes further and speaks of the need for a Legislator prepared 'to change human nature, to transform each individual, who by himself is entirely complete and solitary, into a part of a much greater whole, from which that same individual will then receive, in a sense, his life and his being' (Bk. II, Ch. 7, p. 84). It cannot be assumed from this, however, that Rousseau wanted to turn men into mere creatures of the state, completely subordinating their interests to its purposes. In *A Discourse on Political Economy* Rousseau wrote 'Is the welfare of a single citizen any less the common cause than that of the whole state?' (p. 248), and went on to praise the Romans who 'distinguished themselves above all other peoples by the regard which their government paid to the individual; and by its scrupulous attention to the preservation of the inviolable rights of all the members of the State' (p. 249). Nor were the rights Rousseau was concerned with purely civil rights. In *The Social Contract* he stresses that citizens not only have duties as subjects but 'natural rights which they ought to enjoy as men' (Bk. II, Ch. 4, p. 74). Each man has the right to dispose at will of such goods and liberty as are not required to meet the essential needs of the community. On the other hand Rousseau admits that the community itself, when it speaks with the voice of the general will, is the sole and rightful judge of how much of each man's goods and liberty shall be alienated to its control. What this will amount to will differ from one community to another and from time to time within the same community; but there is little reason to believe that, except in time of dire emergency, Rousseau envisaged the state using its powers to control all aspects of life. In his proposals for Poland for example, he insists, 'We want few laws, but those well classified and above all well enforced.'[1] Nevertheless the absence of any limitations as to what the general will may legitimately

1. *The Government of Poland*, in Rousseau, *Political Writings*, edited by F. Watkins, 1953, p. 223.

require, implicit as it is in the very notion of the concept, is dangerous. It is capable in other hands of being used to fasten a rigid totalitarian system on a people in the name of the will which is claimed to be theirs, but which they are too blind to see. One may perhaps aptly conclude a discussion of Rousseau's view on liberty with these words from *A Discourse on Political Economy*. 'With whatever sophistry all this may be covered over, it is certain that if any constraint can be laid on my will, I am no longer free' (p. 239).

READING

J. J. Rousseau, *The Social Contract*, Bk. I, Chs. 1–8; Bk. II, Chs. 4 and 7.

A. Cobban, *Rousseau and the Modern State*, 2nd edition, 1964, Ch. III, 'Liberty and the General Will'.

4. BENTHAM AND MILL

Liberty for Bentham is simply the absence of restraint and since the imposition of restriction gives rise to pain, restrictions on liberty are always in themselves evil. 'Every law,' writes Bentham, 'is an evil, for every law is an infraction of liberty' (*Theory of Legislation*, p. 48). Consequently no legal restriction can be justified unless it can be clearly demonstrated that the evil consequences of the remedy are less than those of the malady. All too often, in Bentham's view, governments in attempting to suppress one vice have only succeeded in creating other and more dangerous vices and he instances attempts to suppress drunkenness and fornication. Matters of moral prudence and of personal taste should be left to the individuals concerned to decide for themselves.

> As a general rule, the greatest possible latitude should be left to individuals, in all cases in which they can injure none but themselves, for they are the best judges of their own interests. If they deceive themselves, it is to be supposed that the moment they discover their error they will alter their conduct. The power of the law need interfere only to prevent them from injuring each other. It is there that restraint is necessary; it is there that the application of punishment is truly useful,

because the rigour exercised upon an individual becomes in such a case the security of all (p. 63).

Bentham's objection to legal action in matters of moral prudence does not stem from a rooted opposition in principle to interference but to the evil social consequences to which it would give rise. He sees no objection to the moral sanction of public opinion being applied to ensure compliance with the accepted moral code if it can be shown that the action concerned is liable to spread by example, and he is prepared to see the law used in support of popular morality. 'All that the legislator can do in reference to offences of this kind, is to submit to some slight punishment in cases of scandalous notoriety. This will be sufficient to give them a taint of illegality, which will excite the popular sanction against them' (p. 62). He also envisages legislative action aimed at influencing public opinion by the publication of facts and of moral codes based on the principle of utility. But although Bentham lays down no specific checks to the popular moral sanction, it is not to be assumed that he envisaged it as entitled to displace individual judgement and decision in all matters of prudence. Utility as a code of private ethics 'teaches how each man may dispose himself to pursue the course most conducive to his own happiness' (*Principles of Morals and Legislation*, p. 423). If it is plain to Bentham that legislators can know nothing 'concerning those points of conduct which depend upon the personal circumstances of each individual', and 'therefore, that he can determine nothing to advantage' (p. 420), the same considerations would apply to public opinion. 'No man,' wrote Bentham in 1813,

can allow another to decide for him as to what is pleasure, or what is the balance, or the amount of pleasure: and hence a necessary consequence is that every man of ripe age and sound mind ought on this subject to be left to judge and act for himself, and that attempts to give a direction to conduct inconsistent with his views of his own interest is no better than folly and impertinence.[1]

Bentham remains true to the proposition that 'the care of his enjoyments ought to be left almost entirely to the individual' (*Theory of Legislation*, p. 95).

Though Bentham stresses the need to increase the force of the sanction of public opinion he warns of the dangers of strengthening it 'where it is in opposition to the principle of utility' (p. 433). This danger is one of the main themes of John Stuart Mill's celebrated essay

1. Quoted by D. J. Manning, *The Mind of Jeremy Bentham*, pp. 87–8.

On Liberty where it appears in a much graver and more sinister light than it ever did for Bentham. Mill deals with the new form taken by the old problem of the nature and limits of the power which can legitimately be exercised by society over the individual under the new conditions of popular government. Political liberty traditionally meant the setting of limits to the powers which the ruler might exercise over the community, by the establishment of certain political liberties or rights 'which it was to be regarded as a breach of duty in the ruler to infringe, and which if he did infringe, specific resistance, or general rebellion, was held to be justifiable' and by the creation of constitutional checks on the exercise of some of the more important acts of governing (*On Liberty*, p. 66).[1] Under popular government where the governors are responsible to the people these safeguards are held to be unnecessary – for the people do not need protecting against themselves. Mill, however, points out that in practice the will of the people 'means the will of the most numerous or the most active *part* of the people; the majority, or those who succeed in making themselves accepted as the majority; the people, consequently *may* desire to oppress a part of their number; and precautions are as much needed against this as against any other abuse of power' (pp. 67–8). It is consequently as necessary to protect the subjects' political liberty against the tyranny of rulers when the majority are rulers as it was when they were subjects. Moreover under popular government society as a whole comes more and more to exercise social control, as distinct from political control, over all the individual members of the community.

> Protection therefore, against the tyranny of the magistrate is not enough : there needs protection also against the tyranny of the prevailing opinion and feeling; against the tendency of society to impose by other means than civil penalties, its own ideas and practices as rules of conduct on those who dissent from them; to fetter the development, and, if possible, prevent the formation, of any individuality not in harmony with its ways, and compels all characters to fashion themselves upon the model of its own. (p. 68)

In Mill's view protection against social tyranny is the more urgent task in England, since there is a tradition of opposition to legislative and executive encroachment on private conduct, but none against the yoke of popular opinion.

1. All references to Mill in this section are to *On Liberty*, unless specified to the contrary.

But although the most immediate need is to lay down principles which will protect the individual from social interference and control, it is also necessary to determine the principles which should govern governmental influence, both because the anti-government tradition is likely to weaken as the majority learn 'to feel the power of the government their power' instead of as a separate interest to their own, and because the tradition militates against government action in fields where it is both appropriate and necessary.[1] Mill's own conclusion is that the same principle can be used to govern both sorts of intervention.

That principle is, that the sole end for which mankind are warranted, individually or collectively, in interfering with the liberty of action of any of their number, is self-protection. That the only purpose for which power can be rightfully exercised over any member of a civilized community, against his will, is to prevent harm to others. His own good, either physical or moral, is not a sufficient warrant. He cannot rightfully be compelled to do or forbear because it will be better for him to do so, because it will make him happier, because, in the opinion of others, to do so would be wise, or even right. These are good reasons for remonstrating with him, or reasoning with him, or persuading him, or entreating him, but not for compelling him, or visiting him with any evil in case he do otherwise. To justify that, the conduct which it is desired to deter him must be calculated to produce evil to some one else. The only part of the conduct of any one, for which he is amenable to society, is that which concerns others. In the part which merely concerns himself, his independence is, of right, absolute. Over himself, over his own body and mind, the individual is sovereign (pp. 72–3).[2]

1. Mill instances the moral obligation which society has to see that every child is educated where the parents fail in the performance of this duty and the need for state action to reduce the 'almost despotic power of husbands over wives' by giving wives the same legal rights and protection as other members of society (p. 160). Mill concludes that there are three objections, other than objections on the grounds of infringing liberty, which may be raised against governmental interference in any sphere, (i) that individuals are likely to do the job better, (ii) that even though individuals may not do the job as well as officials it is desirable that the former should do it as a means to their mental and political education, (iii) that it is undesirable to add unnecessarily to the already great powers of the government.

2. Mill makes it clear that this rule is not to apply to children or young persons below the legal age of adulthood or to 'those backward states of society in which the race itself may be considered as in its nonage'. For such people despotism is a legitimate form of government 'provided the end be their improvement, and the means justified by actually effecting that end' (p. 73).

What Mill has done is to extend the general rule laid down by Bentham which would restrict *legal* interference to cases where a man's actions harm others (see pp. 156–7 above), to all forms of interference, whether justified on moral, religious, political or social grounds, and to exclude the possibility of the exceptions contemplated by Bentham.[1] Under the rule as Mill applies it a man might be punished, either by law or general disapprobation only if he directly violates some specific public duty or occasions perceptible injury to some assignable person, other than an adult consenting to the act in question. Even if the act falls within one of these restricted categories it does not follow that the offending party ought automatically to be punished; rather the question becomes open to discussion to determine 'whether the general welfare will or will not be promoted by interfering with it' (p. 132). Mill insists that where a man's conduct has only indirect, inferred or incidental adverse effects on others no case arises for the imposition of legal or social sanctions, and his use of the term 'self-regarding' actions to cover actions which should not be interfered with is to be understood as covering such cases. What he does not discuss is whether the notion of 'the general welfare', introduced above, may not be used, as a principle of social conduct in its own right, instead of simply to determine whether an act prejudicial to the interests of others should be actually stopped. Thus the notion of the general welfare is today frequently appealed to to justify interference with people's activities where no question of such activities harming others arises, e.g. I may be required to sell my house for public road-widening purposes.

Mill lists three areas of activity where society has only an indirect interest and where consequently the presumption must be that individuals ought not to be restricted; unless conclusive evidence to the contrary can be adduced in any particular case. Men need first, liberty of inner consciousness (conscience, thought, opinion, sentiment, expression and publication); secondly, liberty of tastes and pursuits; and thirdly liberty of association. 'No society in which these liberties are not, on the whole, respected, is free, whatever may be its form of government' (p. 75)– respected that is by government and popular opinion alike. Mill develops a closely reasoned case in Chapter II of *On Liberty* to show that freedom of thought and expression are essential

---

1. Bentham wrote with regard to legislative action: 'There are few cases in which it *would* be expedient to punish a man for hurting *himself*: but there are few cases, if any, in which it would *not* be expedient to punish a man for injuring his neighbour' (*Principles of Morals and Legislation*, p. 422).

to the ascertaining of truth and knowledge on which the ultimate well-being of mankind depends. The growth of legal and social restrictions on open discussion in any society cramps the minds of great thinkers and ordinary men alike and inhibits both the establishment of new truths and the refutation of old falsehoods.[1]

The second kind of liberty, freedom of tastes and pursuits, is the freedom of men to act upon their opinions and beliefs 'without hindrance, either physical or moral, from their fellow-men, so long as it is at their own risk and peril' (p. 114). Mill develops two separate but related sets of argument in support of this thesis. The first of these is that individuality in behaviour is a good in itself, and the second that it works to the benefit of society. The case for individuality needs, in Mill's view, to be strongly asserted in modern popular states, because it is there more than anywhere else that it is undervalued and regarded with suspicion. 'The majority, being satisfied with the ways of mankind as they now are (for it is they who make them what they are) cannot comprehend why those ways should not be good enough for everybody' (p. 115). Lacking strength of intellect and inclination themselves they are intolerant towards its manifestation in others. They do not ask themselves

> what do I prefer? or, what would suit my character and disposition? or, what would allow the best and highest in me to have fair play, and enable it to grow and thrive? They ask themselves, what is suitable in my position? what is usually done by persons of my station and pecuniary circumstances? or (worse still) what is usually done by persons of a station and circumstances superior to mine? I do not mean that they choose what is customary in preference to what suits their own inclination. It does not occur to them to have any inclination, except for what is customary. Thus the mind itself is bowed to the yoke . . . until by dint of not following their own nature they have no nature to follow: their human capacities are withered and starved: they become incapable of any strong wishes or native pleasures, and are generally without either opinions or feelings of home growth, or properly their own (p. 119).

The tendency of modern democratic society, as seen by Mill a hundred years ago, was to turn men into ape-like creatures incapable of exercising

---

1. Bentham would have strongly concurred with these views. He was an ardent advocate of freedom of the press, insisting that censorship gives rise to 'the danger of stopping the whole progress of the human mind in all its paths. Every new and important truth must of necessity have many enemies, for the single reason that it is new and important' (*Theory of Legislation*, p. 371).

the 'human faculties of perception, judgment, discriminative feeling, mental activity and even moral preference' (p. 116), all of which are dependent on individual choice. Such men 'do not desire liberty, and would not avail themselves of it' (p. 122).[1]

In itself Mill's conception that 'liberty consists in doing what one desires' (p. 152) is simply a positive conception of liberty as action, differing only in emphasis and standpoint from Bentham's negative conception of liberty as the absence of restraint – the absence of restraint being a necessary but not always a sufficient condition for being able to do what one desires. Both conceptions are formulated in empirical not prescriptive terms, although Mill's approach has, as we have seen, strong prescriptive undertones. 'Doing what one desires' and 'pursuing our own good in our own way' (p. 75) are for Mill not simply statements about what men do, but about what men ought to be able to do. One cannot do what one desires if one has no desires of one's own, as distinct from desires 'picked-up' from others. The withered and culturally starved mass, without natures of their own, are not, in Mill's eye, in a state of liberty, because they lack the capacity to choose for themselves. Liberty in this sense is to be found in only the intellectual minority and it is their responsibility to encourage individuality in others so that all men bring 'themselves nearer to the best thing they can be' (p. 121). Liberty for Mill is essentially the capacity of being able to choose for oneself effectively what one will do with one's life, a capacity desirable in itself in all conditions and circumstances, since everything worthwhile in life is dependent on its development.[2]

Mill does not expect that these arguments in support of his case for the development of the capacity for individual self-expression will

1. Mill's views on the nature and future of democracy were considerably influenced by Alexis de Tocqueville's *Democracy in America* published in 1835.
2. In *The Logic of the Moral Sciences*, Bk. VI, Ch. II, 'Of Liberty and Necessity', Mill develops a parallel line of argument with regard to free will. He writes 'this feeling, of our being able to modify our own character *if we wish*, is itself the feeling of moral freedom which we are conscious of. A person feels morally free who feels that his habits or his temptations are not his masters, but he theirs: who even in yielding to them knows that he could resist; that were he desirous of altogether throwing them off, there would not be required for that purpose a stronger desire than he knows himself to be capable of feeling. It is of course necessary to render our consciousness of freedom complete, that we should have succeeded in making our character all we have hitherto attempted to make it; for if we have wished and not attained, we have, to that extent, not power over our own character, we are not free' (p. 427).

suffice to convince those who most need convincing, the masses who rejoice in conformity. He therefore finds it necessary 'to point out to those who do not desire liberty, and would not avail themselves of it, that they may be in some intelligible manner rewarded for allowing other people to make use of it without hindrance' (p. 122). They may expect both the opportunity to learn by example how they too may enrich their lives and the direct benefits which flow from the initiative of outstanding individuals.

For Mill the two arguments in favour of individuality are complementary, since in 'proportion to the development of his individuality, each person becomes more valuable to himself, and is therefore capable of being more valuable to others' (p. 121). The most urgent need is to protect those who have already developed their own distinctive personalities from the tyranny of social opinion; but the more fundamental long-term purpose must be for society to use its education powers over children 'to try whether it could make them capable of rational conduct in life' (p. 139), capable that is of making rational choices instead of blindly following their fellows.[1]

Mill holds firmly to the view that men should be left to their own devices as long as they do not directly injure others. Interference is harmful both to the individual concerned and to society. Mill does not hold, however, that any expression of individuality is necessarily valuable in itself. The furthest that he goes is to assert that in an age of increasing conformity eccentricity should be encouraged. While he defends a man's right to be any sort of creature he likes, as long as he harms nobody but himself, he laments the stupidity of those who injure themselves or who fail to develop their intellectual and artistic capacities. The eccentricity he wishes to encourage is that associated with wise and noble minds who reach out for new ideas which advance the progress of mankind. Individuality which expresses itself in self-regarding acts of sensual pleasure is to be tolerated, but strongly discouraged.

> There is a degree of folly, and a degree of what may be called (though the phrase is not unobjectionable) lowness or depravation of taste, which, though it cannot justify doing harm to the person who manifests it, renders him necessarily and properly a subject of distaste, or in extreme cases, even of contempt; a person could not have the opposite qualities in due strength without entertaining these feelings (p. 134).

1. This analysis owes much to Richard B. Friedman's article, 'A New Exploration of Mill's Essay *On Liberty*', *Political Studies*, Vol. XIV, No. 3, October 1966. The conclusions, however, are different.

Mill tells us that we may not only rightly remonstrate with such a person but we are also entitled to caution others against him. Such action is not regarded by Mill as the exercise of the moral sanction, since these 'inconveniences', in his view, flow simply from the unfavourable judgements of others which the individual's anti-social behaviour inevitably produces. The moral sanction, on the other hand, involves the deliberate use of organized public pressure to compel compliance to its will. For Mill it is the development of one's capacity to choose, not the exercising of that capacity which is an end in itself, for it is the prior condition for becoming an individual human being. The exercise of the capacity of choice needs to be subordinated to the principle of utility to ensure that all persons have the opportunity to develop their capacities and enjoy the best that life has to offer.

READING

John Stuart Mill, *On Liberty*, Chs. I, III and IV.

Richard B. Friedman, 'A New Exploration of Mill's Essay *On Liberty*', in *Political Studies*, October 1966.

5. HEGEL

Freedom is one of the key concepts of Hegel's political philosophy, but as with all Hegel's concepts, its meaning can be understood only in relation to the whole context of his thinking, while its nature and role vary according to the stage of human development one is considering. The true nature of the concept of freedom is to be seen in the role that it is to play in the ultimate. In the concluding paragraph of his *Science of Logic* Hegel speaks of the Absolute Idea as 'absolute *liberation*', where there remains no conflict between the notion or concept of absolute cognition (The Idea) and its reality. 'Absolute *liberation*' must 'be taken to mean that the Idea freely releases itself in absolute self-security and self-repose. By reason of this freedom the form of its determinateness also is absolutely free – the externality of space and time which is absolutely for itself and without subjectivity' (*Science of Logic*, Vol. II, pp. 485–6).

In the *Phenomenology of Mind* Hegel expresses the same approach when he writes:

> Absolute knowledge contains within itself this necessity of relinquish-
> ing itself from the form of the pure notion, and necessarily involves
> the transition of the notion into consciousness. For Spirit that knows
> itself is, just for the reason that it grasps its own notion, immediate
> identity with itself; and this, in the distinction that it implies, is the
> certainty of what is immediate or is semi-consciousness – the beginning
> from which we started. The process of releasing itself from the form
> of its self is the highest freedom and security of its knowledge of itself
> (p. 806).

The realization of the concept of freedom means that the subject ceases to exist as an individual who sees himself as a being apart from and different from the world. The subject will comprehend the objective world in its entirety by abandoning his own subjectivity in the process of overcoming the objectivity of the outside world. It is the realization of this condition which constitutes for Hegel the ultimate fulfilment of freedom – by gathering up the world into the mind of the beholder it abolishes it as an alien restricting force. Hegel's conception is perhaps made most explicit in *Philosophy of History* where he extols freedom as 'the essence of Spirit'. Philosophy teaches 'that all the qualities of Spirit exist only through Freedom; that all are but means for attaining Freedom; that all seek and produce this and this alone'. Spirit and Freedom are equated because they both express the same fundamental quality, that of self-sufficiency.

> Spirit is *self-contained existence*. Now this is Freedom, exactly. For
> if I am dependent, my being is referred to something else which I am
> not; I cannot exist independently of something external. I am free,
> on the contrary, when my existence depends upon myself. This self-
> contained existence of Spirit is none other than self-consciousness –
> consciousness of one's own being (p. 18).

The 'self-contained existence' of the Spirit is only realized in the ulti-mate when the Spirit is absolutely free in its complete knowledge of itself as knowing all. Since Spirit contains within itself the potential which it is to realize, it follows for Hegel that 'the History of the world is none other than the progress of the consciousness of Freedom . . . according to the necessity of its nature . . .' (pp. 19–20). It is only if one keeps firmly in mind that for Hegel the essence of freedom is contained in the nature of the final goal of human development, and that this goal is worked out through different stages and processes of development, that one is able to attain any real understanding of the way in which he discusses the concept.

The origin of freedom is the will of man, for man as a rational creature has the power to give effect to his thoughts. The very notion of will involves, for Hegel, that of freedom. 'Will without freedom is an empty word, while freedom is actual only as will, as subject' (*Philosophy of Right*, para. 4, addition p. 226). Freedom of the will knows no bounds and can abstract itself entirely from the outside world concentrating only on the inner life of the self. This negative freedom of the Understanding as Hegel terms it, finds its expression in destruction, destruction of the true nature of the self as a social being in 'the fanaticism' of pure self-contemplation, destruction of the self as the ultimate act of self-will, or finally as religious and political acts of destruction aimed against the whole subsisting social order. In this last sense what is objected to, as in the French Revolutionary Terror, is particularity itself; the existence of organizations and individuals with any authority or control over the free citizen. Consequently the ideals which religious or political fanaticism claims to serve can never be realized, since realization involves the re-establishment in some form or other of a structure of authority. 'Consequently, what negative freedom intends to will can never be anything in itself but an abstract idea, and giving effect to this idea can only be the fury of destruction' (p. 22). Negative freedom is itself unfreedom, for it restricts the will to an understanding in abstract universal terms without reference to the world in which the subject lives. The will is consequently confined either to pure contemplation, which denies the nature of will as 'thinking translating itself into existence' (para. 4, addition p. 226); or it expresses itself in undesirable actions which frustrate the subject, driving him to destruction and despair. To be free the will must give concrete form to the abstract conceptions of thought. To be free is to be an individual.

Individuality is expressed in action not in thought, but this does not mean that any action is a free action. Those who conceive freedom as 'ability to do what we please' have 'not even an inkling of the absolutely free will' (p. 27). The arbitrary choice of what pleases for the moment is not freedom of choice, but freedom of chance. Freedom cannot consist in merely exercising one's capacity to choose what one wishes from the selection offered in the immediate world of encounter; for without guidance and unity of purpose, this will mean a succession of unrelated acts which are meaningless outside themselves. The will that expresses mere feelings and impulses is the natural will not the free will. The natural will is only implicitly free because lacking the form of rationality it is satisfied with immediate gratification; 'it is only as thinking intelligence that the will is genuinely will and free'. 'The slave does not know his infinity, his freedom; he does not know himself as human in essence and he lacks this knowledge of himself because he does not think himself' (p. 30).

Self-consciousness of oneself as a rational person is a necessary condition of being a free individual, but it is not sufficient in itself. In *Phenomenology of Spirit* Hegel traces the stages in the development of self-consciousness towards absolute freedom. In its simplest form, as stoicism, self-consciousness is taken as being itself freedom. 'In thinking,' it is held, 'I am free, because I am not in another, but remain simply and solely in touch with myself; and the object which for me is my essential reality, is in undivided unity my self-existence; and my procedure in dealing with notions is a process within myself' (p. 243). This subjective notion of freedom is indifferent to the natural existence, taking 'only pure thought as its truth and lacking the concrete filling of life. It is therefore, merely the notion of freedom, not living freedom itself' (p. 245). There is a living truth in stoicism, the truth that man is capable of withdrawing into the inner realm of his own soul, thus removing himself from the possibility of coercion by others; 'the free will cannot be coerced at all except in so far as it fails to withdraw itself out of the external object in which it is held fast, or rather out of its idea of that object. Only the will which allows itself to be coerced can in any way be coerced' (*Philosophy of Right*, p. 66). But my capacity as a self-conscious being to abstract myself from the oppressions and restrictions of the outside world in order to *retain* the core of my subjective freedom, i.e. in order to prevent my becoming the mere tool of another, should not be confused with the *realization* of freedom in positive action. The self ought not to accept the power of withdrawal as its purpose, neither should it, as with Scepticism, find the certainty of its own freedom in the arbitrary and illusory nature of the outside world.

Both the Stoic and the Sceptic wrongly believe themselves to be free in the kernel of their own being. The 'Unhappy Consciousness' or 'Alienated Soul', on the other hand is all too aware of itself as unfree. Those in this condition rightly recognize that freedom cannot be achieved within oneself, but being unable to realize themselves in this world, they turn to the next. The 'Unhappy Consciousness' has transcended the limited notion of freedom as pure thought, only to give itself up to the unattainable 'beyond', the ultimate reality of an absolute universal Being, in whose light the individual is as nothing. In *Philosophy of History* Hegel makes it apparent that it is medieval Christianity which he has particularly in mind in his conception of the 'Unhappy Consciousness', for the medieval church, in his view, had perverted the spiritual message that Christ was the mediator between man and God. It is only on 'the supposition that the human and the divine nature are essentially one, and that Man, so far as he is Spirit, also possesses the essentiality and substantiality that belongs to the idea of Deity' that the individual can attain his Spiritual essence, which is true freedom (p. 392).

Frustrated by the attempt to gain spiritual freedom through the Christian Church, which as ecclesiastical authority demands blind slavish obedience to its will, the Spirit of man turns back to seek salvation in the world below. The upshot is the emergence of three successive stages of individualism. The first of these is the pursuit of pleasure where the individual spirit 'takes to itself life much as a ripe fruit is plucked, which comes to meet the hand that takes it' (*Phenomenology of Mind*, p. 385). The satisfaction of desire, however, while it enables the individual to realize himself objectively in the object desired and to abolish the gap between self and other; does so at the expense of cancelling the existence of the desired object at the very point where it has ceased to be alien and apart from the subject. The fruits of pleasure cannot satisfy. The second form of individualism is romanticism which holds that a man is free when he does what he knows in his heart to be right. In this form self-consciousness 'knows that it has the universal, the law, immediately within itself, a law which, because of this characteristic of being immediately within consciousness as it is for itself, is called the Law of the *Heart*' (p. 391). The purpose of 'the Law of the Heart' is not the private pleasure of the individual, but the realization of its own natural excellence for the benefit of all mankind. But in claiming to express universal purpose immediately through its particular consciousness the individual demonstrates simply his 'frantic self-conceit'.

> When consciousness therefore sets up the law of its heart, it finds itself resisted by others because it conflicts with the equally individual laws of their heart; and the latter in opposing it are doing nothing else but setting up in their turn and making valid their own law. The universal

here presented, therefore, is only a universal resistance and struggle of all against one another, in which each makes good his own individuality, but at the same time does not come off successfully, because each individuality meets with the same opposition and each is reciprocally dissipated by the others (p. 399).

The third form of individualism is that of 'virtuous consciousness' whereby the individual surrenders his own will and desires to the discipline and control of the universal law of truth and goodness; but where that law has still to be sought by the individual within himself, not in the 'course of the world'. The 'course of the world' is seen as one in which universal principles are denied in favour of individual pleasure and enjoyment. The virtuous man must needs set himself up against the world in defence of the universal principles of truth and goodness which he has made his own, in a vain attempt to impose these principles upon it. The world's process is viewed as 'a passive instrument, which is directed by the hand of free individuality and is quite indifferent to the use it is put to, and can be misused for the production of a reality which means its ruin: a lifeless material deprived of any independence of its own – a material that can be formed in this way or that, or even to its own destruction' (p. 405). The puffed-up virtuous individual fails to see that the reality of the world's process, for all its apparent selfishness, is 'in undivided unity with the universal'. Individuality does not have to be sacrificed to abstract morality, nor does the world of reality need to be recast in conformity with such abstraction. On the contrary individuality needs to identify itself with the world of reality and to find its own reality and freedom in that world.

In *Philosophy of Right* Hegel traces out the forms in which the individual may realize his freedom in the spheres of morality, family, civil society and the state, each sphere interlocking with the next and understandable only in terms of the organic unity which they form. Freedom first becomes actual at the moral level where the individual seeks to give effect to the dictates of conscience. Such action, however, will be perverted unless the realm of conscience is firmly fixed in the wider field of ethical life, of family, society and the state. This ethical order provides the individual 'with a stable content independently necessary and subsistent in exaltation above subjective opinion and caprice' (p. 105). When he enters the areas of family, society and state the individual enters the realm of duties arising out of the necessity of the relationship in which he stands to other individuals and the community at large. For Hegel the notion of duty is in no way inconsistent with the notion of freedom; since, as we have seen, freedom is for him a positive objective universal concept, not a negative subjective particular one.

> The bond of duty can appear as a restriction only on indeterminate subjectivity or abstract freedom, and on the impulses either of the natural will or of the moral will which determines its indeterminate good arbitrarily. The truth is, however, that in duty the individual finds his liberation; first liberation from dependence on mere natural impulse and from the depression which as a particular subject he cannot escape in his moral reflections on what ought to be and what might be; secondly liberation from the indeterminate subjectivity which never reaching reality or the objective determinacy of action, remains self-enclosed and devoid of actuality. In duty the individual acquires his substantive freedom (p. 107).

But the spheres of duty are also spheres of rights, for an ethical order recognizes 'the right of individuals to their *particular* satisfaction' (p. 109). While in the areas of morality, family and civil society rights and duties differ in content, in the state they are united and 'individuals have duties to the state in proportion as they have rights against it' (p. 161). Hegel does not deny rights to the individual, on the contrary he argues that the state has responsibilities to its members, but only in so far as these members carry out their duties; indeed unless they carry out their duties the state cannot fulfil its responsibilities. What may be said, however, is that Hegel gives priority to the fulfilment of duty, that there can be no justification for a demand for rights on the part of those who do not carry out their social responsibilities. Men who see society as a provider of goods and services fail to comprehend the truth that it is only in serving the community that a man can realize his true self and be free.

> The *isolated* individual, so far as his duties are concerned, is in subjection, but as a member of *civil society* he finds in fulfilling his duties to it protection of his person and property, regard for his private welfare, the satisfaction of the depths of his being, the consciousness and feeling of himself as a member of the whole; and, so far as he completely fulfils his duties by performing tasks and services for the *state*, he is upheld and preserved (p. 162).

Hegel's conception of the role of the state in relation to the individual is not one of suppression. He does not assert the claim of the state to total control of the life of the community and its members, nor does he conceive the need for the state to impose a single all-embracing pattern of values on individuals by indoctrination and censorship. This is clearly demonstrated in *The German Constitution*, where Hegel attacks

the proposition that 'a state is a machine with a single spring which imparts movement to all the rest of the infinite wheelwork, and that all
institutions implicit in the nature of a society should proceed from the
supreme public authority and be regulated, commanded, overseen, and
conducted by it'. In contradistinction he insists that 'the public authority, i.e. the government, must leave to the freedom of the citizens whatever is not necessary for its appointed function of organizing and
maintaining authority and thus for its security at home and abroad.
Nothing should be so sacrosanct to the government as facilitating and
protecting the free activity of citizens in matters other than this'
(pp. 161–2). Further he argues that the area of free activity must include
the right to elect a body representative of the people to 'share in the
making of laws and the management of the most important affairs of
state'. 'Without such a representative body, freedom is no longer
thinkable' (p. 234).

Freedom is the theme of Hegel's *Philosophy of History*. To understand the history of the world 'we must know what *is essential*; and that
is – the Consciousness of Freedom, and the phases which this consciousness assumes in developing itself. The bearing of historical facts on this
category, is their bearing on the truly Essential' (p. 68). The first great
phase of world history, oriental despotism, is characterized as the condition in which only the ruler has a separate existence and where all
subjects merge their freedom in his being. Even the despot is not truly
free, as he acts simply by caprice. The first men to be conscious of
freedom were the Greeks, although for them only some men, free-born
citizens, were free. They did not perceive the essential truth 'that Man
as such' is free. 'The Greeks, therefore, had slaves; and their whole life
and the maintenance of their splendid liberty, was implicated with the
institution of slavery: a fact moreover, which made that liberty on the
one hand only an accidental, transient and limited growth; on the other
hand, constituted it a rigorous thraldom of our common nature – of the
Human' (p. 19). Hegel contrasts the 'vital freedom' of Athens where
'all diversities of character and talent, and all variety of idiosyncrasy
could assert itself in the most unrestrained manner, and find the most
abundant stimulus to development in its environment' (p. 271) with the
'lifeless equality' to be found in Sparta. Greek freedom is the freedom
of the self-emancipation of Thought which reached its culmination in
the teaching of Socrates that the individual is the final moral judge of all
things, a teaching which inevitably eroded the basis of customary
morality and unreflecting patriotism. The full manifestation of freedom

had to await the appearance of Christianity with its message of spiritual freedom 'God will have *all* men to be saved' (p. 346) and of a people able to give effect to this message in its institutions. It was the destiny of the German peoples[1] 'to be the bearers of that principle . . . from the time of the decline of Rome to the present day'. The decisive event of this whole period is seen by Hegel as the Reformation, personified in Luther. In Luther's Church and teaching 'Christian Freedom is actualized', since it holds the subjective feeling and the conviction of the individual as equally necessary with the objective side of Truth (p. 433). 'Time, since that epoch, has had no other work to do than the formal imbuing of the world with this principle.' The essence of the Reformation is: 'Man is in his very nature destined to be free' (p. 434).

READING

Hegel, *Philosophy of Right*, Introduction.

Hegel, *Philosophy of History*, 'Classification of Historical Data', pp. 109–16.

J. Plamenatz, *Man and Society*, Vol. II, 'Social and Political Philosophy of Hegel', I, pp. 150–73.

6. MARX AND ENGELS

Marx and Engels' conception of freedom has its origins in French materialism and Hegelian idealism. The French materialists had taught that man is the product of his circumstances and that consequently the essence of unfreedom was the absence not of 'the negative capacity to avoid this or that' but of 'the positive power to assert his true individuality' which results from the failure of society to provide the 'social scope for the essential assertion of his vitality'.[2] From Hegel had come the insight that 'freedom is the appreciation of necessity'. 'Freedom,' Engels writes,

1. By the German peoples, Hegel meant the peoples of north-western Europe.
2. *The German Ideology*, Easton and Guddat, op. cit., p. 394.

does not consist in the dream of independence of natural laws, but in the knowledge of these laws, and in the possibility this gives of systematically making them work towards definite ends. . . . Freedom of will therefore means nothing but the capacity to make decisions with real knowledge of the subject. Therefore the *freer* a man's judgment is in relation to a definite question, with so much the greater *necessity* is the content of this judgment determined; while the uncertainty, founded in ignorance, which seems to make an arbitrary choice among many different and conflicting possible desires, shows by this precisely that it is not free, that it is controlled by the very object it should itself control (*Anti-Dühring*, p. 128).

Freedom for Marx and Engels is not a negative quality of being left alone to one's own devices or a subjective feeling of not being conscious of restraints, but a matter of fact about the extent to which any society enables its members to develop their capacities to the full as social and individual beings. In primitive communities men are at the mercy of the forces of nature, in the state they are at the mercy of the ruling class.

Only in community do the means exist for every individual to cultivate his talents in all directions. Only in the community is personal freedom possible. In previous substitutes for the community, in the state etc., personal freedom has existed only for the individuals who developed within the ruling class and only insofar as they belonged to this class (*The German Ideology*, p. 457).

Under conditions of slavery the conditions of servitude are apparent to all, under feudalism the restrictions on the movements and activities of the serf are well-defined and understood, only under capitalism is the subjection of one class to another denied by the exploiter and only partially comprehended by the exploited. 'In imagination, individuals seem freer under the rule of the bourgeoisie than before because their conditions of life seem accidental to them. In reality they are less free, because they are more subjected to the domination of things' (p. 458). The serfs of the Middle Ages, from whom sprang the burghers of the towns – the forerunners of the bourgeoisie – had been able to use and profit from their handicraft skills within the framework of feudal society. They required freedom in order to be able to develop these skills without restriction. They desired to appropriate for themselves the full product of their own labour; but the system they developed was one under which they appropriated the product of the labour of others. The freedom which was demanded by the standard bearers of the bourgeoisie was freedom for all to use their labour as they thought fit, freedom to buy and sell on an open market. The social consequences of the realization

of economic freedom under capitalism were that the workers were free
to determine which master they would allow to appropriate the surplus
value produced by their labour when times were good, and free to
starve when times were bad. Nor were the consequences of bourgeois
freedom quite what that class had expected and desired.

> The 'freedom of property' from feudal fetters, now veritably accom-
> plished, turned out to be, for the small capitalists and small proprietors,
> the freedom to sell their small property, crushed under the overmaster-
> ing competition of the large capitalists and landlords, to these great
> lords, and thus, so far as the small capitalists and peasant proprietors
> were concerned, became 'freedom *from* property'.[1]

The freedom which capitalism establishes is 'not the freedom of one
individual in relation to another, but the freedom of capital to crush the
worker',[2] an operation carried on by an ever-decreasing number of expropriators over an ever-increasing number of expropriated. The
workers under capitalism find themselves cogs in a gigantic machine
which they can neither control nor comprehend. As free workers they
are not tied to an individual master, but to a system of masters since
their condition of life does not alter with their employer. That condition
is completely demoralized and degrading, as well as arduous and ill-
rewarded. Not only is the product of the workers' labour appropriated
by the capitalist, but he does not have the satisfaction of making a whole
product. He becomes an appendage to a machine, performing one
function in a complex process. The objectification of labour as production under conditions of capitalism results in the complete alienation of
the worker, both from the product and from the work process.

> The worker puts his life into the object; then it no longer belongs to
> him but to the object. The greater this activity, the poorer is the
> worker. What the product of his work is, he is not . . . . The *externa-
> lization* of the worker in his product means not only that his work
> becomes an object, an *external* existence, but that it exists *outside him*,
> independently alien, an autonomous power, opposed to him.[3]

He becomes a slave to the objects which he produces, his labour is not
voluntary but forced labour which he carries on solely to live, where life

1. F. Engels, *Socialism, Utopian and Scientific*, 1892, in *Engels: Selected Writings*,
   p. 188.
2. K. Marx, Address on Free Trade, 1848, reprinted in *The Poverty of Philosophy*,
   op. cit., p. 207.
3. K. Marx, *Economic and Philosophic Manuscripts*, 1844, Easton and Guddat,
   op. cit., p. 290.

is seen as what exists outside of work. This position cannot be remedied by attempts to improve the conditions of the workers for even if successful this would mean nothing more than 'a better slave-salary and would not achieve either for the worker or for labour human significance and dignity' (p. 298). To raise the worker to the level of an individual requires the abolition of the whole system of private appropriation of socially produced products. 'In bourgeois society capital is independent and has individuality, while the living person is dependent and has no individuality.' 'And the abolition of this state of things,' declares *The Communist Manifesto*, 'is called by the bourgeois abolition of individuality and freedom! And rightly so. The abolition of bourgeois individuality, bourgeois independence, and bourgeois freedom is undoubtedly aimed at.' [1] This contempt for 'bourgeois freedom' did not extend to contempt for all the institutions and principles of bourgeois rule. Engels, in *Anti-Dühring*,[2] commends the safeguards to personal liberty provided by English law, and in a letter to Bebel speaks of the responsibility of functionaries to the ordinary courts and common law for their official actions as 'the first condition of all freedom'.[3]

Marx and Engels provide us with only a very hazy outline of how communist society will provide all the necessary conditions of freedom by liberating men from subjection to the productive process. In the *Economic and Philosophic Manuscripts*, Marx contrasts true communism with crude communism; where 'the community as universal capitalist' gives effect to envy, and simply abolishes individual private property without fundamentally altering the wages system which subordinates the worker to the productive process. 'Such a system,' Marx insists, 'still remains captive to and infected by private property.'[4] What has to be avoided above all is 'establishing "society" once again as an abstraction over against the individual. The individual *is* the *social being*' (p. 306). The overcoming of private property means 'the complete *emancipation* of all human senses and aptitudes' (p. 308) from subordination to the acquisition of things for personal use. Man's nature must be humanized and socialized so as to produce 'the *rich*, deep and *entirely sensitive* man' in place of the crude consumer and acquirer (p. 310).

In *Capital*, Vol. I, Marx speaks of the need to transform the factory

1. Feuer, op. cit., p. 64.
2. *Anti-Dühring*, p. 127.
3. Engels to Bebel, 18–28 March 1875. *Selected Correspondence*, p. 336.
4. Easton and Guddat, op. cit., p. 304.

system where the workers are incorporated into the machines 'as its living appendages' (p. 451) into 'a process carried on by a free association of producers, under their conscious and purposive control' (p. 54). In *Capital*, Vol. III, Marx makes it clear that his conception of freedom is one which will dispense with the methods used by capitalism to discipline the labour force. Such methods would be superfluous where the labourers work in free association 'for their own accord'.[1] Marx's claim that labour discipline would not be required under socialism, does not necessarily conflict with Engels's insistence that authority would still be necessary. Marx was arguing that under socialism it would no longer be necessary to maintain the factory as 'a mitigated form of convict prison', where 'in place of the slave driver's lash, we have the overlooker's book of penalties'.[2] The workers under socialism would be engaged in a co-operative venture for their mutual benefit. Engels, on the other hand, was concerned to rebut the views of those who condemned all authority in principle, without recognizing that organization, especially large scale industrial organization involves authority. What was necessary was to 'restrict authority solely to the limits within which the condition of production render it inevitable. This requires that, in the last resort, 'the will of the single individual will always have to subordinate itself' to a dominant will, whether this will is represented by a single delegate or a committee charged with the execution of the resolutions of the majority of persons interested'.[3]

Marx recognized with Engels that a man cannot be free to work or not to work as he chooses, nor can he be free to determine for himself how or when he should work. 'The realm of freedom' he wrote in *Capital*, Vol. III, 'only begins, in fact, where that labour which is determined by need and external purposes ceases; it is therefore, by its very nature, outside the sphere of material production proper' –

> Freedom in this field cannot consist of anything else but the fact that socialized mankind, the associated producers, regulate their interchange with Nature rationally, bring it under their common control, instead of being ruled by it as by some blind power, and accomplish their task with the least expenditure of energy and under such conditions as are proper and worthy for human beings. Nevertheless, this always remains a realm of necessity. Beyond it begins that development

1. Quoted in Avineri, op. cit., p. 236.
2. *Capital*, Vol. I, pp. 453–4.
3. F. Engels, *On Authority*, 1874, Feuer, op. cit., pp. 519–23.

of human potentiality for its own sake, the true realm of freedom, which however can only flourish upon that realm of necessity as its basis.[1]

READING

K. Marx, *Economic and Philosophic Manuscripts*, 'Alienated Labour', 'Private Property and Communism', in *Writings of the Young Marx on Philosophy and Society*, edited by Loyd D. Easton and Kurt H. Guddat, pp. 287–314.

F. Engels, *On Authority*, in *Marx and Engels: Basic Writings on Politics and Philosophy*, edited by Lewis S. Feuer, pp. 518–23.

1. Bottomore and Rubel, op. cit., pp. 259–60.

CHAPTER 5

Equality and Property

1. HOBBES

> Nature hath made men so equall in the faculties of body, and mind; as
> that though there bee found one man sometimes manifestly stronger in
> body, or of quicker mind than another; yet when all is reckoned to-
> gether, the difference between man, and man, is not so considerable,
> as that one man can thereupon claim to himselfe any benefit, to which
> another may not pretend, as well as he (*Leviathan*, p. 63).

Because men are roughly equal by nature they are difficult to govern for
they do not recognize any claims to rule based on superiority in strength
or wisdom. Hobbes does not accept that mankind can be naturally
divided into leaders and led, as Plato does. His arguments for a strong
sovereign are based not on the qualities of the ruler, but the urgency
of man's social condition. It is precisely because men are roughly
equal that they stand in need of firm government. 'From this equality
of ability, ariseth equality of hope in the attaining of our Ends. And
therefore if any two men desire the same thing, which neverthelesse
they cannot both enjoy, they become enemies; and in the way to their
End – endeavour to destroy, or subdue one an other' (p. 63). The fact
that all men are basically motivated by the same desires and are roughly
the natural equals of each other means that the natural condition of
mankind is one of conflict which if unrestrained will result in death or
injury.

By the natural condition of men Hobbes meant not so much the
condition men were in before entering civil society as the condition they
would find themselves in if the restraining arms of law and order were
removed. Consequently it can be argued, as Professor Macpherson
does, that

> Hobbes's state of nature is a description neither of the necessary be-
> haviour of primitive men (though primitive men approximate to it
> more nearly than do men under established civil governments) nor of
> the necessary behaviour of the human animal stripped of all his socially

acquired appetites. The state of nature is a deduction from the appetites and other faculties not of man as such but of civilized men.[1]

Professor Macpherson's thesis is that Hobbes's theory of political obligation is a theory of and for rational men in possessive market societies, i.e. in capitalist or bourgeois societies. This interpretation of Hobbes has aroused such interest and controversy that it has been made the focal point for discussing Hobbes's views in this section. The key to Professor Macpherson's assertions is to be found in his reading of three passages of Hobbes taken from *Leviathan*, *Rudiments* and *Elements*. The first of these is that quoted at the beginning of this section (p. 178, above). The second passage from *Rudiments* reads 'there is no reason why any man trusting to his own strength should conceive himself made by nature above others, they are equals who can do equal things',[2] and the third from *Elements*, 'if we consider . . . with how great facility he that is the weaker in strength or in wit, or in both, may utterly destroy the power of the stronger . . . we may conclude that men considered in mere nature, ought to admit amongst themselves equality'.[3] Macpherson argues that in these passages Hobbes assumes that an equality of fact sets up an equality of right, without bringing in any outside value judgement or moral premise. Hobbes, that is to say, deduces 'right' from the fact that every man has wants which he must and does seek to satisfy. In Macpherson's view it is precisely because Hobbes treats these equal rights as moral rights that he is able to regard the obligations created by the transfer of these rights to the sovereign as moral obligations binding on all members of the community, and this it is which constitutes Hobbes's 'revolution in moral and political theory' (Macpherson, p. 78).

When we examine closely the passages which Professor Macpherson uses we find, however, that they do not establish that Hobbes was concerned to show that the fact of natural equality creates an obligation or duty for one man to trust another as his equal. Macpherson imposes an interpretation on these three passages which is neither required nor intended. The statement from *Leviathan* (p. 63) that 'the difference between man, and man, is not so considerable, as that one man can

1. C. B. Macpherson, *The Political Theory of Possessive Individualism*: *Hobbes to Locke*, 1962, p. 29.
2. T. H. Hobbes, *Rudiments*, Ch. 1, section 3, quoted by Macpherson, op. cit., p. 74.
3. T. H. Hobbes, *Elements*, Part I, Ch. 14, section 2, quoted by Macpherson, op. cit., p. 74.

thereupon claim to himselfe any benefit, to which another may not pretend, as well as he' is one of fact about men's natural equality not a statement about how men *ought* to handle others' claims to equality of treatment. Similarly the assertion that 'there is no reason why any man should conceive himself made by nature above others' (*Rudiments*) is not a negative moral imperative, i.e. it does not tell us what we should not do, in the sense of ought not to do. It is a factual statement that points out that it would be foolish for any man to consider himself above another, because all are equally at each others' mercy. Finally the 'ought' in the conclusion that 'men considered in mere nature, ought to admit amongst themselves equality' (*Elements*) is not a moral ought. Men are told to accept that they are equal, not that they have an obligation to treat men equally. Hobbes does not speak of men having natural obligations to treat each other equally or to recognize claims to equality of treatment, except with reference to the responsibility of judges to apply the natural law principle of equity in cases which come before them. (See pp. 95–6 above.)

The second point which needs to be made is that Macpherson uses the term 'right' in the sense of a moral claim which is quite different from the sense in which Hobbes uses the word 'The RIGHT OF NATURE . . . is the Liberty each man hath, to use his own power, as he will him-selfe, for the preservation of his own Nature' – liberty being defined as 'the absence of externall Impediments' (*Leviathan*, p. 66). Thus a man's right is for Hobbes, not a moral claim, but the actual power he possesses to do what he judges best for himself. This power may be voluntarily laid aside, but only where this is necessary for 'the security of a man's person, in his life, and in the means of so preserving life' (p. 68). A voluntary transfer of Right to another consists not in a transfer of claims or obligations but in the divestment of power. 'For he that renounceth, or passeth away his Right, giveth not to any other man a Right which he had not before . . . but onely standeth out of his way, that he may enjoy his own originall Right, without hindrance from him' (p. 67). Hobbes is quite specific that it is the voluntary act of abandonment of his Right, not the nature of the Right itself, which creates obligations and duties. Just as in scholarly disputation 'it is there called an Absur-dity, to contradict what one maintained in the Beginning: so in the world, it is called Injustice, and Injury, voluntarily to undo that, which from the beginning he had voluntarily done' (p. 68). For Hobbes the natural equality of men provides not the basis for the establishment of an equality of right which all men feel obliged to acknowledge (as

Macpherson argues); but the grounds for his assertion that the natural condition of man is continuous war, which can only be ended if men recognize the need to put on one side their natural power to do what they please.

Professor Macpherson's secondary purpose is to establish that the type of model society depicted by Hobbes exhibits 'a kind of equality; the equal subordination of every individual to the laws of the market', so that

> every man's entitlements are determined by the actual competitive relationship between the powers of individuals. If the determination of values and rights by the market is accepted as justice by all members of the society, there is a sufficient basis for rational obligation, binding on all men, to an authority which could maintain and enforce the market system (Macpherson, p. 86).

Macpherson derives this interpretation principally from the following short passage in *Leviathan*.

> The *value*, or WORTH of a man, is as of all other things, his Price; that is to say, so much as would be given for the use of his Power: and therefore is not absolute; but a thing dependent on the need and judgement of another. (An able conductor of Souldiers, is of great Price in time of War present, or imminent; but in Peace not so. A learned and uncorrupt Judge, is much Worth in times of Peace; but not so much in War.)[1] And as in other things, so in men, not the seller, but the buyer determines the Price. For let a man (as most men do) rate themselves at the highest Value they can; yet their true Value is no more than it is esteemed by others (p. 44).

The passage in itself is ambiguous. It might mean, as Macpherson suggests that 'Every man's value is established as prices are established in the market', (Macpherson, p. 39), but it would not thereby follow that 'there is no room in Hobbes's model . . . for an assessment of the merit of different men in terms of the contribution they make to the purposes of the whole society, or in terms of their needs as functioning parts of a social organism' (p. 64). As Keith Thomas has pointed out,[2] value is only one of the criteria which Hobbes uses in assessing men. Hobbes speaks of a man's merit or desert as what he is entitled to receive under the terms of a contract, and of his worthiness when he possesses the qualities required to fulfil an office or function. Value itself he sees as

1. Words in parentheses omitted by Macpherson.
2. Keith Thomas, 'The Social Origins of Hobbes's Political Thought', in *Hobbes Studies*, pp. 230–1.

being manifested in honouring and dishonouring (i.e. judging another at high or low value in comparison with oneself). Although it is true that in the main Hobbes expresses these manifestations in terms of power relationships, this is not true in all the cases instanced. Hobbes tells us that men may be praised for their goodness or felicity, trusted for their virtue, harkened to for their wisdom, agreed with for their judgement – none of which fit in with Professor Macpherson's conception that value for Hobbes is established by and in a competitive market for power. Moreover Hobbes makes it clear that the sovereign has power to grant honours to whom he will and that these arbitrary acts create a special public expression of value 'which men commonly call DIGNITY' (*Leviathan*, p. 44).

If one turns to the actual picture which Hobbes paints of his model society it corresponds at some points only with Macpherson's model of a possessive market society. While Hobbes will have no truck with the medieval notion of the 'just price' as something separate from the market price and while he speaks of men's labour as a commodity and opposes internal monopolies, there are other features of his model which do not accord with the market society model. The most important of these, and the least acceptable to men of property, was his insistence that no man had an unqualified claim to or control over his own property. Hobbes argues that since propriety (or ownership) could not exist outside civil society, the distribution of wealth stems from the creation of the state. In terms of his model this means that 'the Sovereign assigneth to every man a portion according as he, and not according as any Subject, or any number of them, shall judge agreeable to Equity, and the Common Good'. 'From whence we may collect, that the propriety which a subject hath in his lands, consisteth in a right to exclude all other subjects from the use of them; and not to exclude their Soveraign' (p. 131). Hobbes claims that the false but widely held opinion that every Subject has the right to complete and full enjoyment of his goods and property is the reason why rulers find difficulty in raising money 'for the necessary uses of the Common-wealth' (p. 176). But there are other aspects of the Hobbesian model which either do not meet or which conflict with the requirements of a free market society. Thus Hobbes talks of the right of the Sovereign to control foreign trade and to decide the terms and form which economic contracts are to take and of his duty to provide for the aged and infirm, to compel the indolent to work, to transport the surplus poor to other lands and to encourage all manufacture that requires labour (pp. 132–3 and 185). Hobbes, as Keith

Thomas points out, was championing a medieval cause, in opposition to bourgeois values and thinking, when he argued that it was no crime for a man to steal in order to keep himself alive (p. 160). Hobbes's views on contract were not orthodox bourgeois views, for not only did he grant the sovereign the right to determine the conditions under which contracts might be made, but he held that contracts made under duress or through fear were as binding as those freely entered into (p. 72).

Hobbes's prime concern is not with the preservation of property rights but the preservation of the individual's life. He does not assume that the former is always the means to the latter, for he makes express provision for the invasion or curtailment of property rights by the sovereign (where the sovereign holds this necessary to the carrying out of his functions), and in extremity by the individual. Not only does Hobbes give the sovereign power to act as he wills in the economic field, as in all spheres, but his views on economic policy are far from being simple *laissez-faire* views. They are rather a blend of traditional and bourgeois notions, laced with notions of his own derived from the conceptual scheme of the *Leviathan* state. The equality which the Hobbesian state affords is not that of equal subjection to the laws of the market but equal subjection to the laws of the sovereign. 'The safety of the People, requireth further, from him, or them that have the Sovereign Power, that Justice be equally administered to all degrees of People' (p. 183). A sovereign who ignores this precept fails to discharge the obligations of his office and risks the collapse of civil society through internal strife.

READING

Hobbes, *Leviathan*, Ch. 24.

C. B. Macpherson, *The Political Theory of Possessive Individualism*, Ch. 2, sections 3–5.

Keith Thomas, 'The Social Origins of Hobbes' Political Thought' in *Hobbes Studies*, edited by K. C. Brown.

2. LOCKE

When Locke writes that men are 'in Nature equal' he does not mean that they are equal in capacity or even potentiality, but that they all 'share in the same common, Nature Faculties and Powers'. (I, s. 67). They are all men, distinguished from beasts by their possession of the faculty of reason and this common and distinctive feature provides the basis for human morality. Because we are all aware of other men as fellow creatures to ourselves with the same needs and desires, we ought to recognize their right to exist on the same terms as ourselves. In particular we ought to recognize 'that *equal Right* that every Man hath, *to his Natural Freedom*, without being subjected to the Will or Authority of any other Man' (II, s. 54). It is precisely because of the oneness and sameness of men's nature that any differentiation in treatment between one man and another needs justifying. Men are entitled 'to partake in the same common Rights and Priviledges' (I, s. 67) on the same terms as other men unless it can be shown that God's manifest will or men's own consent determines to the contrary, or unless one can demonstrate inequality of capacity. Locke lists a number of areas in which men are not equal and which therefore may qualify the claim to equal rights and privileges, namely age, virtue, physical excellence, birth. He insists however that none of these conflicts with the right not to be subordinated to the will of another (II, s. 54): indeed he goes so far as to argue that no man has the right to enslave himself or put himself under the absolute arbitrary power of another (II, s. 23). Those who lack reason, like children and lunatics, may be placed under the authority of others but only for their good, not the advantage of their mentors. For the rest, a man may only have authority over others by their consent and for expressly understood and limited purposes –

> The Authority of the Rich Proprietor, and the Subjection of the Needy Beggar began not from the Possession of the Lord, but the Consent of the poor Man, who preferr'd being his Subject to starving. And the Man he thus submits to, can pretend to no more Power over him, than he has consented to, upon Compact (I, s. 43).

Even a wife, for Locke, is not subject to the arbitrary despotism of her husband. She possesses rights, including 'in many cases, a Liberty to *separate* from him' (II, s. 82).

Since all men have an equal right to life they must be accepted as having in the beginning an equal claim to the fruits of the earth. Indeed

Locke spends a considerable time in the *First Treatise* refuting Filmer's biblical evidence for private property stemming from God's donation of the world to Adam. In Locke's view reason and revelation both demonstrate that God gave the earth to mankind in common, but its fruits have to be appropriated for the exclusive use of individuals, before they can be of benefit to man. The questions which arise are how can one justify private appropriation of commonly available goods and how much may be appropriated? The answers are to be found in Locke's theory of property which is perhaps the most distinctive feature of his political thinking.

> Though the Earth, and all inferior Creatures be common to all Men, yet every Man has a *Property* in his own *Person*. This no Body has any Right to but himself. The *Labour* of his Body, and the *Work* of his Hands, we may say, are properly his. Whatsoever then he removes out of the State that Nature hath provided, and left it in, he hath mixed his *Labour* with, and joyned to it something that is his own, and thereby makes it his *Property*. It being by him removed from the common state Nature placed it in, it hath by this *labour* something annexed to it, that excludes it from the common right of other Men. For this *Labour* being the unquestionable Property of the Labourer, no Man but he can have a right to what that is once joyned to, at least where there is enough, and as good left in common for others (II, s. 27).

It is labour which creates property rights by removing the fruits of the earth from the common state. Consent is not necessary to create property rights because it was God's gift not 'any express Compact of all the Commoners' (II, s. 25), which established the common availability of the earth's fruits. Moreover it would be an impossible task to obtain the consent of all mankind to any proposed appropriation and such universal consent would be required since all were equally entitled to share in the earth's benefits. To insist on consent would be to condemn men to starvation in the midst of God's plenty (II, s. 28).

I have a natural right to the product of my own labour, even if that labour consists simply in picking apples from a tree. The mere act of picking makes the apples mine because it 'added something to them more than Nature, the Common Mother of all, had done' (II, s. 28). This claim to the use of what I have appropriated and created by my own labour is not, however, for Locke an absolute and unconditional one. It is subject to there remaining a sufficiency of fruits available for others which they too may appropriate and to my not wasting what I have myself appropriated. To waste is to offend against the common Law of

Nature for no man has a right to take more than he can himself consume (II, s. 37). All men have an equal claim on these terms to appropriate from the commonstock of nature; no man has a claim to appropriate what has become the private property of another by appropriation. What applies to fruits and beasts applies to the land and he that 'subdued, tilled and sowed any part of it, thereby annexed to it something that was his Property, which another had no Title to, nor could without injury take from him' (II, s. 32). Thus the private labour of individual men transforms the common lands into private estates. But the moral injunction against waste to ensure that a sufficiency is left for others, applies equally in the case of land. I may only enclose land which I can put to use and if I fail to cultivate the land or consume its products my claim to possess it, based on the labour of my act of enclosure is nullified and any man in need may take possession of it for his own use.

If Locke had left the argument at this point he would have associated himself with the social revolutionary doctrines of Gerard Winstanley and the Diggers of the English Commonwealth, who proclaimed the right of the landless to take over and cultivate unkept and unused land.[1] But the whole position is transformed for Locke by the introduction of money as a means of exchange. Money solved the problem of waste, for it enabled men to store up wealth in a non-perishable form, and made possible a great increase in production and commerce. It also had the effect of creating great disparities in wealth and possessions, in place of 'the equality of a simple poor way of liveing' (II, s. 107). The use of money is justified negatively on the grounds that it does not involve any invasion of other's rights and positively because men have mutually consented to its use. They must therefore be understood to have given their consent to its consequences – the 'disproportionate and unequal Possession of the Earth' (II, s. 50). The widespread use of money vastly accelerates the process of differentiation of wealth begun when men of different degrees of capacity and industry began to appropriate the fruits of the earth.

It will be noted that while Locke argues that the limitation of waste is removed by the introduction of wealth nothing is said about the second limitation of sufficiency. Professor Macpherson argues that this limitation is inoperative when its purpose, to secure to each man a means of subsistence by his labour, is otherwise met.

---

1. An entertaining study of Digger philosophy is to be found in David Caute's novel, *Comrade Jacob*, 1961.

In short the appropriation of land in excess of what leaves enough and as good for others is justified both by the implied tacit consent to the necessary consequences of the introduction of money, and by the assertion that the standards of those without land, where it is all appropriated and used, are higher than the standards of any where it is not generally appropriated.[1]

Macpherson's second argument is a doubtful one for, if all Locke had been concerned with was the possession of an adequate standard of life for all, there would have been no necessity for him to have introduced the sufficiency principle. For he proclaims it as a general rule 'that he who appropriates land to himself by his labour, does not lessen but increase the common stock of mankind' (II, s. 37). Yet this very passage occurs immediately after a reiteration of the need for the appropriator to leave 'the same plenty' to those 'who would use the same Industry'. Appropriation is important to Locke, not simply because it enables men to survive, but as the means of establishing property rights. Consequently the requirement to abide by the sufficiency principle when one appropriates land from the common stock is a guarantee that others too may acquire rights of land proprietorship. Locke accepts that the sufficiency principle could still apply in the modern world 'since there is Land enough in the World to suffice double the Inhabitants' (II, s.36), but argues that the possibility of a world of small-scale proprietors was destroyed by the invention and use of money, which 'altered the intrinsick value of things' (II, s. 37). Money unleashed the desire for possessions by making it possible for a man to hold more than he could possess or use. This principle of sufficiency only becomes of importance when land begins to become scarce and it does not become scarce until population increases under a money-based economy. The sufficiency principle is then taken up in a form familiar to many men of Locke's generation, of landless men laying claim to part of the land appropriated by those who possess far more than they need or even use.

It is perhaps because Locke recognizes that the alteration of 'the intrinsick value of things' results in most men having no effective rights of land proprietorship that he seeks to justify it in terms of consent: consent to the use of money and consent to the establishment of political societies which protect existing established property rights. It was where the increase of people and the use of money had made land scarce and valuable that men settled in distinct communities 'and by Laws within

1. C. B. Macpherson, *The Political Theory of Possessive Individualism: Hobbes to Locke*, p. 213.

themselves, regulated the Properties of the private Men of their Society, and so, *by Compact* and Agreement, *settled the Property* which Labour and Industry began' (II, s. 45). But although the civil power has the authority to pass laws to 'regulate the right of property' (II, s. 50), it cannot undermine and upset the established system of property relations, for 'the chief end' of civil society 'is the preservation of property' (II, s. 85). It is therefore impossible for Locke to recognize any claim of the propertyless to land already appropriated by others, whether on the grounds that because the appropriators have taken more than they need there is none left for others, or that they are not cultivating all the land they have (i.e. are wasting it). One of the effects of the institution of civil society, according to Locke's formulation, is that claims of this sort which might be made in terms of natural law rights can no longer be sustained. The civil law decides disputes as to what rights men have.

> For the Law of Nature being unwritten, and so no where to be found but in the minds of Men, they who through Passion or Interest shall mis-cite, or misapply it, cannot so easily be convinced of their mistake where there is no establish'd Judge: And so it serves not, as it ought, to determine the Rights, and fence the Properties of those that live under it, especially where every one is Judge, Interpreter, and Executioner of it too, and that in his own case: And he that has right on his side, having ordinarily but his own single strength, hath not force enough to defend himself from Injuries, or to punish Delinquents. To avoid these Inconveniences which disorder Mens Properties in the state of Nature, Men unite into Societies, that they may have united strength of the whole Society to secure and defend their Properties and may have *standing Rules* to bound it, by which every one may know what is his (II, s. 136).

Political society is conceived by Locke as having as one of its main purposes the defence of the established system of property rights; natural law can only be urged against an existing government if it attacks and undermines these established rights.

This is not to say, however, that Locke believes that men in society have an unqualified right to do what they like with their own property. Property rights are natural rights and as such cannot be arbitrarily abrogated by society, but they are subject to regulation –

> every Man, when he, at first incorporates himself into any Commonwealth, he, by uniting himself thereunto, annexed also, and submits to the Community those Possessions, which he has, or shall acquire, that do not already belong to any other Government. For it would be a direct Contradiction, for any one, to enter into Society with others for the securing and regulating of Property: And yet to suppose his

Land, whose Property is to be regulated by the Laws of the Society, should be exempt from the Jurisdiction of that Government, to which he himself the Proprietor of the Land, is a Subject (II, s. 120).

Locke distinguishes sharply between the power which governments have to regulate property from the power to expropriate it. Rulers, he insists, 'can never have a Power to take to themselves the whole or any part of the Subjects *Property*, without their own consent' (II, s. 139), but in the next paragraph, in accepting that a man ought to pay taxes out of his estate for the protection of government, he writes 'still it must be with his own Consent i.e. the Consent of the Majority, giving it either by themselves, or their Representatives chosen by them' (II, s. 140). Do these two passages taken in conjunction mean that Locke held that a man might be legitimately deprived of his property by the decision of a majority vote in a representative legislative? It is difficult to believe that this was his intention, especially in the light of his earlier insistence that the legislative power 'is *not*, nor can possibly be absolutely *Arbitrary* over the Lives and Fortunes of the People'.

> A Man, as has been proved, cannot subject himself to the Arbitrary Power of another; and having in the State of Nature no Arbitrary Power over the Life, Liberty or Possessions of another, but only so much as the Law of Nature gave him for the preservation of himself, and the rest of Mankind; this is all he doth, or can give up to the Common-wealth, and by it to the *Legislative Power*, so that the Legislative can have no more than this (II, s. 135).

Moreover it would make nonsense in terms of Locke's philosophy to equate the consent of the majority with the consent of the individual who is to have his property expropriated. It is only possible to make this equation in political terms (logically of course they cannot be equated), on the assumption that the individual to be taxed has consented to the system of representation and to the election of the representatives who have responsibility for determining what level of taxes should be levied on all property, to defray the cost of protecting the goods and persons of the members of the community. Nevertheless it is clear that in other hands Locke's doctrine of majority consent could be used to justify, not the defence of established property rights, but their redistribution in the interests of the majority.[1]

In addition to legal restrictions imposed by society on property rights Locke also recognized moral restrictions. Locke did not deny,

1. For a discussion of Locke's conception of the majority see Chapter 6, section 2, below.

even if he did not give pride of place to, the right and the duty of charity.
God, he writes,

> has given no one of his Children such a Property, in his peculiar
> Portion of the things of this World, but that he has given his needy
> Brother a Right to the Surplusage of his Goods; so that it cannot justly
> be denied him, when his pressing Wants call for it. . . . As *Justice* gives
> every Man a Title to the product of his honest Industry, and the fair
> Acquisitions of his Ancestors descended to him; so *Charity* gives every
> Man a Title to so much out of another's Plenty, as will keep him from
> extream want, where he has no means to subsist otherwise (I, s. 42).

While this doctrine could not be used to justify a revolution aimed at
altering the existing system of property relations in favour of the dis-
possessed; it would, in the absence of public relief provisions, seem to
justify stealing food and clothes from the rich who refuse charity. Again
Locke argues that while a selling merchant may take advantage of a
Buyer's needs or fancies 'yet he must not make use of his necessity to
his destruction, and enrich himself so as to make another perish. He is
so far from being permitted to gain to that degree, that he is bound to
be at some loss and impart of his own to save the other from perishing'.[1]
Property rights, even within the framework of regulation by law, are
not exclusive, they are circumscribed by the moral obligation to preserve
the life of others.

Finally it is important to note that Locke uses the term property in
two senses, a narrow one of goods and possessions and an extended one
to cover 'life, liberty and estate' (II, ss. 87 and 123). Thus when Locke
in one passage (II, s. 85) says that the preservation of property is 'the
chief end' of civil society and in another (II, s. 94) that 'Government
has no other end', he is almost certainly using the narrow sense of
property in the first case and the extended sense in the second. Failure
to distinguish between the two senses is liable to result in overestimating
the importance which Locke attached to the preservation of goods and
chattels as distinct from life and liberty. What is more interesting to
note, however, is the very close links which Locke establishes between
a man's possessions on the one hand and his rights and liberties on the
other. What he appears to argue is that the basic tangible characteristics
of property rights in the narrow sense are applicable to property rights
in the extended sense. A man can make compacts and arrangements

1. John Locke, *Venditio*, printed in full as an addendum to 'Justice and the
Interpretation of Locke's Political Theory' by John Dunn, *Political Studies*,
xvi, February 1968, pp. 86–7.

concerning his natural law rights and liberties on the same terms and conditions as he can his goods and possessions. Thus, while no man has the right to make himself the slave of another, he may consent to put himself in the service of another and be subject to all manner of limitations on his personal freedom. Locke does not hold, however, that a man who possesses no property possesses no rights. Since the propertyless man is subject to the restrictions of the law he is entitled to the benefits of its protection. Locke goes out of his way to insist that there should be but 'one Rule for the Rich and Poor, for the Favourite at Court, and the Country Man at Plough' (II, s. 142).

On the other hand there can be little doubt that Locke accepted the established view that only men of property were entitled or required to directly exercise political rights. Non-voters were not excluded under the seventeenth century theory of representation, for the elected member of the Commons represented an area and its interests rather than its voters. Moreover non-voters were regarded as being virtually represented indirectly through the voters who were in theory responsible to the unenfranchised for the way they cast their votes. When Locke in the *Second Treatise* talks of the desirability that 'true reason' not 'old custom' should determine 'the *number of Members*, in all places, that have a right to be distinctly represented, which no part of the People however incorporated can pretend to, but in proportion to the assistance which it affords to the publick' (II, s. 158); he is not, as Professor Seliger suggests,[1] arguing that all those who pay taxes should have a right to vote and that the more taxes a man pays, the more votes he should have. Locke is here referring, in typical seventeenth century terms, to the representation of places in the English House of Commons through acts of incorporation which gave towns the right to return one or more Members of Parliament. He is taking the moderate reform view that past incorporation does not justify present representation, except in relation to the contribution made by the area to the general welfare of the community measured in terms of wealth and number of inhabitants. Sections 157 and 158 are in fact both concerned with the problem of reforming 'the rotten boroughs'. Locke argues that the king has prerogative power to alter the system of representation for the public good. He speaks of 'The Power of Erecting new Corporations, and therewith *new Representatives*' which in time might lead to some places, not persons, losing their right to be represented and others gaining it.

1. *The Liberal Politics of John Locke*, p. 286.

Locke is studiously quiet on the issue of who should have the right to
vote, but his very silence shows that he favours no change.[1]

READING

John Locke, *Second Treatise of Government*, Ch. V.

C. B. Macpherson, *The Political Theory of Possessive Individualism*, Ch. 5, Locke:
The Political Theory of Appropriation.

M. Seliger, *The Liberal Politics of John Locke*, Chs. 5 and 6.

3. ROUSSEAU

Rousseau in *A Discourse on the Origin of Inequality* distinguishes two
kinds of inequality, the natural inequalities of age, health, bodily
strength and the qualities of mind and soul with which men are born;
and man-made political inequalities which create privileges of wealth,
honour and power. Rousseau contemptuously dismisses the view that
the two kinds of inequality are necessarily linked together:

> for this would be only asking, in other words, whether those who com-
> mand are necessarily better than those who obey, if strength of body or
> of mind, wisdom, or virtue are always found in particular individuals,
> in proportion to their power or wealth: a question fit perhaps to be dis-
> cussed by slaves in the hearing of their masters, but highly unbecoming
> to reasonable and free men in search of the truth (*Inequality*, p. 160).

In the original state of nature natural inequalities are of little moment
both because there is no shortage of means to meet man's simple needs
and because his self-sufficient, solitary, wandering existence does not
lend itself to dependence on others, or even to awareness of their
condition.

1. In a letter to Edward Clarke dated 8 February 1689, on the coming meeting
of the Convention Parliament Locke wrote: 'The settlement of the nation is
put into their hands, which can no way so well be done as by restoring our
ancient government; the best possible that ever was, if taken and put together
all of a piece in its original constitution'. Quoted by John Dunn 'Consent in
the Political Theory of John Locke', *Historical Journal*, Vol. X, No. 2, July
1967.

But from the moment one man began to stand in need of the help of another; from the moment it appeared advantageous to any one man to have provisions enough for two, equality disappeared, property was introduced, work became indispensable, and vast forests became smiling fields, which man had to water with the sweat of his brow, and where slavery and misery were soon seen to germinate and grow with the crops (p. 199).

Whereas the physical inequalities between men in the natural state had little effect and were of little concern, the social inequalities brought about by living in the political communities which developed were far-reaching and, for most men, undesirable and oppressive. The lot of the vast majority of mankind was to live in drudgery and subjection to 'a few rich and powerful men on the pinnacle of fortune and grandeur, while the crowd grovels in want and obscurity' (p. 217).

In *The Social Contract* Rousseau set out to show that this dependence and slavishness was not an inevitable and necessary consequence of social existence: that the alternative to the narrow and spiritually un-satisfying condition of natural man was not social bondage but social freedom; the substitution of 'a moral and lawful equality for whatever physical inequality that nature may have imposed on mankind; so that however unequal in strength and intelligence, men become equal by covenant and by right' (*The Social Contract*, Bk. I, Ch. 9, p. 68). 'Moral and lawful equality' was attainable, however, only on certain stringent conditions which would be very difficult to realize in practice. Considered in terms of forming an ideal society of free and equal men (rather than in terms of the gradual reform of existing societies in the light of the ideal form, as in the projects for Poland and Corsica) this involves a unanimous act of will of all those who are to be its members. 'Each one of us puts into the community his person and all his powers under the supreme direction of the general will; and as a body, we incorporate every member as an individual part of the whole' (*The Social Contract*, Bk. I, Ch. 6, p. 61). The ideal community is a community of equals where no man is subordinate to any other, but where all are equally subject to the laws which each participates in making. In this way a 'reciprocal commitment' is established between society and the individual which ensures that the commands of the sovereign body of the state can never be contrary to the interests of its subjects; for these same subjects under the law are the citizens who make it. Because the general will springs from all and applies equally to all there is the pos-sibility of a complete identification of interest between society and the individual; in so far as the will of the former expresses the general will, and not just the will of all, and the latter the enlightened self-interest of a citizen and not the narrow particular interest of an egoist.

> The commitments which bind us to the social body are obligatory only because they are mutual; and their nature is such that in fulfilling them a man cannot work for others without at the same time working for himself. How should it be that the general will is always rightful[1] and that all men constantly wish the happiness of each but for the fact that there is no one who does not take that word 'each' to pertain to himself and in voting for all think of himself? This proves that the equality of rights and the notion of justice which it produces derive from the predilection which each man has for himself and hence from human nature as such (*The Social Contract*, Bk. II, Ch. 4, p. 75).

The general will derives its being from the common interest which unites the members of a community together, and consequently it can only be expressed in relation to matters of common concern – 'every authentic act of the general will binds, or favours all the citizens equally' (p. 76). But although Rousseau insists that the general will is a will 'towards equality' (Bk. II, Ch 1), he does not mean by this that the ultimate objective it seeks to realize is a society of men politically and socially equal in all respects. The application of the general abstract rules of law expressing the general will of the community requires the institution of government, and, except under the rarefied conditions of strict democracy, this involves special powers being given to the few to be exercised over all in accordance with the law. The law, he tells us, may itself lay down privileges by establishing several classes of citizen, as long as it does not nominate who are to be the actual beneficiaries. Such privileges will, however, only be accorded in the ideal society if they are required by the common interest and not by the particular interest of those who receive them. Political equality does not require that all shall exercise the same degree of power but 'that power shall stop short of violence and never be exercised except by virtue of authority and law' (Bk. II, Ch. 11). Rousseau never departs from this principle, even though he recognizes that circumstances may require the postponement of its full operation. Thus in his proposals for Poland he accepts the practical impossibility of the immediate abolition of serfdom, but he insists that the noblemen will never be free as long as

---

1. Rousseau's term 'droite' in the phrase 'la volonté' générale est toujours droite' is very difficult to translate. Alternatives would be 'unbiased' or 'well-intentioned' or 'fair'. The problems of translating Rousseau are discussed in an article by J. H. Burns and A. Cobban in *Political Studies*, x, June 1962, pp. 203–7.

they hold their 'brothers' in chains, and puts forward proposals for their gradual manumission so that the more numerous part of the nation may be able to 'attach its affections to the fatherland' (*Poland*, p. 251).

If men are consciously to attach their affections to the community of which they are a part they must not only be given a direct stake and interest in it, they must also be educated to become citizens and patriots. Both in *A Discourse on Political Economy*, written four years before *Émile*, and *Considerations on the Government of Poland*, written ten years afterwards, Rousseau comes out strongly in favour of a system of public education for all. In the former he writes with reference to men's passions,

> If, for example, they were early accustomed to regard their individuality only in its relation to the body of the State, and to be aware, so to speak, of their own existence merely as a part of the State, they might at length come to identify themselves in some degree with this greater whole, to feel themselves members of their country, and to love it with that exquisite feeling which no isolated person has save for himself; to lift up their spirits perpetually to this great object, and thus to transform into a sublime virtue that dangerous disposition which gives rise to all our vices (p. 251).

In *Considerations on Poland* he declares: 'All, being equal under the constitution of the state, ought to be educated together and in the same fashion' (p. 177). 'It is education that must give souls a national formation, and direct their opinions and tastes in such a way that they will be patriotic by inclination, by passion, by necessity' (p. 176). In these passages public education appears to take the form of paternalist indoctrination aimed at producing uniform responses, rather than that concern for the child's individual bent and nature which characterizes the private education process in *Émile*. There is indeed more than a difference of emphasis here, but it is arguable whether the views are incompatible. Émile's tutor is more than the guardian and prompter of the natural talents of the developing child. The individual bent of the child has to be thoroughly known in order that the tutor may choose the 'fittest moral training' for him. 'Every mind,' he writes, 'has its own form, in accordance with which it must be controlled' (*Émile*, p. 58). In *Émile*, Rousseau presumes an all-wise entirely devoted tutor, just as he supposes an all-wise, public-spirited legislator in *The Social Contract*. In the absence of these god-like figures in the real world, men must be satisfied with less ambitious objectives. Moreover, the educational issues are quite different in *Émile* on the one hand and in *Considerations on*

Poland and *A Discourse on Political Economy* on the other. The former is concerned exclusively with showing the best way to educate any child to 'best endure the good and evil of life' (*Émile*, p. 9), while the latter are only interested in education in so far as it can be used to promote social unity and public-spiritedness. In theory these two approaches are not exclusive, and in the ideal state they might well be synthesized. In the hard world of reality the dangers of uniformity in patriotic education are for Rousseau outweighted by the benefits; especially in Poland whose survival depended on the maintenance and strengthening of its national sentiment and awareness.

In the *Considerations on Poland* Rousseau develops one of his favourite themes, the need to turn men from the search for wealth to the search for honour and service. He inveighs against the evils of the acquisitive society in words which ring more sharply each decade that passes. 'As long as luxury reigns among the great, cupidity will reign in all hearts ... and if one must be rich in order to shine, to be rich will always be the dominant passion' (p. 174). He calls on the Polish nation to choose between devotion to 'material luxury' which will create 'a scheming, ardent, avid, ambitious, servile and knavish people' like all the rest in Europe; and devotion to 'simple customs and wholesome tastes', contemptuous of money-making, which will produce 'a free, wise and peaceful nation ... self-sufficient and happy' (p. 224). Public offices should be filled on the basis of merit not wealth, so that 'everyone may see the road to any attainment open before him' (p. 257), while public service should be rewarded with honours not profit. Exactly the same egalitarian principles are commended by Rousseau to the Corsicans. 'All should be equal by right of birth; the state should grant no distinctions save from merit, virtue and patriotic service; and these distinctions should be no more hereditary than are the qualities on which they are based' (*Corsica*, p. 289). Even worse than power and privilege based on hereditary descent is power derived from the possession of wealth, for wherever wealth predominates in a community one finds 'apparent power' in the hands of the lawful authorities but 'real power in those of the rich' (p. 327).

Rousseau's distrust of the rich and distaste for wealth accumulation dominates his economic thinking. Inequality of wealth is seen as having its origin in natural physical inequalities which enable one man to produce with his labour much more than another; but it is not until this natural inequality is harnessed to insatiable ambition and a multiplicity of new wants that there arises 'rivalry and competition on the one hand, and conflicting interests on the other, together with a secret desire on both of profiting at the expense of others. All these evils were the first effects of property, and the inseparable attendants of growing inequality' (*Inequality*, p. 203). It is not property as such, however, which Rousseau objects to but the present evil consequences of its mal-distribution. It is 'plainly contrary to the law of nature, however defined, that . . . the privileged few should gorge themselves with superfluities, while the starving multitudes are in want of the bare necessities of life' (p. 221).

In *A Discourse on Political Economy*, published three years later, in 1758, Rousseau appears to strike a different chord. He speaks of the right of property as 'the most sacred of all the rights of citizenship' – 'the true foundation of civil society' (p. 254) and argues, like Locke, that no man may be taxed to pay for the maintenance of the state and its services without his voluntary consent. But whereas Locke equates the consent of elected representatives with the consent of those he repres-ents, Rousseau makes it dependent on the general will. Since the general will (through law) 'dictates to each citizen the precepts of public reason and teaches him to act according to the rules of his own judg-ment, and not to act inconsistently with himself' (p. 240), a man's property may be legitimately taxed to the extent that the common good requires, not to the extent that the citizens are willing to accept. Further Rousseau lays down three principles of taxation designed to ensure equity, first that the taxation paid should be proportional to the property owned, secondly that necessities should not be taxed at all 'while the tax on him who is in possession of superfluities may justly be extended to everything he has over and above mere necessaries', and thirdly that the greater the advantage derived from the state the greater the contribu-tion that should be levied for 'Are not all the advantages of society for the rich and powerful?' (pp. 262–3). The government for Rousseau should not act simply as the 'nightwatchman of the state', confining itself to the maintenance of law and order, but should protect the poor 'against the tyranny of the rich' and 'prevent extreme inequality of fortunes' (p. 250).

This insistence on the need for and responsibility of governments to reduce the inequalities of wealth and fortune to be found in European societies is the central theme of all Rousseau's economic writings, although the emphasis and the particular remedies he puts forward vary from work to work. Wealth must be so distributed and society so organized 'that no citizen shall be rich enough to buy another and none so poor as to be forced to sell himself', he tells us in *The Social Contract*. Extremes of wealth undermine the coherence of the state, corrupt both rich and poor, turning them into traders in the public freedom which 'the one buys, the other sells' (Bk. II, Ch. 11, p. 96). The right of any man to property is derived from the natural right which every man has to what is necessary for his survival, and when land came to be divided up this principle found common expression in 'the right of first occupant'. The institution of civil society changed these individual acts of appropriation into valid rights and 'mere enjoyment into legal ownership' (Bk. I, Ch. 9, pp. 67–8). But Rousseau is far from asserting that any system of land distribution by first occupation is acceptable or that once established it cannot be altered. He lays down three conditions which must be met to justify the right of first occupation: 'first, that the land shall not already be inhabited by anyone else; secondly, that the claimant occupies no more than he needs for subsistence; thirdly, that he takes possession, not by an idle ceremony, but by actually working and cultivating the soil – the only sign of ownership which need be respected by other people in the absence of a legal title' (p. 66). It is clear that these principles are binding for Rousseau in society as well as in the state of nature and that he would expect them to be given effect to in order to bring about the ideal society without rich or poor. To this end he lays down that the initial social contract involves the total surrender of every man's goods and property to the community. This does not mean that the state takes possession of everyone's land, but by making the legal owner 'a trustee of the public property' and 'the right of any individual over his estate ... subordinate to the right of the community over everything' (p. 68), he ensures that the state will not lack the means to prevent the natural drift to inequality inherent in society.

In the *Constitutional Project for Corsica* Rousseau goes further than anywhere else in developing his conception of the positive role of the state in the economy. He writes there as one who shares in the socialist vision of society. 'Far from wanting the state to be poor, I should like, on the contrary, for it to own everything, and for each individual to share in the common property only in proportion to his services' but since it is impossible to destroy private property completely he proposes 'to confine it within the narrowest possible limits' and to 'keep it ever subordinate to the public good'. 'In short, I want the property of the state to be as large and strong, that of the citizens as small and weak, as possible' (p. 317). This objective is to be realized not by depriving existing owners of their land but by setting up a public domain from reclaimed waste land and by purchases. The land would either be made available to the landless for a limited number of years or worked in common by members of the community who would give their labour instead of paying taxes. In spite of his declaration of socialist principles Rousseau's proposals for Corsica are dependent not on communal ownership but on the creation of a prosperous independent community of farmers secure in the possession of their own lands and producing primarily for their own consumption. He remains true to his original conception – 'Everyone should make a living, and no one should grow rich; that is the fundamental principle of the prosperity of the nation' (p. 308).

READING

J. J. Rousseau, *The Social Contract*, Bk. I, Ch. 9.

J. J. Rousseau, *Considerations on the Government of Poland*, Chs. 4 and 11.

J. Plamenatz, *Man and Society*, Vol. I, Ch. 10, section iv, pp. 418–33.

A. Cobban, *Rousseau and the Modern State*, Ch. 5.

4. BENTHAM AND MILL

The notion of equality lies at the heart of utilitarianism, for without Bentham's dictum 'everybody to count for one, nobody for more than one', the greatest happiness principle is unworkable. In the *Essay on Representation*, written in 1788 for the French National Assembly, Bentham argues that since a benevolent unbiased superior being would have no reason for promoting the interests of one man rather than another and since men lack 'the power to determine the relative degree of happiness that different individuals are susceptible of, it is necessary to start with the *assumption* that the degree is the same for all'.[1] He also assumes that 'each has an equal desire for happiness', because it is impossible to compute differences in desire and because it is impossible

---

1. Translated and printed in Appendix D to Mary Mack, op. cit., p. 449, (my italics).

to produce any other usable proposition which is likely to be as near
to the truth. It will be seen that Bentham does not claim to have
shown that all men equally desire happiness and are equally capable of
enjoying it, he simply *assumes* it as a self-evident rough and ready proposition that can be used *for calculation purposes.* He is not interested
in abstract propositions about the equality of men or the equal rights of
men. The goal of social action is not equality of happiness between men,
but the greatest happiness of all the members of the community. To
the benevolent ruler or legislator 'the happiness of any of them has no
more value in his eyes than the equal happiness of any other. Nevertheless any greater happiness obtained by any one among them has more
value in proportion to its quantity, than a lesser happiness obtained by
another' (ibid., p. 449).

In his *Theory of Legislation* Bentham puts forward what amounts to a
rudimentary law of diminishing marginal utility with regard to happiness
in general and to wealth as a happiness producer in particular.

> Put on one side a thousand farmers, having enough to live upon, and a
> little more. Put on the other side a king . . . as rich as all the farmers
> taken together. It is probable, I say, that his happiness is greater than
> the average happiness of the thousand farmers; but it is by no means
> probable that it is equal to the sum total of their happiness . . . It
> would be remarkable if his happiness were ten times, or even five times
> greater (pp. 104–5).

Bentham concludes that the nearer the distribution of wealth in a community '*approaches to equality, the greater will be the total mass of
happiness*' (p. 104). Bentham does not, however, conclude from this
that a redistribution of wealth to secure equality would bring about the
maximization of happiness. This is partly because, in his view, the pain
incurred through loss is always greater than the pleasure felt from the
corresponding gain; but more importantly because any forced redistribution would completely undermine the vital sense of security of the
members of the community. His own objective is the reduction of existing wealth inequalities by ensuring that an increasing proportion of new
wealth produced goes to the poor rather than to the rich. '*Among
participants of unequal fortunes, the more the distribution of new wealth
tends to do away that inequality, the greater will be the total mass of
happiness*' (p. 105).

In the final analysis equality of wealth must always give way to
security, which is itself the creation of law. 'Without law there is no
security; and, consequently no abundance, and not even a certainty of

subsistence; and, the only equality which can exist in such a state of things is an equality of misery' (p. 109). Security requires that the existing distribution of wealth and property be not disturbed, for if it is men will have no inducement to labour and produce goods surplus to those required for immediate satisfaction. Should this happen the spirit of industry and labour will be deadened and all will sink into a fatal lethargy. Even if perfect equality of wealth were to be established by revolution it would require a permanent army of levellers to maintain it and to ensure that the disagreeable functions of society were carried out. 'What an apparatus of penal laws would be necessary as a substitute for the sweet liberty of choice, and the natural recompense of labour! One half the society would not suffice to regulate the other half' (pp. 121-2).

Bentham calls on men to turn their eyes away from the chimera of perfect equality. If they do this they will find that the principles of equality and security are reconcilable, in the sense that a steady reduction in inequality is compatible with security. Bentham holds that 'a continual progress towards equality' (p. 123) is to be found in all modern states where law does not interfere with the natural economic processes by seeking to regulate trade and industry. Great properties and estates are continually being broken up as new able men of moderate fortune come to the fore. The only important artificial means which Bentham advocated for bringing about a redistribution of existing wealth was 'by limiting in certain respects the testamentary power, in order to prevent too great an accumulation of wealth in the hands of an individual; or by regulating the succession in favour of equality in cases where the deceased has left no consort, nor relation in the direct line, and has made no will' (p. 122). The wealth so accumulated as public funds would be used to meet the dire claims of 'the deserving poor' to exist, which had to come before even the claims of the rich to enjoy the fruits of their own efforts. 'For the pain of death, which would presently fall upon the starving poor, would be always a more serious evil than the pain of disappointment which falls upon the rich when a portion of his superfluity is taken from him' (p. 132). The scheme Bentham outlined in *Supply without Burthen, or Escheat vice Taxation* (1795)[1] was designed to meet this need without endangering security, in a situation

1. Bentham proposes that half the estate only should go to the beneficiaries of any bequest where the beneficiaries are not close relations and that in the case of intestacy the whole estate should go to the public funds. *Jeremy Bentham's Economic Writings*, edited by G. W. Stark, 1952, Vol. I.

where in Bentham's view 'a considerable portion of the aggregate number of the members of the community there will always be, in whose instance a subsistence cannot have place without provision made by the legislator to that effect'.[1] In time Bentham moved away from his initial view that the role of the government in the social and economic field should be restricted to simply preventing the poor from starving, removing restrictions on trade and commerce, and encouraging education and the dissemination of information. He came to recommend positive government action to control inflation, avoid depressions (by bulk purchase of surplus durables in periods of overproduction) and make public capital available at low rates of interest to promising undercapitalized industries.[2]

John Stuart Mill takes up this theme where Bentham leaves off and one can trace in successive editions of *Principles of Political Economy* between 1848 and 1871 the shift in Mill's own views more and more in a direction sympathetic to what later became reformist socialism. If one looks at the final expression of his economic thinking in the seventh edition one finds that, whereas Bentham defends the existing distribution of private property in terms of the undesirable consequences for the sum total of human happiness which would flow from its disturbance, Mill is concerned to justify the principle of private property as it might with equity be applied. He accepts that,

> if the institution of private property necessarily carried with it as a consequence, that the produce of labour should be apportioned as we now see it, almost in an inverse ratio to the labour – the largest portions to those who have never worked at all . . . the remuneration dwindling as the work grows harder and more disagreeable, until the most fatiguing and exhausting bodily labour cannot count with certainty on being able to earn even the necessaries of life; if this or Communism were the alternatives, all the difficulties, great or small, of Communism would be but as dust in the balance (*Principles of Political Economy*, p. 208).

Mill contends, however, that the true principles of private property have never been given a fair trial and that private property has been blamed for characteristics which it need not and should not have. Mill was all too aware that the natural tendency towards equality in the distribution of wealth, which Bentham had pointed to, had not been borne

1. 'The Philosophy of Economic Science', *Jeremy Bentham's Economic Writings*, Vol. I, p. 109.
2. See D. J. Manning, *The Mind of Jeremy Bentham*, Ch. 17, 'The Business of Government'.

out by later developments. Mill blames the laws of property for this in that they

> have not held the balance fairly between human beings, but have heaped impediments upon some, to give advantage to others; they have purposely fostered inequalities, and prevented all from starting fair in the race. That all should start on perfectly equal terms is inconsistent with any law of private property: but if as much pains as has been taken to aggravate the inequality of chances arising from the natural working of the principle, had been taken to temper that inequality by every means not subversive of the principle itself; if the tendency of legislation had been to favour the diffusion, instead of the concentration of wealth – to encourage the subdivision of the large masses, instead of striving to keep them together; the principle of individual property would have been found to have no necessary connexion with the physical and social evils which almost all Socialist writers assume to be inseparable from it (p. 209).

Whereas Bentham had seen the primary role of the laws of property as upholding the established expectations of the existing system of property relations; Mill saw the law as an instrument for bringing about 'that equitable principle, of proportion between remuneration and exertion' by which alone in his view private property might be vindicated (p. 209). To this end he proposes a limitation on the amount of wealth any man might inherit and a recognition that the state has the right to take possession of such land as it requires for public purposes, on payment of compensation. In the longer run he foresees the development of a mixed economy which will obliterate the sharp line of division between workers and capitalists. On the one hand exclusive ownership and control would be replaced by co-partnership and profit sharing; on the other he expected a great extension of the co-operative movement and above all of what we might term guild socialism – 'the association of the labourers themselves on terms of equality, collectively owning the capital with which they carry out their operations, and working under managers elected and removable by themselves' (p. 773). What he is rigidly opposed to is any direct intervention by the state in the economic affairs of the nation and to any extension of public ownership of the means of production of wealth, apart from the land. He rejects the complete communist solution to societies' problems on the grounds that 'the absolute dependence of each on all, and surveillance of each by all' would be likely to 'grind all down into a tame uniformity of thoughts, feelings, and actions' (p. 211). If for Bentham equality must give way to security, for Mill it must give way to liberty.

Mill sees equality in terms of claims which men may justifiably make on society for equality of treatment. 'The equal claim of everybody to happiness in the estimation of the moralist and the legislator, involves an equal claim to all the means to happiness, except in so far as the inevitable conditions of human life, and the general interest, in which that of every individual is included, set limits to the maxim . . .' (*Utilitarianism*, pp. 58–9). But Mill stresses that men's conception of what 'the inevitable conditions of human life . . . and the general interest' requires in the way of restrictions on the principle of equality is a matter of social expediency which varies from age to age and he looks forward to the 'aristocracies of colour, race, and sex' joining the discarded distinctions between slave and freeman, noble and serf. Mill himself struck hard blows against sexual discrimination in Victorian England. He argued for full equality of married persons before the law as a step towards the full social recognition and acceptance of marriage as an association of equals, and for women to have the same freedom to choose for themselves what to do with their lives as men had. In the meantime women should be given the vote on the same terms as men 'as their guarantee of just and equal consideration' by Parliament. 'Even if every woman were a wife, and if every wife ought to be a slave, all the more would these slaves stand in need of legal protection: and we know what legal protection slaves have, where the laws are made by their masters' (*The Subjection of Women*, p. 269).[1]

The need to ensure the representation in Parliament of interests which would otherwise be ignored was one of the main themes of Mill's *Representative Government* (1861).[2] He supports the case for universal suffrage in Britain on the grounds that a legislature which excludes working people altogether is incapable of appreciating their point of view on any matter vitally affecting their interest such as strikes. 'It is an adherent condition of human affairs that no intention, however sincere, of protecting the interests of others can make it safe or salutary to tie up their own hands' (*Representative Government*, p. 210). But the extension of the franchise in 1861 to the totally excluded working class would, in Mill's eyes, give rise to the opposite danger that the legislative body would be swamped with completely inexperienced working class representatives. Such a result would not be democratic in Mill's view, for the 'pure idea of democracy, according to its definition, is the govern-

---

1. J. S. Mill, *The Subjection of Women*, 1869, Everyman's Library edition, 1929.
2. Everyman's Library edition, 1910.

ment of the whole people by the whole people, equally represented', not 'the government of the whole people by a mere majority of the people, exclusively represented' (p. 256). It is to avert this danger that Mill advocates the adoption of a scheme of proportional representation designed to secure representation for minorities, in particular of that minority of middle class intellectuals so beloved by Mill, whose task it would be to guide a legislature composed mainly of persons of limited intellectual capacity. The great advantage of Mr Hare's scheme of representation for John Stuart Mill is that it would enable every or any section of opinion in the community to be proportionately represented in Parliament. Under this scheme each elector would have the right to use his vote for any candidate standing in any constituency and to cast second or third preference votes if his first preference is not elected or if his vote is surplus to quota requirements.[1] In this way 'real equality of representation' (p. 261) would be secured, since every individual's vote would count for exactly as much as every other individual's vote in determining the nature of the representative assembly. More particularly Mill hoped that the outcome would be that 'the minority of instructed minds scattered through the local constituencies would unite to return a number, proportional to their own numbers, of the very ablest men the country contains' (p. 266). The people would thus be provided with 'leaders of a higher grade of intellect and character than itself' who might be expected 'to keep popular opinion within reason and justice' and to take 'more than their numerical share of the actual administration of government' (p. 269).

The right to vote itself would, under Mill's proposals, be made conditional on ability to read, write and do simple arithmetic tests, ('universal teaching must precede universal enfranchisement') (p. 280) and on the payment of direct taxes in a form designed to include the poor. Persons on parish relief and bankrupts would be disqualified from voting. But these disqualifications, designed to ensure that everyone had a direct stake in defraying a share of the public expenses and was capable of understanding what was at issue, were not regarded by Mill as adequate. He assumed, as did most supporters and opponents of universal suffrage at the time, that the great mass of meanly educated manual labourers would vote solidly for representatives from their own class, and that without adequate guidance they would introduce legislation designed

1. To be elected, a candidate under Mr Hare's scheme would have to receive a quota arrived at by simply dividing the total number of electors in the county by the total number of seats to be contested.

to further their own interest at the expense of other groups in the community. He therefore interprets 'real equality of representation' as requiring that 'every one ought to have a voice' in determining how the country is to be governed but not that 'every one should have an equal voice'.

> When two persons who have a joint interest in any business differ in opinion, does justice require that both opinions should be held of exactly equal value? If, with equal virtue, one is superior to the other in knowledge and intelligence – or if, with equal intelligence, one excels the other in virtue – the opinion, the judgment, of the higher moral or intellectual being is worth more than that of the inferior (p. 283).

It is in terms of these arguments that Mill defends his proposals for plural votes for those with greater capacity for the management of the community's affairs. Mill would like to rely on educational attainment as the sole criteria for additional votes, but until a fully developed national education scheme is working, this would be supplemented by extra votes for skilled labourers, foremen, managers and employers as well as members of the liberal professions. Voluntary examinations would be available to enable other persons to secure the privilege. 'The plurality of votes must on no account be carried so far that those who are privileged by it, or the class (if any) to which they mainly belong, shall outweigh by means of it all the rest of the community' (p. 286). Plurality of voting is designed to secure the return of a sufficiently strong minority of educated capable representatives that they will be able to guide the mediocre working class members. Mill makes his position quite clear when he writes:

> I do not look upon equal voting as among the things which are good in themselves, provided they can be guarded against inconveniences. I look upon it as only relatively good; less objectionable than inequality of privilege grounded on irrelevant or adventitious circumstances, but in principle wrong, because recognizing a wrong standard, and exercising a bad influence on the voter's mind. It is not useful, but hurtful, that the constitution of the country should declare ignorance to be entitled to as much political power as knowledge (p. 288).

Mill's ideal of democracy is one of meritocracy by consent.

READING

D. J. Manning, *The Mind of Jeremy Bentham*, Ch. 17.

J. S. Mill, *Representative Government*, Chs. 7 and 8.

5. HEGEL

The most striking feature of Hegel's conception of property is the way he derives it from man's distinctive characteristic, his will. Property is not something which has to be justified, it simply needs to be understood as an inevitable consequence of the nature of man. To be free a man must give effect to his will in the world outside himself; in the first place in and then through his own body, for will itself is an aspect of mind. While to others there is no distinction between 'me as mind' and 'me as body' my body is only mine in so far as I make a conscious effort of will to possess it. If for any reason I do not will to possess it, my body is not mine for me. If for example I regard my body as the incarnation of evil, then I may reject or mortify the body as something alien to my true self. Alternatively if through physical defect some parts of the body refuse to respond to my will they cease as such to be mine in any meaningful sense. But although I may withdraw myself out of my bodily existence and make my body something external to me, I only exist as a person through by body, just as my body can exist only as something other than a thing or object if I will it so.

> As a person, I am myself an *immediate* individual; if we give further precision to this expression, it means in the first instance that I am alive in this bodily organism which is my external existence, universal in content and undivided, the real pre-condition of every further determined mode of existence. But, all the same, as person, I possess my life and my body, like other things only in so far as my will is in them. . . . In so far as the body is an immediate existent, it is not in conformity with mind. If it is to be the willing organ and soul-endowed instrument of mind, it must first be taken into possession by mind (*Philosophy of Right*, p. 43).

I possess my body because I will to possess it and I will to possess it because I can only become myself through my body. The particular acts of will are only understandable in terms of the nature and necessity of willing. In giving expression to my will through my body I enter the external world. My will is translated into action which transforms that world. Just as my body becomes alive and purposive under the charge of my will so 'things' too are transformed by my actions. Inert objects are given an end which as mere objects they could not have, while living plants and creatures have their unconscious purposes subordinated to my conscious will. 'A person has as his substantive end the right of putting his will into any and every thing and thereby making it his, because it has no such end in itself and derives its destiny and soul from his will. This is the absolute right of appropriation which man has over all "things"' (p. 41). Whatever I put my will into becomes my property, because until my will is applied to it it has no meaningful existence and unless my will is translated into the external world and brought to bear on objects, I can have no meaningful existence. But it is not only material objects which can become immediately subject to my will and so Hegel's category of property is much broader than the category of material possessions.

'Property is the first embodiment of freedom and so is in itself a substantive end' (p. 42) writes Hegel. Its purpose is the universal one of enabling the free will to actualize itself. This, however, is not the way in which acts of appropriation will appear to the actor. For him taking possession is a means of satisfying his own particular and immediate needs and desires.

> To have power over a thing *ab extra* constitutes possession. The particular aspect of the matter, the fact that I make something my own as a result of my natural need, impulse, and caprice, is the particular interest satisfied by possession. But I as free will am an object to myself in what I possess and thereby also for the first time am an actual will, and this is the aspect which constitutes the category of *property*, the true and right factor in possession (p. 42).

It is this factor which requires that the normal form which property should take is private property, as it is only in this form that I can express and exercise my own personal free will. Unless the universal character of property is seen as the immediate agency for the realization of the will as freedom, private property will appear as the expression of impulse and caprice. Moreover as Hegel pointed out in *Phenomenology of Spirit* the case of property private as against communal property cannot be substantiated in terms of logical consistency, since neither is self-contradictory (pp. 447-9). To make anything mine it is not sufficient that I should will it so – I must take possession and occupy it, thus giving a recognizable sign of its embodiment in me. I may take possession of a thing in one of three ways. The first and simplest is simply by directly grasping hold of it, but this method is not only limited in scope but unclear in intent for it is not apparent whether I will the object to be mine permanently or simply for the moment. These doubts are removed in the second and third methods. If I impose a form on something, if I mould it to my will through my own efforts it now bears my mark and is distinguishable from the thing it was before I subjected it to my will.

Thirdly I may mark an object as mine by my persistent permanent use of it in its entirety. Once an object has become marked as mine, once that it is apparent that my will has become permanetly embodied in it, no other person may take possession of it, except with my consent or agreement.

> The reason I can alienate my property, [Hegel argues] is that it is mine only in so far as I put my will into it. Hence I may abandon (*derelinquere*) as a *res nullus* anything that I have or yield it to the will of another and so into his possession, provided that the thing in question is a thing external by nature. Therefore those goods, or rather substantive characteristics, which constitute my own private personality and the universal essence of my self-consciousness are inalienable and my right to them is imprescriptible. Such characteristics are my personality as such, my universal freedom of will, my ethical life, my religion (*Philosophy of Right*, pp. 52–3).

My personality is not something external to myself, it is myself and as such it cannot become the property of another. It is contrary to the whole nature and purpose of the will, which is the embodiment of man as individual, for the personality to be alienated to another in any of its aspects, whether that alienation occur unconsciously or intentionally.

The most extreme example of alienation of personality is to be found in slavery, which Hegel regarded as an inevitable stage in the development of man to a self-conscious independent existence. But since slavery denies the very notion of freedom he held that a slave has 'an absolute right to free himself', even though the system under which he lived might be regarded as 'necessary and inevitable' (*Philosophy of Right*, additions 36 & 43, pp. 239 and 241). Hegel devoted a complete section of *Phenomenology of Spirit* to an analysis of the slave-master relationship, an analysis which in its broad outlines is applicable to any condition where one man's self is subordinated to that of another. The conceptual basis of slavery is the need of the self-conscious mind to be acknowledged or recognized by another self. It is only through recognition that an individual can gain assurance not merely of his own worth but of his very existence as a self-conscious being. The need for recognition is mutual, however, and expresses itself in both parties concerned as a demand made upon that self by the other. Each is solely conscious of his own self as a being and sees the other simply as an object capable of giving recognition. The conflict is immediately resolved through the establishment of a relationship in which 'one is independent, and its essential nature is to be for itself; the other is dependent, and its essence is life or existence for another. The former is the Master, or Lord, the latter the Bondsman' (*Phenomenology of Mind*, p. 234).

The essential feature of this new relationship is that the Master's independence is now asserted through the dependence of the slave on him for existence and his independence from the need to labour. By being required to work for his master the slave gives recognition. The recognition, however, is not a recognition by the slave of the self of the master but of his own lack of self. The slave no longer exists as a person but only a means for satisfying the needs of his lord. Such 'one-sided and unequal' recognition cannot satisfy the master – 'for recognition proper there is needed the moment that what the master does to the other he should also do to himself, and what the bondsman does to himself, he should do to the other also' (p. 236). The master is able to obtain confidence in himself as a person only through receiving the abject recognition of a completely dependent depersonalized being. But this means that the master, instead of attaining conscious assurance of himself as an independent being, has become dependent on another whom he must treat as an object. The slave on the other hand is a submerged conscious being and this submerged consciousness of self is brought to the surface through work and labour. Unlike the master who stagnates, detached as he is from the world of action and design, the slave develops an awareness of his distinctive character. 'The consciousness that toils and serves accordingly attains by this means the direct apprehension of that indepedent being as its self' (p. 238). The bondsman discovers that he has a mind of his own and this discovery breaks down his absolute inward fear of the master, for he now realizes that while the master needs him, he does not need his master. This section of the *Phenomenology* made a great impression on Karl Marx who himself wrote in *Capital*, 'As man . . . works on nature outside himself and changes it, he changes at the same time his own nature'.[1] What Marx rejected was Hegel's qualitative distinction between alienating part of one's time to another in the form of working for him and alienating one's whole self as a slave. For Hegel, 'the use of my powers differs from my powers and therefore from myself . . . as it is quantitatively restricted' and consequently the position of the domestic servant or day labourer is not one of servitude (*Philosophy of Right*, p. 54).

Although Hegel regards property as essential to man as a medium for the expression of will, he does not see its acquisition as the most

1. Quoted by Kaufmann, op. cit., p. 153.

important form of that expression. Consequently the amassing of wealth cannot be accepted as an end in itself. In the *Phenomenology of Spirit* Hegel exposes both the hypocrisy of those who, while loudly proclaiming their service to the state, use that service for the purpose of amassing wealth and the blindness of those whose reaction is to reject both state power and wealth. Both the barren pursuit of wealth and its equally barren outright rejection are characteristic of what Hegel calls 'spirit in self-estrangement'; a stage of development in which man seeks to resolve the conflict between the individual and the universal spirit by imposing his personality on an alien world, by taking it into his possession. A man is here judged in terms of the power which he wields and the wealth he has amassed, the extent to which he has 'mastered' the world.

> This world, although it has come into being by means of individuality, is in the eyes of self-consciousness something that is directly and primarily estranged, and, for self-consciousness, takes on the form of a fixed, undisturbed reality. But at the same time self-consciousness is sure this is its own substance, and proceeds to take it under control. . . . For the power of the individual consists in conforming itself to that substance, i.e. in emptying itself of its own self, and thus establishing itself as the objectively existing substance (pp. 516–17).

It is because of the ambiguous nature of its approach to the outside world that the 'spirit in self-estrangement' fails to see the proper relationship between the realms of wealth and state power. The rich and noble come in practice to make the pursuit and protection of wealth the main purpose of the state and the poor and base to decry wealth and state alike. The rich refuse to see that the universal quality of state power as 'the simple spiritual substance, as well as the achievement of all the absolutely accomplished fact, wherein individuals find their essential nature expressed, and where their particular existence is simply and solely a consciousness of their own universality' (pp. 519–20). They identify the existence of the state with the existence of themselves as a class apart. The poor, on the other hand, fail to see the positive role which wealth plays in setting men to realize themselves in work, as well as in producing means of enjoyment for all.

> Each individual doubtless thinks he is acting in his own interests when getting his enjoyment, for this is the aspect in which he gets the sense of being something on his own account, and for that reason he does not take it to be something spiritual. Yet looked at even in external fashion, it becomes manifest that in his own enjoyment each gives enjoyment to all, in his own labour each works for all as well as for

himself, and all for him. His self-existence is therefore, inherently universal. . . . (p. 520).

The sphere of property, though essential to the ethical life of the community, must be harmonized with that of the community and be subject to the overall authority of the state. Consequently 'the specific characteristics pertaining to private property may have to be subordinated to a higher sphere of right (e.g. to a society or the state) . . .' but 'such exceptions to private property cannot be grounded in chance, in private caprice, or private advantage, but only to the rational organism of the state' (*Philosophy of Right*, p. 42). The right to property has to be seen to be subordinate to the right to life. Thus an individual has in extremity the right of distress against another's property, while the state itself has a responsibility for organizing public relief. Both the individual's life and the individual's property, however, may need to be sacrificed to the needs of the community. The state, as the embodiment of the universal and infinite, must take precedence over the finite and the accidental.

READING

Hegel, *Philosophy of Right*, Part I, section i, 'Property'.

Hegel, *Phenomenology of Mind*, Part IV, A, 'Lordship and Bondage'.

6. MARX AND ENGELS

The importance of property for Marx and Engels lies in the role which it plays in the productive process. It is with property as the producer of wealth, not property as the means of personal gratification, that they are concerned. In *The German Ideology* (1845–6) Marx and Engels had argued that the earliest form of ownership had been tribal communal ownership and that the social structure which this supported had declined as the division of labour and the use of slaves had been introduced.[1] In *The Origin of the Family* (1884) Engels suggested that private

1. Easton and Guddat, op. cit., pp. 410–11.

ownership had emerged following on the domestication of animals and breeding of herds, as this new and rich source of wealth had 'passed out of the common possession of the tribe or the gens into the ownership of individual heads of families'.[1] While slavery existed under conditions of barbarism, wherever and whenever the techniques of production of the means of life enabled captured prisoners of war to produce more than their own keep, it did not become the dominant form of wealth production until classical antiquity.

Contrary to popular belief Marx and Engels did not argue that conditions of primitive society always gave rise to its supercession by slave society, which in its turn necessarily gave way to feudal society. In *Capital*, Vol. I, Marx points to the existence of small, ancient communities in India 'based upon the communal ownership of the land, upon a direct linking up of agriculture and handicraft, and upon a fixed form of the division of labour which is adopted as a cut-and-dried scheme whenever new communities are formed' (p. 377). The very simplicity of the productive organism in these self-sufficient communities 'unlocks for us the mystery of the unchangeableness of Asiatic society, which contrasts so strongly with the perpetual dissolutions and reconstructions of Asiatic States and with the unceasing change of dynasties. The structure of the economic elements of the society remains unaffected by the storms in the political weather' (p. 379). It is apparent that for Marx it is only under certain conditions that a communal society, with its characteristic forms of property and property relations, will break down. In notes written in 1857–8 on *Pre-Capitalist Economic Formations*[2] Marx writes: 'The Asiatic form necessarily survives longest and most stubbornly. This is due to the fundamental principle on which it is based, that is, that the individual does not become independent of the community; that the circle of production is self-sustaining, unity of agriculture and craft manufacture, etc.' (p. 83). The dependent relationship is weaker in ancient Roman society 'where conditions arise which allow the individual to become a private proprietor' (p. 72), and which undermine 'the precondition for the continued existence of the community – the maintenance of equality among its free self-sustaining

1. F. Engels, *The Origin of the Family, Private Property and the State*, translated from the 4th Russian edition, 1964, by Alick West and Dona Torr, London, 1942, p. 183.
2. K. Marx, *Pre-Capitalist Economic Formations*, translated by Jack Cohen, edited with an introduction by Eric Hobsbawm, 1964. First published in Moscow, 1939–41.

peasants and their individual labour as the condition of the continued existence of their property' (p. 73). Marx instances foreign conquest, evolution of slavery, concentration of landed property, development of exchange and a monetary economy as factors which beyond a certain point necessarily led to the decay and disintegration of Roman society. What Marx does not provide is any discussion of the economic contradictions of slave society or of feudalism and this omission is not remedied by Engels. In *The Origin of the Family* he fails to show why slavery should become the predominant basis of production in one society and not in another. When Engels turns to a consideration of the reasons for the collapse of Roman society he finds the cause in the economic *policies* pursued by the Empire rather than in the nature of the productive process itself. The Roman state undermined the very society it was supposed to uphold by its oppressive taxation and appropriation policies which ruined the large slave estates and brought about the decay of the towns. The estates were therefore divided up and rented out to stewards, tenants and above all to *coloni*, 'the forerunners of the medieval serfs'. 'The slavery of classical times had outlived itself. Whether employed on the land, in large-scale agriculture or in manufacture in the towns, it no longer yielded any satisfactory return – the market for its products was no longer there' (p. 169). But it was not the *coloni* from within who brought about the overthrow of Roman society but the German barbarians from without who had no claims to represent a higher form of economic or social organization. Engels accepts that the level of agricultural and industrial production had neither risen nor fallen significantly in the four hundred years following the collapse of the Roman Empire. As for the 'free' German peasants they had been transformed into serfs, subject to forced labour and tribute. The distinctive progressive element which Engels is able to discern in feudal society is not economic superiority or technological advance but a milder form of servitude centred on the village community which gave to 'the oppressed class, the peasants, even under the harshest medieval serfdom, a local centre of solidarity and a means of resistance such as neither the slaves of classical times nor the modern proletariat found ready to their hand' (p. 177). In consequence the medieval bondsman, unlike the slave of antiquity, gradually won their liberation as a class. 'And to what do we owe this if not to their barbarism, thanks to which they had not reached the stage of fully developed slavery, neither the labour slavery of the classical world nor the domestic slavery of the Orient ?' (p. 178).

There is nothing in this formulation, or in the other writings of Marx and Engels, to show any real parallel between the emergence of feudal society and capitalist society. The new feudal lords, unlike the bourgeoisie, did not emerge from an oppressed class who found existing productive relations economically restrictive, nor did they play a progressive role in developing the productive forces once they were in power. The relations of production under feudalism do not appear to correspond to 'a definite stage of development of their material powers of production' as Marx had laid down in the famous Preface to *A Contribution to the Critique of Political Economy*.[1] This classic formulation would only seem to be applicable to the emergence of the bourgeoisie within feudal society.

In the well-known section of *Capital* on 'The Historical Tendency of Capitalist Accumulation', Marx summarizes his views on the relationship which develops between productive forces and property relations within feudal society.

> Private property, as contrasted with social or collective property, exists only where the means of labour and the external conditions of labour belong to private individuals. But the character of private property differs according as the private individuals are workers or non-workers. The innumerable shades which, at the first glance, seem to be exhibited by private property, are merely reflexions of the intermediate conditions that lie between these two extremes.
>
> The worker's private ownership of the means of production is the basis of petty industry; and petty industry is an indispensable condition for the development of social production and of the free individuality of the worker. Of course, this method of production is also found within the slaveholding system, within the system of serfdom, and within other dependent relationships. But it only flourishes, only manifests its full energy, only assumes its adequate and classical form, where the worker is the free private owner of the means of labour which he uses; only when the peasant owns the land he tills, and when the handicraftsman owns the tools which he handles as a virtuoso.
>
> This method of production presupposes a parcelling-out of the soil, a scattered ownership of the instruments of production. Just as it excludes concentration of these means into a few hands, so does it exclude co-operation, the division of labour within the process of production, the social mastery and regulation of the forces of nature, the free development of the social energies of production. It is only compatible with narrow limits for production and society, limits that are the outcome of spontaneous growth. The desire to perpetuate the existence of such limits would be, as Pecqueur has rightly said: 'a decree for the perpetuation of universal mediocrity'. At a certain level

---

1. See Appendix to Ch. 1, section vi, pp. 45–6, above.

of development, this method of production brings into the world material means which will effect its own destruction. Thenceforward there stir within the womb of society forces and passions which feel this method of production to be a fetter. It must be destroyed, it is destroyed. Its destruction, the transformation of the individual and scattered means of production into socially concentrated means of production, the transformation of the pygmy property of the many into the titan property of the few, the expropriation of the great masses of the people from the land, from the means of subsistence, and from the instruments of labour – this terrible and grievous expropriation of the populace – comprises the prelude to the history of capital. It comprises a series of forcible measures, of which we have passed in review those only that have been epoch-making as methods of the primary accumulation of capital. The expropriation of the immediate producers is effected with ruthless vandalism; and under the stimulus of the most infamous, the basest, the meanest, and the most odious of passions. Self-earned private property, the private property that may be looked upon as grounded on a coalescence of the isolated, individual, and independent worker, with his working conditions, is supplanted by capitalist private property, which is maintained by the exploitation of others' labour, but of labour which, in a formal sense, is free (pp. 844–5).

Capitalist private property is capital: the means of production of wealth in an economic system where ownership and work, producer and product are divorced from each other. Under capitalism the capitalist as capitalist is simply the embodiment of capital and plays no positive role in the productive process; while the worker is simply a cog in the process. Working becomes simply a means to living, instead of being a creative part of it. The worker is dominated by the commodities which he has to produce, commodities which appear to him, not as objects of use for satisfying human needs, but as tasks which he has to perform under degrading and onerous conditions in order that he may be permitted to live. The alienation of the worker from his product is increased by the continuous subdivision of labour processes and the increasing range of luxury goods produced for upper-class consumption.

With the dominance of production for exchange over production for consumption the labour product assumes two forms, as a thing of use and a thing of value. The latter dominates the former so that the essential characteristic of a product appears as its exchange value, first in terms of other commodities and then in terms of money as the universal expression of exchange values. 'But this finished form of the world of commodities, this money form, is the very thing which veils instead of disclosing the social character of private or individual labour, and therewith hides the social relations between the individual producers' (*Capital*, p. 49). The monetary exchange value of one object to another appears as a relationship between objects, instead of an expression of the relationships that exist between those engaged in the respective production processes. What is concealed is what determines the level at which goods exchange with one another, their relative money prices. The answer is that 'in the chance and ever-varying exchange relations between products the labour time socially necessary for their production exerts its coersive influence like an over-riding law of nature' (pp. 48–9). While bourgeois economists, and Ricardo in particular, had come to understand this, their understanding was imperfect since they failed to distinguish between labour as it finds expression in use value and the same labour as it finds expression in exchange value. The first is common to labour employed under all social conditions and situations, the second is characteristic of commodity production only.

It is the relationship between the use value and exchange value of labour which for Marx is the key to capitalist production for exchange. On the basis of the labour theory of value it can be shown that there is a gap between the use value of labour power and its exchange value. The use value is simply transferred over directly and proportionately to the product; but the exchange value of the labour power, the price for which the labour is hired, is determined by what is necessary for the labourer's cost of maintenance. 'The daily cost of maintenance of labour power, and the daily output of labour power, are two very different things. The former determines the exchange-value of labour power; the latter, its use value. – The value of labour power, and the value which that labour power creates in the labour process are, therefore, two completely different magnitudes' (pp. 187–8). The seller of labour power 'realizes its exchange value and alienates its use value' (p. 188), while the owner, having paid for the exchange value of a day's labour power has the use-value of the labour during the whole of that day. This means that he appropriates the surplus value created in excess of the cost (exchange value) of the labour power purchased. Surplus-value is the basis of the capitalist economy, the source of accumulated capital and profit. Thus it becomes apparent that capitalism is a system of economic exploitation, equally with slavery and feudalism, since the capitalist appropriates the use value he can extract from the whole labour time expended, while only paying for its exchange value. The expropriation is masked under capitalism, where the existence of an unpaid portion of labour-time expended is less evident than under other economic class systems. Marx claimed to have torn away this mask, to have shown both the need, and possibility of, the workers ending the private class expropriation of the social product of their labour.

But what form is the socialization of production to take? It is clear to both Marx and Engels that state ownership of selected industries and services will not in itself suffice, since this will simply lead to state industries and services buttressing the capitalist system. Engels even suggests that capitalism is developing to a stage where it no longer requires capitalists, that 'the state – will ultimately have to undertake the direction of production'. This, however, will not alter, in Engels's view, the fundamental nature of the economic system.

> The modern state, no matter what its form, is essentially a capitalist machine, the state of the capitalist, the ideal personification of the total national capital. The more it proceeds to the taking over of productive forces, the more does it actually become the national capitalist, the more citizens does it exploit. The workers remain wage workers – proletarians. The capitalist relation is not done away with.[1]

Marx describes how this exploiting relationship can be abolished in his *Critique of the Gotha Programme*, of the German Social Democratic Party written in 1875.[2] Marx characterizes the conditions which will exist in the first stage of communist society when it is 'in every respect, economically, morally and intellectually, still stamped with the birthmarks of the old society from whose womb it emerges. Accordingly the individual producer receives back from society – after the deductions have been made – exactly what he gives to it' (p. 563). Instead of receiving the value of his labour power (i.e. his social maintenance cost) and leaving all the surplus value he produces to the capitalist, he will receive the full value of his labour, measured both quantitatively and qualitatively; minus what is required for the economic and social purposes of society, i.e. for himself as a social being. These deductions will cover the cost of replacement, insurance and expansion of productive resources, the provision of social amenities and services and their administration.

In this phase of communism the equal legal right to own property is replaced, not by equality of wealth, but by equal reward for equal effort, measured by an equal standard, labour. All will equally be

---

1. *Socialism: Utopian and Scientific*, pp. 143–4, in Feuer, op. cit.
2. The work was published by Engels in the newspaper *Neue Zeit* in 1891. The edition used here is that in *Karl Marx: Selected Works*, Vol. 2.

required to work, but inequality will remain since men have unequal physical and mental endowments and different needs and responsibilities. These defects are only remediable in the higher phase of communist society,

> after the enslaving subordination of individuals under division of labour, and therefore also the antithesis between mental and physical labour, has vanished, after labour has become not merely a means to live but has become itself the primary necessity of life, after the productive forces have also increased with the all-round development of the individual, and all the springs of co-operative wealth flow more abundantly – only then can the narrow horizon of bourgeois right be fully left behind and society inscribe on its banners: from each according to his ability, to each according to his needs (p. 566).

To achieve this higher stage of communism men have to transcend the notion of equality of rights, a notion which has relevance only in a society still dominated by bourgeois conceptions of property and exchange. Under conditions of capitalism the proletarian demand for equality has been either a spontaneous reaction against crying social inequalities, or against the failure to apply bourgeois conceptions of equality to the relationship between the bourgeoisie and the proletariat. 'In both cases the real content of the proletarian demand for equality is the demand for the *abolition of classes*'.[1]

With the abolition of classes and the establishment of a full communist society, the concept of equality will have become historically redundant.

READING

K. Marx, *Capital*, Vol. I, Everyman's Library edition, Ch. 1, 'Commodities', Ch. 24, 'Primary Accumulation'.

K. Marx, *Value, Price and Profit*.

F. Engels, *Socialism: Utopian and Scientific*, extracts in Feuer, op. cit.

F. Engels, *The Origin of the Family, Private Property and the State*, Ch. 8, in *Engels: Selected Writings*, edited by W. O. Henderson.

Joseph A. Schumpeter, *Ten Great Economists from Marx to Keynes*, (1952).

1. Engels, *Anti-Dühring*, p. 121.

CHAPTER 6

The Form of the State

1. HOBBES

A Commonwealth for Hobbes is a state in which sovereign power is exercised according to the model conditions which Hobbes finds necessary for the maintenance of civil society. These conditions have been discussed in Chapter 3, section 1. In dealing therefore with the various kinds of Commonwealth which might be instituted Hobbes deals not with the various forms of state which exist, but with the forms which a strictly sovereign state in his terms might assume. These are monarchy, aristocracy or democracy. 'Other kinds of Common-wealth there can be none: for either One, or More, or All, must have the Sovereign Power . . . entire' (p. 97). Hobbes is at great pains to insist that the sovereign must possess and directly control all major powers (or rights as Hobbes terms them) of government for 'if he transferre the *Militia*, he retains the Judicature in vain, for want of execution of the Lawes: Or if he grant away the Power of raising Mony; the *Militia* is in vain' (p. 95). The important thing for Hobbes is that there should be a fully effective sovereign power not the form that it takes. The importance he attaches to this point is borne out in the following passage:

> If there had not first been an opinion received of the greatest part of *England*, that these Powers were divided between the King and the Lords, and the House of Commons, the people had never been divided, and fallen into this Civill Warre; . . . which have so instructed men in this point of Soveraign Right, that there be few now (in *England*) that do not see, that these Rights are inseparable (p. 95).

When Hobbes uses the term democracy he is not thinking of liberal representative democracy, with its emphasis on the rule of law, protection of individual liberties and the election of a legislature to which the executive is constitutionally responsible; but direct government by assembly of all the people, possessed of all powers, executive and judicial as well as legislative. Our conception of representative democracy comes under Hobbes's category of aristocratic government with an elective assembly.[1] Hobbes, however, is not concerned, as we are, with the number or categories of people who qualify for electing the assembly; indeed he sees little distinction between democracy and aristocracy as forms of government, contrasting them both with monarchy. Again monarchy was not simply the term applied to a state which had one person as its named head but a state in which the full sovereign power was in one man's hands.

Hobbes attacks what he calls 'mixt Monarchy' where the power of levying money required the assent of one body, that of making laws the affirmation of another and where executive power was in the hands of a third.[2] He insists 'that such government, is not government, but division of the Common-wealth into three Factions' (p. 176). A limited sovereign is for Hobbes a contradiction in terms – 'that king whose power is limited is not superior to him, or them, that have the power to limit it . . . that is to say not Soveraign'. The conclusion he draws from this is that 'The Soveraignty therefore was alwaies in the Assembly which had the Right to Limit him: and by consequence the government not Monarchy, but either Democracy, or Aristocracy' (p. 101). Hobbes here provides us with a different definition of these forms of government to those used above. Instead of democracy being defined as unqualified rule by general assembly we now have the term applied to states where the *ultimate* power lies in the hands of the people, even though such power may not be exercised and though the monarch may possess many of the rights of the sovereign which Hobbes himself lists. Democracy as Hobbes uses the term in the latter sense comes closer to our present notion of popular sovereignty, where ultimate power

1. Hobbes talks of a democracy as a state governed by any Assembly, into the which, any of them, had right to enter': and aristocracy as a state 'governed by any Assembly, into which, any man could enter by their Election' (p. 101).
2. Hobbes's 'mixt Monarchy' is similar to the form of government advocated by Locke in the *Second Treatise of Government* and to the popular conception of the form adopted in Britain after the Glorious Revolution. The Marquis of Halifax wrote in 1685, 'Our Trimmer admireth our blessed constitution, in which dominion and liberty are so happily reconciled. It giveth to the Prince the glorious power of commanding freemen, and to the subjects the satisfaction of seeing that power so lodged as that their liberties are secure. . . . And though in some instances the King is restrained, yet nothing in the government can move without him.' From the *Character of a Trimmer* quoted in *The Law and Working of the Constitution Documents 1660–1914*, Vol. I, edited by W. C. Costin and J. Steven Watson, 1952.

resides in the electors to shape both the form of the constitution and to decide the person of its office-holders.

Hobbes draws a sharp distinction between sovereign and non-sovereign politically representative bodies. The former are, as we have seen, democratic and aristocratic forms of sovereign state, using these terms in Hobbes's former sense; the latter exist at the discretion of the sovereign.

> For example, if a Soveraign Monarch, or a Soveraign Assembly, shall think fit to give command to the towns, and other severall parts of their territory, to send to him their Deputies, to enforme him of the condition, and necessities of the Subjects, or to advise with him for the making of good Lawes, or for any other cause . . . such Deputies having a place and time of meeting assigned them, are there, and at that time, a Body Politique representing every Subject of the Dominion; but it is onely for such matters as shall be propounded unto them by that Man, or Assembly, that by the Soveraign Authority sent for them; and when it shall be declared that nothing more shall be propounded, nor debated by them, the Body is dissolved (p. 123).

Whereas a man may rightly openly protest against the decree of a non-sovereign Representative Assembly 'because otherwise they may be obliged to pay debts contracted, and be responsible for crimes committed by other men'; this right to opt out is logically denied in a sovereign assembly because it would mean questioning the authority of a sovereign power which the would-be protester had himself instituted to act on his behalf in all things as is thought fit (p. 120). It is important to stress that a sovereign monarch in an instituted state is for Hobbes representative of the people – 'a *Common-wealth* is said to be *Instituted*, when a *Multitude* of men do Agree, and *Covenant, every one, with every one,* that to whatsoever *Man,* or *Assembly of Men,* shall be given by the major part, the *Right* to *Present* the Person of them all, (that is to say to be their *Representative)*' (p. 90). Hobbes makes use of the representative character of instituted sovereigns to rebut certain claims which might be made against the rights and powers of monarchs.

He refutes the view that a 'Monarch receiveth his Power by Covenant, that is to say on Condition' (p. 91), by pointing to the illogicality of applying it to government by Sovereign Assembly (democracy).

> But when an Assembly of men is made Soveraigne; then no man imagineth any such Covenant to have past in the Institution; for no man is so dull as to say, for example, the People of *Rome,* made a Covenant with the Romans, to hold the Soveraignty on such or such conditions; which not performed, the Romans might lawfully depose the Roman people (p. 92).

Again he argues that the view that the collective body of subjects is superior in power to the sovereign is nonsense, as is easily seen if we consider the case where the people in assembly is itself the sovereign body (p. 95). More importantly he argues that

> as it is absurd, to think that a Soveraign Assembly, inviting the People of their Dominion, to send up their Deputies, with power to make known their Advise, or Desires, should therefore hold such Deputies, rather than themselves, for the absolute Representative of the people: so it is absurd also, to think the same in a Monarchy (p. 97).

The sovereign is the 'Representative unlimited' (p. 119) of the People, and as such the people are to accept both the form of rule and the person of the ruler as long as these are extant.

While the three forms of model state discussed by Hobbes are models of his own construction they correspond in outward form to the classification of states commonly accepted in the western world since classical Greek times. The only classificatory change which Hobbes introduces is to do away with the distinction between 'just' and 'unjust' forms of each kind of state, for instance monarchy – tyranny, aristocracy – oligarchy – democracy – anarchy. He does so on the grounds that the latter are not different forms of government at all, but 'the same Formes misliked' (p. 97). At the time of writing the great majority of states in Europe were classifiable under the heading of monarchies in that almost all of them had an emperor, prince, king or monarch as their titular head. Thus most men in reading what Hobbes had to say about different forms of state would identify their own state with his category of monarchy; though as we have seen few if any of them possessed the powers and rights which he thought necessary to the proper functioning of that office. In holding up monarchy therefore as the form best fitted to produce peace and security, Hobbes was approving in *name* the most common form of government that existed. He reassured existing heads of state of the validity of their titles and positions, while urging on them the need to ensure that their rule conformed to the true requirements of the role of a sovereign.

Hobbes sets out at some length the advantages of monarchy as the most effective of the three possible forms of sovereign power. A monarch unites the public and private interests so that 'the riches, power, and honour of a Monarch arise onely from the riches, strength and reputation of his Subjects' (p. 98), whereas in a democracy or an aristocracy a corrupt ruler will gain more from his anti-social practices than he will, as an individual, gain from promoting the general prosperity of the commonwealth. Again a monarch can take counsel from whom he pleases, while decisions are his alone; whereas assemblies will take no heed of non-members, are subject to inconstancy brought about by the changing number of those participating, are liable to disagree amongst themselves and equally with monarchs are subject to seduction by flattery. The vexed problem of the succession in a monarchy is met if it is recognized 'that by the Institution of Monarchy, the disposing of the Successor, is alwaies left to the Judgment and Will of the present Possessor' (p. 102), even if this involves the 'inconvenience' that the monarch may sell or give his right of governing to a stranger. Hobbes firmly rejects, however, what was at the time thought of, as the chief plank of a monarch's claim to rule, his heredity right by succession. 'As if, for example, the Right of the Kings of England did depend on the goodnesse of the cause of *William* the Conquerour, and upon their lineall, and directest Descent from him; by which means, there would perhaps be no tie of the Subjects obedience to their Soveraign at this day in all the world' (p. 387). In spite of its logical force, arguments like this did not endear Hobbes to royalists, while his strictures against those who would attempt to make monarchs responsible to representative assemblies damned him in the eyes of Parliament men.

READING

Hobbes, *Leviathan*, Ch. 19.

2. LOCKE

The main burden of Locke's argument in the *Treatises of Government* is directed against arbitrary rule; that is unconstitutional rule in the original sense of unlimited government which denies fundamental rights and liberties.[1] He keeps returning to the twin themes that absolutism is a form of government incompatible with man's nature as a rational creature and that steps need to be taken to prevent absolutist tendencies

1. See G. G. Sartori, 'Constitutionalism: A Preliminary Discussion', *American Political Science Review*, December 1962.

developing within constitutional forms of government. The great protection which Locke offers against absolutism is the doctrine of consent. If the consent of the people is accepted as the only ultimate justification for any form of government then absolutism in its seventeenth century form is disqualified since it claims God as the sole authority for both its position and its unqualified powers. 'Kings,' wrote James I in *Trew Law of Free Monarchies*, 'are breathing images of God upon earth', and as 'God's lieutenants upon earth' they may make such laws as they think fit to govern the people.[1] Since absolutism is associated with monarchy Locke finds it necessary to show how men came to adopt a form of government so fraught with possible dangers to their rights and liberties. Locke's answer is that monarchy was a natural development from paternal government, but he stresses that the authority which a father exercised over his adult children did not proceed from direct grant of God but by 'the express or tacit Consent of the Children' who merely permitted a continuance of the authority exercised in their infancy (II, s. 74). 'Thus the natural *Fathers of Families* by an insensible change, became the *politick Monarchs* of them too' (II, s. 76), and this accustomed pattern of the rule of one man was adopted by most communities of men because it was familiar, simple and adapted to their immediate needs and conditions. In consequence 'the first Beginners of Common-wealths generally put the Rule into one Man's hand, without any other express Limitation or Restraint, but what the Nature of the thing, and the End of Government required' (II, s. 111). Thus Locke insists that monarchical rule was only ever absolute in the sense that the power of ruling was not shared with any one else; it was not, and could not, be absolute in the sense that it might be used without regard to the interests of the ruled. When men experienced the rule of an oppressive monarch devoted to his own private interests they 'found it necessary to examine more carefully *the Original* and Rights of *Government*; and to find out ways to *restrain the Exorbitances*, and *prevent the Abuses* of that Power which they having intrusted in another's hands only for their own good, they found was made use of to hurt them' (II, s. 111).

The danger of a degeneration into arbitrary rule exists under all forms of government, although it is greatest in a monarchy. To meet this danger Locke introduces his notion of continuing consent which requires all those who come of age to decide for themselves whether they wish to live under the same laws and constitution as their fathers,

1. Quoted by George H. Sabine, *A History of Political Theory*, 1948 edition, p. 337.

and which permits those who have not 'expressly' consented to the form
of government to emigrate if they find conditions intolerable.[1]

Since the notion of tacit consent is derived from the stronger and
clearer notion of express consent it is the latter which Locke uses for his
model showing how a political society might be established. Membership of the community is therefore restricted to those who actually agree
together 'to join and unite into a community'; in contrast to Hobbes
where the majority of assenters bind not only the minority of dissenters
but absentees as well. The act of incorporation does not create in
Locke's conception a 'body Politick' with power to act on behalf of its
members in matters of common interest. All that each and every
individual does in his initial common act of consent is to enter society
on the understanding that some form of political organization will be
necessary for its proper functioning – *the beginning of Politick Society*
depends upon the consent of the Individuals, to joyn into and make one
Society; who, when they are thus incorporated, might set up what form
of Government they thought fit' (II, s. 106). The decision as to *the* form
of Government, unlike the decision *to* form a government need not be
unanimous – a majority will suffice.

Locke's discussion of the use of the majority principle in connection
with 'the beginning of political societies' is somewhat confusing. When
he writes 'For when any number of Men have, by the consent of every
individual, made a *Community*, they have thereby made that *Community*
one Body, with a Power to Act as one Body, which is only by the will
and determination of the *majority*' (II, s. 96), one might be excused for
thinking he is insisting that the only acceptable forms of government
are democratic ones which embody the majority principle. But Locke
is concerned to make the quite different point that the act of agreeing
to live together in an organized society necessarily involves acceptance
of collective decisions. To insist on the right of any individual to deny
any obligation to abide by collective decisions with which he personally
disagrees would nullify the whole conception of the original compact
of society.

> For what appearance would there be of any Compact? What new
> Engagement if he were no farther tied by any Decrees of the Society,
> than he thought fit, and did actually consent to? This would be still
> as great a liberty, as he himself had before his Compact, or any one

---

1. See Chapter 3, section 2, pp. 100–104 above, for a full discussion of Locke's
theory of consent.

else in the State of Nature hath, who may submit himself and consent to any acts of it if he thinks fit (II, s. 97).

Locke asserts the claims of the majority to bind the whole but he produces no real arguments to back up the assertion that the majority has 'by the Law of Nature and Reason' the right to act on behalf of the whole. Indeed it is difficult to see what moral arguments, as distinct from arguments of social convenience or necessity, one could put forward in its support. What is important to note is that Locke uses the majority principle to establish the legitimacy of any particular form of government by reference to the way in which it was constituted, not to the form it takes. In other words a political régime is legitimate by reference to the majority principle, for Locke, if the majority agree to establish it, even if the régime they set up is one in which the majority of the people have no direct say at all.

> The Majority having, as has been shew'd, upon Mens first uniting into Society, the whole power of the Community, naturally in them, may imploy all that power in making Laws for the Community from time to time, and Executing those Laws by Officers of their own appointing; and then the *Form* of the Government is a perfect *Democracy*: Or else may put the power of making Laws into the hands of a few select Men, and their Heirs or Successors; and then it is an *Oligarchy*: Or else into the hands of one Man, and then it is a *Monarchy* (II, s. 132).

Once a particular form of government is established the majority have such 'Right to act and conclude the rest' (II, s. 95) as the constitution itself allows; unless a revolutionary situation arises which results in the dissolution of government,[1] when the people resume their right to determine by majority decision the form of government they wish to live under. It is almost certain that 'the people' to whom Locke refers are 'Freemen' (II, s. 99), a category which would probably exclude all those directly under the authority of others, viz. servants, agricultural and industrial labourers, apprentices, common seamen and soldiers, as well as paupers, vagrants, women and children. Using Professor Macpherson's estimates it would seem that only about one in three of all adult males in England at the time would have come within the category of 'freemen'.[2] Consequently even the ultimate power

---

1. See Chapter 3, section 2, pp. 104-6 above, for a discussion of the conditions under which revolt may be justified.
2. C. B. Macpherson, op. cit; Appendix, 'Social Classes and Franchise Classes in England, c. 1648'.

residing in the people to determine the form of the government would rest in the hands of a majority of a minority of the male population. The 'undemocratic' limitation or even negation of the majority principle, as it appears to us, would not have appeared undemocratic to most seventeenth century readers. Indeed the Levellers themselves, who constituted the 'left wing' within the Commonwealth army had taken up an analogous position.[2] To most radicals of the time to extend voting rights to persons who were economically, socially or officially dependent on others would mean, under conditions of open voting, placing extra votes in the hands of their masters.

Locke's interest does not lie in classifying different forms of political system, but in examining the implications of the relationship between the various arms of government. It is clear to Locke that the 'Supreme Power' in any political community is the legislative power and consequently it is with the proper location and nature of this power that he is chiefly concerned. The legislative power for Locke is sovereign in the sense that it alone has the power to make laws which members of the community are required to obey; but it is not politically sovereign in the sense that one is under an obligation to obey it irrespective of the nature of what is commanded. It is only so long as it keeps within the limits of its authority as laid down by the constitution and does not neglect its duties or interfere with the liberties and properties of the subjects that the legislative has rightful power to act. It is precisely because Locke recognizes the human frailty of those who wield the powers of state that he insists on the need not only to provide an ultimate check on those who have the 'supream' legislative power, but also to ensure that those who make the laws shall not also execute them (II, s. 143). Since in Locke's day executive power was normally vested in one man, king, prince or magistrate, Locke argues against a monarchic form of government, that is one in which the 'supream' legislative power is vested solely in one man's hands.

> Therefore in well order'd Commonwealths, where the good of the whole is so considered, as it ought, the *Legislative* Power is put into the hands of divers Persons who duly Assembled, have by themselves, or jointly with others, a Power to make Laws, which when they have done, being separated again, they are themselves subject to the Laws, they have made; which is a new and near tie upon them, to take care, that they make them for the publick good (II, s. 143).

2. See C. B. Macpherson, op. cit., Ch. 3, 'The Levellers: Franchise and Freedom'.

Such a form of government does not preclude the head of the executive from sharing in the legislative power; as occurred under the English system which accorded the monarch the power to withhold consent to legislation. In such circumstances, however, the monarch as head of the executive is still subject to the laws which he helps to frame.

Locke does not argue for a strict separation of the powers of government but for the subordination of the executive to the legislative power whose main constituent would be an elected legislature capable of initiating proposals of its own and frustrating the designs of the executive. While Locke stresses the need for *'indifferent* and upright *Judges'* (II, s. 131), he does not regard the judiciary as a separate arm of government. His third arm, the federative power, is concerned with relations with other states, defence, foreign relations, and foreign trade. He makes the pertinent point that such matters are 'much less capable to be directed by antecedent, standing, positive Laws' since 'what is to be done in reference to *Foreigners* depending much upon their actions, and the variation of design and interests, must be *left* in great part *to* the *Prudence* of those who have this Power committed to them,' which is invariably the body wielding the executive power (II, s. 148). The distinction was an important one for Locke, since it was historically accepted that British monarchs had authority to do what they thought necessary to defend the realm and further its interests overseas; subject only to the need to get authorization for any moneys required for these objectives.

Perhaps the most surprising feature to modern eyes of Locke's discussion of the relationship between the arms of government is his attitude towards the prerogative rights of the ruler. 'This Power to act according to discretion, for the publick good, without the prescription of the Law, and sometimes even against it, is that which is called *Prerogative'* (II, 160). Far from objecting to the existence of wide prerogative powers Locke accepts them as not only necessary but desirable – 'a good Prince, who is mindful of the trust put into his hands, and careful of the good of his People, cannot have too much *Prerogative'* (II, s. 164). But the prerogative power stems ultimately from the people, if only in the negative sense of their tacit consent to its use. Consequently it may be withdrawn if it is abused. Misuse 'gives the People an occasion, to claim their Right, to limit that Power, which, whilst it was exercised for their good, they were content should be tacitly allowed' (II, s. 164). Moreover such abuse entitles the People not merely to limit the extent of the prerogative as far as the transgressing ruler is concerned, but to permanently restrict the prerogative 'by positive Laws'

(II, s. 163), which defines how and when it may be used in relation to a specific area of government. In the case of dispute between the people and the ruler over prerogative rights,

> tho' the *People* cannot be *Judge*, so as to have by the Constitution of that Society any Superiour power, to determine and give effective Sentence in the case; yet they have, by a Law antecedent and paramount to all positive Laws of men, reserv'd that ultimate Determination to themselves, which belongs to all Mankind, where there lies no Appeal on Earth, *viz* to judge whether they have just Cause to make their Appeal to Heaven [that is, to revolt—my note] (II, s. 168).

Locke's treatment of prerogative right makes it clear that the ultimate principle for him is not what the constitution or the law requires but what the people judge to be for the public good. Since the only power which the people as such have is the right of revolt, acquiescence in the use of the prerogative may be taken as signifying that it is being rightly used. 'For the People are very seldom, or never scrupulous, or nice in the point: they are far from examining *Prerogative*, whilst it is in any tolerable degree imploy'd for the use it was meant; that is, for the good of the People, and not manifestly against it' (II, s. 161). On the basis of Locke's argument, (though not one might hazard in accordance with his intentions), it would always be possible for a ruler to claim, except where the legislative had specifically withdrawn or restricted the use of the prerogative, that 'Salus Populo Suprema Lex'[1] justified him taking any extra-constitutional or unconstitutional action which he thought necessary, as long as the people acquiesced in its use.

READING

John Locke, *Second Treatise of Government*, Chs. 10–14.

J. W. Gough, *John Locke's Political Philosophy*, Ch. 3, 'Government by Consent'.

M. Seliger, *The Liberal Politics of John Locke*, Ch. 10, 'Popular Consent', Ch. 11, 'Executive and Legislature'.

1. "The welfare of the people is the highest law."

3. ROUSSEAU

In the *Confessions*, written in the years between 1762 and 1770, Rousseau wrote with reference to the composition of *The Social Contract*,

> I had realized that everything was basically related to politics, and that no matter how one approached it, no people would ever be anything but what the nature of its government[1] made it. Therefore the great question of the best possible government seemed to me to reduce itself to this: which is the form of government fitted to shape the most virtuous, the most enlightened, the wisest, and, in short, the 'best' people, taking that word in its noblest meaning?[2]

Rousseau had little faith in the ability of men to carve out for themselves a worthwhile and satisfying life, although he had some sympathy, as both *Émile* and his own life shows, with the view that a wise and sensitive being might do well to cut himself off from the worst evils of the corrupt society that surrounded him. But as far as the mass of the people were concerned, they will be what society makes them and, within limits, society will take its shape from what those who control the state want it to be or allow it to become. 'It is certain,' he writes in *A Discourse on Political Economy*, 'that all peoples become in the long run what the government makes them: warriors, citizens, men, when it so pleases; or merely populace and rabble, when it chooses to make them so', and he contrasts ancient governments which took care to lay down 'public rules of conduct' with 'our modern governments, which imagine they have done everything when they have raised money' (p. 243). In *The Social Contract* he adduces general universally applicable principles of good government and discusses the problems of applying them to different peoples in different times and conditions. It is because he passionately believes that valid principles of good government are deducible, and that the neglect of these principles has led to the corruption of modern states, that he insists in his foreword to the *Constitutional Project for Corsica* that it is necessary to shape the nation to fit the government and not the government to fit the nation. It is the nation

---

1. It is necessary to note that Rousseau is here using the term government in its wide general sense as the whole apparatus of the state, instead of as simply the executive arm of the state machine, which is the way he normally employs the term.
2. Quoted in E. Cassirer, *The Question of Jean Jacques Rousseau*, edited by Peter Gay, p. 65.

as it might be, not the nation as it now is, that should be the concern of the constitution-maker.

The most important general principle which Rousseau puts forward in *The Social Contract* is that of popular sovereignty. Sovereignty resides in the whole body of the members of the community meeting in public assembly for the purpose of enacting laws as 'authentic acts of the general will' (Bk. III, Ch. 12, p. 136). This sovereignty is not for Rousseau an original or theoretical sovereignty, it is an actual power which only the people can exercise; although it does not follow that every act of the public assembly would constitute an authoritative expression of sovereignty. The sovereign body of assembled citizens must, if they are to express the general will, confine themselves to matters of common concern and each citizen must ask himself not whether any proposition is to his own advantage but whether it is advantageous to the state. He insists that the sovereign expression of the general will 'can act only when the people is assembled' (p. 136) and that this power cannot be alienated to any other body or represented by any other body, 'for either the will is general or it is not; either it is the will of the body of the people, or merely that of a part' (Bk. II, Ch. 2, p. 70). Consequently he will have no truck with the modern conception of a representative legislature, such as existed in England at that time. 'Any law which the people has not ratified in person is void; it is not law at all' (Bk. III, Ch. 15, p. 141). This forthright declaration marks a sharp break with the views which Rousseau had himself put forward only four years earlier in *A Discourse on Political Economy*. There he writes:

> But how, I shall be asked, can the general will be known in cases in which it has not expressed itself? Must the whole nation be assembled together at every unforseen event? Certainly not. It ought the less to be assembled, because it is by no means certain that its decision would be the expression of the general will; besides the method would be impracticable in a great people, and is hardly ever necessary where the government is well-intentioned: for the rulers well know that the general will is always on the side which is most favourable to the public interest, that is to say most equitable; so that it is needful only to act justly, to be certain of following the general will (p. 242).

It must be remembered, of course, that the *Discourse on Political Economy* contains only the embryo of Rousseau's thinking on the general will. It would appear that further consideration led him to the conclusion that the nature of the general will, as the true will of each citizen and the source of all law, required it to have a recognized and authoritative mode of expression if rulers were to be prevented from claiming their own selfish policies as being in the public interest. As far as the practical problem was concerned, Rousseau argued in *The Social Contract* that the example of the Roman Republic, with its 400,000 citizens in Rome and 4,000,000 in the Empire, showed it was not insoluble if the will were there.

The assembled citizens were for Rousseau the only body with any valid claim to lay down the constitution of the state as well as to approve the laws made under it. By framing a constitution the people as sovereign determine the form which the executive or government of the state shall take. But since the executive cannot operate until particular individuals have taken office, the sovereign must transform itself from a legislative body into a democratic executive in order to make the necessary appointments (Bk. III, Ch. 17). Consequently it follows 'that the holders of the executive power are not the people's masters but its officers; and that the people can appoint them and dismiss them as it pleases' (Bk. III, Ch. 18, p. 146) at fixed and periodic assemblies which nothing can abolish or prorogue (p. 137). The Assembly will pass, amend or revoke such laws as it thinks fit, including the laws of the constitution itself. Rousseau accepts that there are practical difficulties in making the whole body of the people the legislature in any but the smallest state, and he suggests that large states might contract their boundaries or move the seat of government round the country, making the people in each locality in turn the legislative body. When ten years later he produced *Considerations on the Government of Poland* he urged the Poles both to contract their boundaries and to establish a federal form of government based on the thirty-three districts into which the country was divided for administrative purposes (pp. 182–3). More importantly he reluctantly put aside his insistence on the need for the legislative power to be in the hands of the people and reverts to the principle of a representative legislature which he had so scornfully rejected earlier. He has not, however, altered his fundamental position, for he makes clear his view that

One of the greatest disadvantages of large states, the one which above all makes liberty most difficult to preserve in them, is that the legislative power cannot manifest itself directly, and can only act only by delegation. That has its good and its evil side; but the evil outweighs the good. A legislature made up of the whole citizen body is impossible to corrupt, but easy to deceive. Representatives of the people are hard to deceive, but easy to corrupt; and it rarely happens that they are not so corrupted (*Poland*, p. 192).

In *The Social Contract* Rousseau introduced the 'legislator' to ensure that the people were not deceived. In *Considerations on Poland* he requires representatives in the legislature to be mandated by the electorate who would examine their representatives' record on the limited number of occasions on which he might submit himself for re-election at polls held at frequent intervals. These restrictions were necessary in Rousseau's view if representatives were to be held to their duties, for unlike Burke, Rousseau held that representatives were elected 'not to express their own private sentiments, but to declare the will of the nation' (*Poland*, p. 194).

Rousseau recommends these proposals for Poland as the best practicable solution for dealing with the constitutional problems of a particular state. In *The Social Contract* he discusses the general problem of the form of the state, on the presumption that the state is kept small. 'It is no use complaining,' he says, 'about the evils of a large state to someone who wants only small ones' (Bk. III, Ch. 13, p. 138). In the small state a vital role is played by the 'legislator' or 'law-giver'.

> By themselves the people always will what is good, but by themselves they do not always discern it. The general will is always rightful, but the judgment which guides it is not always enlightened. It must be made to see things as they are, and sometimes as they should be seen; it must be shown the good path which it is seeking, and secured against seduction by the desires of individuals; it must be given a sense of situation and season, so as to weigh immediate and tangible advantages against distant and hidden evils. Individuals see the good and reject it; the public desires the good but does not see it. Both equally need guidance. Individuals must be obliged to subordinate their will to their reason; the public must be taught to recognize what it desires. Such public enlightenment would produce a union of understanding and will in the social body, bring the parts into perfect harmony and lift the whole to its fullest strength. Hence the necessity of a lawgiver (Bk. II, Ch. 6, p. 83).

It is precisely because Rousseau is so pessimistic about the capacity of ordinary people to know what they really want or to decide where their true interest lies, that he insists on the need to protect them against themselves and against those who would take advantage of them. This need is met by the all-wise philosopher-king who possesses the qualities of understanding lacking in the public at large and whose own will embodies the general will. But since even the most virtuous of men are creatures of passion Rousseau insists that the legislator should not himself possess either direct legislative or executive power, in spite of the fact that this may well result in his wise counsel being ignored. 'For a newly formed people to understand wise principles of politics and to follow the basic rules of statecraft, the effect would have to become the cause; the social spirit which must be the product of social institutions would have to preside over the setting up of those institutions' (Bk. II, Ch. 7, pp. 86–87). He therefore calls on the legislator to clothe himself with divine authority 'which can compel without violence and persuade without convincing' (p. 87) and to use that authority to mould the morals, customs, and beliefs of the people so that they may come to obey the law through force of habit instead of the force of authority (Bk. II, Ch. 12, pp. 99–100).

The considerations outlined above are, in Rousseau's view, of general application, in that they must form the foundation for any well-run state; but 'apart from those principles which are common to all, each people has its own special reasons for ordering itself in a certain way and for having laws that are fitted to itself alone' (Bk. II, Ch. 11, p. 97). In giving such weight to natural, economic, social and cultural conditions Rousseau is following the lead of Montesquieu whose great work *L'Esprit des Lois* was published in 1748. But these local empirical considerations do not replace or obliterate for Rousseau the theoretical prescriptive principles which he had adduced; they simply modify their application. 'It is in the light of such factors that one must assign to each people the particular form of constitution which is best, not perhaps in itself, but for that state for which it is destined' (p. 97). Few people in Rousseau's view were fit to receive laws and it was only with those few that Rousseau was concerned.

Since the legislative power in any free state or republic[1] must be in the hands of the people, the different forms of republic are to be distinguished by differences in the nature of the governments, i.e. executives, to be found in each case. Rousseau follows the traditional classification of states into democracy, aristocracy and monarchy according to whether the executive power is in the hands of the whole or greater part of the people, a few people or one person. Democracy would be the perfect form of government, if men themselves were perfect; but

---

1. In a footnote (Bk. II, Ch. 6, p. 82) Rousseau explains that by a republic he understands 'any government directed by the general will, which is law' i.e. the subordination of the government to the sovereign people, so that 'even a monarchy can be a republic'. However, in Bk. III, Ch. 6, he uses the term republic in a more conventional and restricted sense as an elected, non-monarchical form of state.

since they are not it is the most difficult of all governments to establish and maintain, as well as being the form most susceptible to civil war and internecine strife. 'In the strict sense of the term, there has never been a true democracy, and there never will be' (Bk. III, Ch. 4, p. 112), for it is impossible that the whole body of the people should sit constantly in session to deal with every item of public business that arises. Moreover such a procedure would cut right across Rousseau's principle that the executive and legislative powers should be kept separate.[1] The conditions necessary for the establishment of even a rudimentary form of democracy are difficult to meet, namely a very small state, simplicity of manners, a large measure of equality in rank and fortune and little or no luxury. In the *Constitutional Project for Corsica* Rousseau states that 'a purely democratic government is suitable rather to a small town than to a nation' (p. 286). Aristocracy is, for Rousseau, 'the best and most natural' form of government since it allows 'the wisest to govern the multitude' in accordance with the sovereign will of the people (Bk. III, Ch. 5, p. 115). In practice, however, it is difficult to ensure that the few govern the state to the general advantage rather than their own. In modern states the choice lies between elective and hereditary aristocracies, the former being for Rousseau the best and the latter the worst form of government.[2] Elective aristocracy requires less exacting qualities than democracy and is suitable, in Rousseau's view, for medium-sized and moderately wealthy states which do not exhibit too wide a gap between rich and poor.

Finally for large opulent states the appropriate form of government is monarchy, for the larger the state the more necessary it is to have strong effective government. But such is Rousseau's distaste both for large states and for kings that this section of *The Social Contract* (Bk. III, Ch. 6) develops into an attack on the whole institution of monarchy. 'It is deliberate self-deception,' he thunders, 'to confuse royal government with the government of a good king. To understand what

1. Like Locke, Rousseau makes no provision for a separate judiciary. In *Considerations on Poland* (p. 220) he argues against the institution of a permanent body of judges.
2. Rousseau recommends for Corsica a form of elected aristocracy with a popular legislative assembly and a small executive changed at frequent intervals. Instead of speaking of this as an elected aristocracy he calls it a 'modified' form of democracy and speaks of aristocracy as a form of government where the supreme authority (i.e. legislative power) is in the hands of delegates.

this form of government is inherently, one must consider it as it is under
mediocre or evil princes, for either princes will be such when they
accede to the throne or such is what occupying the throne will make
them' (p. 122). While in theory the community might validly determine
to 'set up a royal government and an hereditary succession' (Bk. II, Ch. 6,
p. 82) to give effect to the sovereign will of the people, experience
showed that this would not work. The reason is to be found in the 'inevitable tendency' for 'a part of the executive power to escape the domain
of law' (Bk. III, Ch. 5, p. 115). This tendency exists under all forms of
government but it is strongest under monarchy where it expresses itself
as the claim of the king to be an absolute ruler above the law. The
tendency is irreversible. Rulers develop a corporate will as rulers which
is in conflict with their own particular individual wills on the one hand
and the general will on the other. 'In the order of nature ... these
different wills become the more active as they are the more concentrated.
Hence, the general will is always the weakest, the corporate will
takes second place, and the particular will comes first of all' (Bk. III,
Ch. 2, p. 108). Under monarchy the particular and the corporate wills
are united in one person which produces the most active but the most
perverse form of government in direct conflict with the general will.
The same fundamental conflict between the general will and the will
of the government is to be found in all states, although 'the more
numerous the magistrates, the closer their corporate will approaches the
general will' (p. 110).

> Just as the particular will acts unceasingly against the general will, so
> does the government continually exert itself against the sovereign. And
> the more this exertion increases, the more the constitution becomes
> corrupt, and ... sooner or later it is inevitable that the prince[1] will
> oppress the sovereign and break the social treaty. This is the inherent
> and inescapable defect which, from the birth of the political body,
> tends relentlessly to destroy it, just as old age and death destroy the
> body of a man (Bk. III, Ch. 10, p. 131).

The natural tendency of states is one of decline from democracy to
aristocracy and from aristocracy to monarchy for the body politic 'bears
within itself the causes of its own destruction' (p. 134). The most that
men can hope to do is to prolong the life of the state as long as possible

---

1. By the term prince or magistrate, Rousseau means the man or the body
   charged with the administration of the government (*The Social Contract*,
   p. 102).

by giving it the best possible constitution, while recognizing that decay
and death are its certain destiny.

READING

Rousseau, *The Social Contract*, Bk. III.

C. E. Vaughan, *Jean Jacques Rousseau: The Political Writings*, Vol. I, Introduction, pp. 71–86.

4. BENTHAM AND MILL

In *A Fragment on Government* Bentham argues that the difference
between a free government and a despotic one does not turn on the
latter having more power than the former, but on the way that power
is exercised –

> on the *manner* in which the whole mass of power, which, taken to-
> gether, is supreme, is, in a free state, *distributed* among the several
> ranks of persons that are sharers in it: on the *source* from whence their
> titles to it are successively derived: on the frequent and easy *changes*
> of conditions between gover*nors* and gover*ned*; whereby the interests
> of the one class are more or less indistinguishably blended with those
> of the other: on the *responsibility* of the governors; or the right which
> a subject has of having the reasons publicly assigned and canvassed
> of every act of power that is exerted over him: on the *liberty of the
> press*; or the security with which every man, be he of the one class or
> the other, may make known his complaints and remonstrances to the
> whole community: on the *liberty of public association*; or the security
> with which malcontents may communicate their sentiments, concert
> their plans, and practise every mode of opposition short of actual revolt,
> before the executive power can be legally justified in disturbing them
> (pp. 94–5).

It is clear however from Pt. IV, Ch. XXI of *Theory of Legislation* on
'General Precautions against Abuses of Authority' that by a free state
Bentham simply meant at this time (1776) one that is not despotic, for he
praises the freedom of the press existing in Austria and Prussia and
argues that the establishment of the right of association 'might become

one of the principal means of government, in the most absolute monarchies' (p. 465). It is not with the form of government but its effects in terms of human happiness that Bentham is concerned. The principle of utility is dangerous to and directed against the selfish autocrat not the benevolent enlightened autocrat who has the interest of his people at heart.

In time, however, Bentham became disillusioned, not only with benevolent despots like Catherine II of Russia, but with aristocratic governments in Britain which failed to live up to his reforming expectations. He came to the conclusion that there was a fundamental conflict of interest between rulers and ruled and asserted that 'the end pursued by the ruling few was the greatest happiness of the ruling few. And the interest of the ruling few is, in the greater part of the field of government, in a state of continual opposition to that of the great number' (*The Handbook of Fallacies*, p. 207). The French Revolution of 1789 provided a strong stimulus to Bentham's move to radicalism and led him to associate the interests of the governors with that of the class to which they belonged. The only constitutional way out of this situation was to put the sovereign power 'in the hands of persons placed and displaceable by the body of the people' for 'the stricter the dependence of the governors on the governed, the better will the government be, the larger and securer the measure of liberty'.[1] In the same year he produced a scheme for Britain, *Parliamentary Reform*, which proposed franchise rights for all who could read, voting by secret ballot, prohibition of canvassing and frequent elections.[2] He remained true to these principles for the rest of his long life, although his diplomatic silence during the Napoleonic Wars and his own forgetfulness led to the legend that he was converted to representative democracy in 1809 by James Mill.

The core of Bentham's theory of government is the simple assertion that the ruling group has to be made responsible to the ruled in order to prevent it from consciously furthering its own. This assertion John Stuart Mill categorically rejects. On the contrary the actions of all rulers are

> largely influenced (independently of personal calculation) by the habitual sentiments and feelings, the general modes of thinking and acting, which prevail throughout the community of which they are members; as well as by the feelings, habits, and modes of thought which char-

---

1. *On the Efficient Cause and Measure of Constitutional Liberty*, 1790, Mary Mack, op. cit., Appendix E, pp. 453–7.
2. ibid., Appendix G, pp. 462–6.

acterise the particular class in that community to which they themselves belong . . . They are also much influenced by the maxims and traditions which have descended to them from other rulers, their predecessors; which maxims and traditions have been known to retain an ascendancy during long periods, even in opposition to the private interests of the rulers for the time being (*A System of Logic*, Vol. II, Bk. VI, p. 484).

Nor does he accept that 'responsibility to the governed is the only cause capable of producing in the rulers a sense of identity of interest with the community' (p. 485). The suppression of anarchy and resistance to law, for example, is one of the strongest interests shared by rulers and people alike. Moreover a strong sense of common interest between ruler and subjects is to be found in many non-democratic states, for instance Elizabethan England. While Mill accepts that constitutional checks are required as a security against the selfish interests of rulers, and that in modern Europe identity of interest can be achieved only if governments are made responsible to the people, he insists on the need to retain or introduce 'arrangements tending to check the impetus of popular will' (p. 551).

Mill opens his book *Representative Government* by rejecting the exclusive claims of the mechanistic and organic theories of the state. The first regards government 'as wholly an affair of invention and contrivance' (p. 175) and the second as an 'organic growth from the nature and life of that people' (p. 176). Governments are made by men and worked by men but what they make, and how they use what they make, is in large part a consequence of the state of development of the community concerned and the particular nature of its customs, habits, beliefs and needs. On the other hand the form of government itself has a marked effect on the future development of the community concerned. 'Government is at once a great influence acting on the human mind, and a set of organized arrangements for public business' (p. 195). Both as a historian and as a utilitarian Mill was committed to a belief in progress and he consequently saw the role of government as the promotion of progress in civilization, 'the one indispensable merit of a government, in favour of which it may be forgiven almost any amount of other demerit compatible with progress, is that its operation on the people is favourable, or not unfavourable, to the next step which it is necessary for them to take, in order to raise themselves to a higher level' (p. 197). But since change is not synonymous with progress it is necessary to determine what is the ideal form of government and what conditions are required for its establishment, so that one may judge whether any particular community is fitted for it or whether some 'inferior' form of polity will best carry them through the necessary 'intermediate stages' before they become fit for the best form of government (p. 202).

For Mill the ideal form of government is that

> in which the sovereignty, or supreme controlling power in the last resort, is vested in the entire aggregate of the community; every citizen not only having a voice in the exercise of that ultimate sovereignty, but being, at least occasionally, called on to take an actual part in the government, by the personal discharge of some public function, local or general (p. 207).

He adduces two arguments in favour of this claim. Firstly that the rights and interests of any person or group are only secure from being disregarded or sacrificed if they have the power to assert those rights and interests not merely on the government but as part of the government. The second is that intellectual, practical and moral excellence will be the best stimulated by a form of government which requires the active participation of all its citizens, and Mill cites the examples of the Athenian democracy which raised the intellectual standard of its citizens to a level far beyond anything existing today. Representative government cannot subsist, however, unless these conditions are met. '1. That the people should be willing to receive it. 2. That they should be willing and able to do what is necessary for its preservation. 3. That they should be willing and able to fulfil the duties and discharge the functions which it imposes on them' (p. 218). With regard to the first two conditions, indifference and inability rather than outright opposition are the main obstacles to be expected. Unless they are removed no popular government can be set up or established popular government sustained. 'Representative institutions necessarily depend for permanence upon the readiness of the people to fight for them in case of their being endangered', and danger always exists in the shape of an encroaching executive (p. 219). The third condition is threatened if the majority of citizens fail to exercise their right of suffrage or exercise it only to serve some private or local interest; for then representative government becomes a mockery – either the nation's interests are subordinated to those of corrupt representations or the executive takes over control whilst retaining the parliamentary façade.

The number of communities which are suited to representative institutions is relatively small. Most primitive peoples are excluded as they have still to learn 'the first lesson of civilization, that of obedience' (p. 220). What they require is despotic rule or preferably subjection to a foreign government which will guide them rapidly through progressive stages until they become fit for representative institutions of their own. Extreme passivity and ready submission to tyranny itself militates against the introduction of representative government, as does inveterate attachment to the spirit of locality, while a desire for foreign dominion and the conception of democracy as an open scramble for an ever-increasing number of public posts, seriously restricts the benefits to be derived from it.

Mill has a number of proposals to make about the way in which representative institutions should work. He makes a distinction between the function of controlling the business of government and actually doing it, and insists that it is the former not the latter which is appropriate to a legislature. 'The proper duty of a representative assembly in regard to matters of administration is not to decide them by its own vote, but to take care that the persons who have to decide them shall be the proper persons' (p. 233). But even this it should not do directly, according to Mill, who accepts without question the current British practice whereby 'the only thing which Parliament decides is, which of two, or at the most three, parties or bodies of men, shall furnish the executive government: the opinion of the party itself decides which of its members is fittest to be placed at the head' (p. 234). The detailed work of administration should be carried out by a bureaucracy of trained officials appointed by public examination.

More controversially Mill argues that a legislative assembly is 'as little fitted for the direct business of legislation as it is for that of administration' (p. 235). He proposes the creation of a Commission of legislation appointed by the Crown whose job it would be to draw up bills, either on its own initiative or on instruction from both Houses of Parliament. Such bills would be subject to ratification or rejection, but not to amendment, by Parliament. 'By such arrangements as these, legislation would assume its proper place as a work of skilled labour and special study and experience; while the most important liberty of the nation, that of being governed only by laws assented to by its elected representatives, would be fully preserved. . . .' (p. 239). Mill proceeds to set out his views as to what are the proper functions of a representative assembly in words which have a familiar ring a hundred years later:

> to watch and control the government: to throw the light of publicity on its acts: to compel a full exposition and justification of all of them which any one considers questionable; to censure them if found condemnable, and, if the men who compose the government abuse their

trust, or fulfil it in a manner which conflicts with the deliberate sense of the nation, to expel them from office, and either expressly or virtually appoint their successors . . . to be at once the nation's Committee of Grievances, and its Congress of Opinions (p. 239).

A properly constituted legislature in a representative democracy being 'a fair sample of every grade of intellect among the people' (p. 241), is well fitted to carry out these tasks but not the vital and skilled roles of legislation and administration.

READING

John S. Mill, *Representative Government*, Chs. 1–5.

5. HEGEL

'The state,' declares Hegel, 'is the actuality of the ethical Idea' (*Philosophy of Right*, p. 155). It is in and through the state that the individual is given the opportunity to live the good life and to realize his potentialities; for it is the destiny of man to identify himself with what is universal and true, not with the false individuality which consists in negative rejection of social values and the empty assertion of personal eccentricities. 'The state is the divine will, in the sense that it is mind present on earth, unfolding itself to be the actual shape and organization of a world' (p. 166). It is the most sublime of all human institutions, the physical embodiment of mind or spirit. The great strength of the state lies in its ability to put the particular interests and purposes of individuals 'in correspondence' with its own universal ends, so that members of the state are able to gain personal satisfaction in ways which further the interests of the community as a whole. In this way the citizens come to identify themselves with the state and to consciously will its ends and purposes in preference to any of their own which conflict with it. The state is both spirit and form. The spirit is what moves and guides the purposes of all the members of the community; the form is the constitution of the state, which Hegel calls 'the political state'. The form of the state must be organic not mechanical, since it has to fulfil the universal purpose of creating the conditions in which individual citizens may realize their true selves.

Hegel is at pains to point out that not all states have fulfilled this role. There have been times when 'the state was a mere mundane rule of force, caprice, and passion' (p. 171), but Hegel does not regard states of this sort as strictly states at all, since they fail to carry out the state's fundamental purposes. So for Hegel 'an oriental despotism is not a state, or at any rate not the self-conscious form of state which is alone worthy of mind, the form which is organically developed and where there are rights and a free ethical life' (p. 173). Hegel's philosophy leads him to assert, however, that as states have developed they have become more complete and adequate embodiments of the Idea of the state. He distinguishes between the 'immature states' of the past where 'the Idea of the state is still veiled' and the modern state whose 'essence' is that 'the universal be bound up with the complete freedom of its particular members' (addition, p. 280).

The modern state for Hegel was constitutional monarchy, which provided for the division of the powers of the political state into three separate branches, the legislature, the executive and the crown. The most important of these is the crown for through it the separate powers are bound together in a unity. Hegel severely criticizes those who would turn the doctrine of the separation or division of powers into 'the false doctrine of the absolute self-subsistence of each of the powers against the others'. This view implies that it is only by each power treating the others as evils, which it must oppose and restrain, that equilibrium can be secured. 'If the powers ... become self-subsistent ... the destruction of the state is forthwith a *fait accompli*. Alternatively, if the state is maintained in essentials, it is strife which through the subjection by one power of the others, produces unity at least, however defective, and so secures the bare essential, the maintenance of the state' (p. 175). But while constitutional monarchy is the most developed and advanced form of state it cannot be simply imposed on a people. Napoleon's attempt to provide the Spaniards with a more rational constitution failed because they saw it as something alien. 'A nation's constitution must embody its feeling for its rights and its position, otherwise there may be a constitution there in an external way, but it is meaningless and valueless' (addition, p. 287). Hegel's conclusion that 'every nation has the constitution appropriate to it and suitable for it' (p. 179) ill-accords with this analysis and with his own denunciation of pre-revolutionary France (see p. 130 above).

The fundamental characteristic of the state as a political entity is its sovereignty which 'depends on the fact that the particular functions and powers of the state are not self-subsistent or firmly grounded either on their own account or in the particular will of the individual functionaries, but have their roots ultimately in the unity of the state as their single self' (pp. 179–80). Sovereignty is not to be found in despotisms where the resources of the state are devoted to the caprices of the despot, nor in feudal states where 'the particular functions and powers of the state and civil society were arranged . . . into independent Corporations and societies so that the state as a whole was rather an aggregate than an organism' (p. 180). Sovereignty requires constitutional government which directs all the spheres of the state for the benefit of the whole, but more specifically it requires a person to embody that unity. 'It is only as a person, the monarch, that the personality of the state is actual' (p. 182). Hegel does not base the claim of monarchs on Divine Right – 'we cannot be content with saying God has appointed kings to rule over us, since God has made everything, even the worst of things' (addition, p. 289) – but on the need for the embodiment of the essential unity of the state in a subjective person with the power of ultimate decision. He insists on the hereditary nature of monarchy since the exercise of the power of final decision is dependent on the immediate recognition of the dignity and majesty of the office, not on the personal capacities of the holder. Yet he requires that the conduct of foreign affairs, the command of the armed forces, the making of peace and war, the choice of public officials, the rectification of maladministration, shall devolve on the monarch, although the proper exercise of such important functions clearly requires high capacity, skill and experience. On the other hand Hegel lays great stress on the need for a permanent civil service recruited on the basis of ability and knowledge, not of birth. Such a body will develop a marked *esprit de corps* and its members will find their satisfaction in 'the dutiful discharge of their public functions' (p. 191). Hegel's conception of a vigorous nation state depends on the emergence of energetic capable monarchs who devote themselves to building up a public-spirited state bureaucracy.

The third aim of the state, the representative assembly, is for Hegel the most distinctive feature of the modern state; but by this Hegel meant not the democratically elected legislature of our own time but an Assembly of Estates representing the various interests and classes which

had something directly of value to contribute to the discussion of
matters of public concern. In *The German Constitution* (*c.* 1802) he
argued that the management of national affairs had become

> more and more closely concentrated in a centre consisting of the
> monarch and of the Estates, i.e. of one part of the nation consisting of
> (a) the nobility and the clergy speaking personally in discussion on
> their own account and (b) the third estate, [speaking] as representative
> of the rest of the people. The monarch manages national affairs,
> especially in so far as they concern foreign relations with other states;
> he is the centre of the state's power; from him everything issues which
> requires legal compulsion. The legal power is thus in his hands; the
> Estates participate in legislation and they pass the budget which sup-
> ports the state's power (*Political Writings*, pp. 202–3).

Hegel insists on the need for an active Third Estate representing the
people as a condition of freedom, and he attacks the Prussia of his own
time where the estates have lost their significance owing to the growth
in the arbitrary power of the monarch, especially in matters of taxation.
'The guarantee that the government will proceed in accordance with
law, and the co-operation of the general will in the most important
affairs of state which affect everyone, the people finds in the organization
of a body representative of the people – Without such a representative
body, freedom is no longer thinkable' (p. 234). In *Philosophy of Right*,
written twenty years later, Hegel moderates his enthusiasm for the
Estates as *the* guarantee of general welfare and public freedom. He
argues that all the political institutions of the state share in this task,
which is indeed more effectively performed by the monarch and the
judiciary than by the estates. The Estates cannot claim to have a greater
insight or understanding of public affairs than the officers of state, but
they can keep a check on the latter's activities. In this way officials,
especially those in the lower ranks, will be induced through fear of
public criticism, to devote themselves wholly to their public duties.
Hegel goes so far in 1821 as to characterize the matters with which the
Estates should deal as 'rather specialized and trifling' (p. 197), in spite
of his declaration that they should possess the power to pass laws, subject to the confirmation of the monarch and to raise taxes.

The fundamental purpose of the Estates for Hegel is not to carry
specific functions as a legislature but to act as 'a mediating organ' between the government and the people. It is through the Estates that
the private will and judgements of individual men are integrally related
to the state. The Estates are

a middle term preventing both the extreme isolation of the power of the crown, which otherwise might seem a mere arbitrary tyranny, and also the isolation of the particular interests of persons, societies, and Corporations. Further, and more important, they prevent individuals from having the appearance of a mass or an aggregate and so from acquiring an unorganized opinion and volition and from crystallizing into a powerful *bloc* in opposition to the organized state (p. 197).

It follows therefore that if the Estates come to regard themselves as the spokesmen for the people against the executive they become a danger to the state, instead of a buttress. This does not mean, as we have seen, that the Estates may not legitimately criticize public officials and policies, but only that their criticism must be creative and directed to assisting the other branches of the state to carry out their responsibilities. In *The Wurtemberg Estates* (written in 1817), Hegel had contrasted unfavourably the tendency of the German Estates to set itself up in opposition to the state, with that of the opposition party in the English Parliament which sought to gain control of those powers for itself. What the English opposition is charged with 'namely that all it wants is to form a Ministry itself, is in fact its greatest justification' (p. 258).

The *Philosophy of Right* contains no reference to either parties or opposition groups, instead Hegel returns to the *Wurtemberg Estate* theme of the need to ensure that the Estates represent interests not citizens as isolated atoms. The people who need to be represented are the members of the agricultural and business classes, although individual members of the executive ought not to be precluded from participating in Assembly affairs. Although the agricultural class includes everybody connected with the land, it is to be represented solely through the members of the class of landed aristocracy, all of whom are to be entitled by birth to direct membership of the Estates. He rightly sees that an Estate constituted in this way would become 'a support at once of the throne and society' (p. 200). The business class, which comprises all who work in industry, trade or commerce, is for Hegel too unstable, ignorant, heterogeneous and large for its members to have a direct share in deliberating and deciding on matters of general concern. It must therefore be represented through deputies summoned by the crown from the various associations, communities and corporations set up to further the particular interests of the different trades and professions. Such representatives would be appointed by their particular associations and would bring to the Assembly wide experience and knowledge of the needs and roles of the groups concerned. Moreover such persons would have attained in their positions as officers of their associations and societies skill in the actual transaction of business which would stand them in good stead in carrying out their duties as scrutineers of the state executive. They would not act as agents bound by mandates but as representatives carrying the confidence of their members.

Hegel rejects outright the notion that deputies should be elected by the populace at large, whether on a wide or restricted franchise. He insists that 'the concrete state is the whole, articulated into its particular groups. The member of a state is a member of such a group, i.e. of a social class, and it is only as characterized in this objective way that he comes under consideration when we are dealing with the state' (p. 200). It is clear from this that the representatives of the Lower House would consist of members of the middle classes, leading members of professional and business organizations which claimed to speak on behalf of all engaged in their particular pursuit, even though labourers would be precluded from membership and small traders from any effective part in their deliberations. The people considered apart from their social organizations are for Hegel 'a formless mass whose commotion and activity could therefore only be elementary, irrational, barbarous, and frightful' (p. 198). The notion that 'the wild idea of the "people"' could form the basis for any valid notion of sovereignty is for Hegel an indication of the utter confusion and vacuousness of republican thinking. The right of everyone to participate in public affairs is limited to the right of 'having and expressing their own private judgments, opinions, and recommendations on affairs of state' (p. 204).

Hegel lays considerable stress on the value of public opinion as the repository of the genuine needs and tendencies of common life and of the underlying principles of justice, which he regards as the substantial heart of public opinion. On the other hand he stresses that the particular form which public opinion may take at any time may be highly injurious to the true interests of the state. Public opinion lacks any power of discrimination. He declares that 'to be independent of public opinion is the first formal condition of achieving anything great or rational whether in life or in science' (p. 205). He advocates freedom of the press, but not at the expense of the state. He would not permit 'traducing the honour of anyone, slander, abuse, the contemptuous caricature of government, its ministers, officials, and in particular the person of the monarch' (p. 207). Hegel cannot accept that any individual has the right to express opinions which are liable to undermine the state's authority. Public opinion can only play a constructive role if it identifies

the interests of the individual members of the public with the true
interests of the community.

READING

Hegel, *Philosophy of Right*, Part III, 'The State', pp. 174–208.

Hegel's Political Writings, an Introductory Essay of Z. A. Pelczynski, Chs. 4–7.

6. MARX AND ENGELS

Marx derived his early conceptions of the nature of the state from a
critical analysis in 1843 of Hegel's *Philosophy of Right* and these conceptions profoundly influenced his whole later approach. Marx's
criticism of Hegel is that his proposals completely fail to provide for
the realization of the state as the 'completely existent universal'. Instead
we have in constitutional monarchy the creation of 'two hostile armies',
the state and civil society which are united only through the abstract
unity of the monarch, as the personal embodiment of the sovereignty
of the state, and the bureaucracy, as the universal class of state servants
which all might aspire to join irrespective of rank or wealth. Marx,
however, insists that one has to choose between the concept of the
sovereignty of the state, personified in the monarch and the sovereignty
of the people. One cannot meaningfully talk, as Hegel does, of the
sovereignty of the people being realized through the state as a monarchy.
The truth of monarchy as conceived by Hegel, is its reliance on the
notion of sovereignty residing in the people, its falsity is the assertion
that this sovereignty is expressed through one person, the monarch.
Under the constitutional monarchical form of government the state
simply assumes a political form and the people fulfil such limited roles
as the constitution provides for them. In general this means that a
prescribed section of the people take part, either directly or indirectly
through delegates, in the exercise of the legislative power. It is precisely
because the political state is separated from civil society, and exists apart
from it, that the problem of popular sovereignty appears in the form of

whether all as individuals should participate in deliberating and deciding on political matters of general concern to the community. Such an arrangement leaves the concrete governmental power, the power to act and direct, in the hands of the bureaucracy and distorts the whole purpose of the state. 'Bureaucracy considers itself the ultimate finite purpose of the state' and consequently 'the purposes of the state are changed into purposes of bureaus and vice versa'.[1] The bureaucracy uses the political state as a private tool for furthering its own particular interests as a group within civil society.

The antithesis between the bureaucracy and the people, between the political state and civil society can only be overcome if the democratic element 'acquires its *rational form* within the state organism as a *whole*' (p. 196). This involves 'The essential demand that every social need, law, etc., be *politically* evolved and *determined by the entire state* in the *social* sense' (p. 201); a demand which is only realizable by 'the greatest possible *universalization* of *voting*, of *active* as well as *passive* franchise' (p. 202). The conclusion which Marx draws from this analysis is both radical and unexpected.

> Only in *unlimited voting*, active as well as passive, does civil society *actually* rise to an abstraction of itself, to *political* existence as its true universal and essential nature. But the realization of this abstraction is also the transcendence of the abstraction. By making its *political existence* actual as its *true* existence, civil society also makes its civil existence *unessential* in contrast to its political existence. And with the one thing separated, the other, its opposite, falls. Within the *abstract political state* the reform of voting is the *dissolution* of the state, but likewise the *dissolution* of *civil society* (p. 202).

By involving the whole community in settling community affairs by universalized voting the whole basis of the existing form of political state, with its separation of formal legislative from concrete executive powers, its powerful caste of professional bureaucrats, and its personal sovereign, will be superseded. At the same time civil society, in the shape of separate institutions and classes not subject to any effective social control, will also disappear. In a further article, written in the same year, Marx returns to this theme and proclaims 'the negation of private property' to be the key to the realization of democracy, and the proletariat the class destined to bring this about; since its demand for the abolition of private property is simply a demand for the universalizing

1. *Critique of Hegel's Philosophy of the State*, 1843, in Easton and Guddatt, op. cit., p. 185.

of its own propertyless position. Thus the realization of the proletariat's demand will mean 'the *dissolution of the existing order of things*', both socially and politically.[1]

The significant feature about this analysis is that the private spheres of modern bourgeois civil society are regarded by Marx as having an independent existence from the political state, in contrast with the medieval state where 'the life of the people and the life of the state were identical' and 'the political constitution was the constitution of private property but only because the constitution of private property was political'[2]. In modern bourgeois society the form of the political state is alienated from the form of social organization and property ownership. Thus Marx notes that 'Property etc., in short, the entire content of law and state is the same in North America and in Prussia, with few modifications', in spite of the fact that one is a Republic and the other a monarchy. The reason is that 'the content of the state remains outside these constitutions. . . . The political state is the constitution, that is, the material state is not political' (p. 175). Five years later, however, in *The Communist Manifesto* Marx insisted that the bourgeoisie had 'conquered for itself, in the modern representative state, exclusive political sway. The executive of the modern state is but a committee for managing the common affairs of the whole bourgeoisie'.[3] 'Political power, properly so called, is merely the organized power of one class for oppressing another' (p. 70). There would be no particular significance in this change in Marx's attitude towards the state were there no evidence to suggest that Marx did not hold consistently to the new view. John Plamenatz argues that Marx developed two different theories of the state, as the instrument of class rule and as a parasite on society,[4] while Shlomo Avineri suggests that while Engels saw the state simply in the former role, Marx's concept remained true to the conceptions he developed in his critical analysis of Hegel's writings.[5]

Neither of these explanations seems very plausible. It is difficult to believe either that Marx and Engels could have collaborated together without realizing that they differed from each other on such a fundamental question as the nature of the state, or that they produced two

1. *Towards the Critique of Hegel's Philosophy of Law: Introduction*, Easton and Guddat, op. cit., p. 263.
2. *Critique of Hegel's Philosophy of the State*, ibid., p. 176.
3. Feuer, op. cit., p. 51.
4. John Plamenatz, *German Marxism and Russian Communism*, 1954, pp. 135–51.
5. Shlomo Avineri, *The Social and Political Thought of Karl Marx*, pp. 202–3.

quite separate theories of the state without noticing it. The answer is to be found I suggest in Engels's *The Origin of the Family, Private Property and the State,* which contains the most detailed treatment of the theme. Engels writes:

> As the state arose from the need to keep class antagonisms in check, but also arose in the thick of the fight between the classes, it is normally the state of the most powerful, economically ruling class which by its means becomes also the politically ruling class, and so acquires new means of holding down and exploiting the oppressed class. The ancient state was, above all, the state of the slave-owners for holding down the slaves, just as the feudal state was the organ of the nobility for holding down the peasant serfs and bondsmen, and the modern representative state is the instrument for exploiting wage-labour by capital. Exceptional periods, however, occur when the warring classes are so nearly equal in forces that the state power, as apparent mediator, acquires for the moment a certain independence in relation to both. This applies to the absolute monarchy of the seventeenth and eighteenth centuries, which balances the nobility and the bourgeoisie against one another; and to the Bonapartism of the First and particularly of the Second French Empire, which played off the proletariat against the bourgeoisie and the bourgeoisie against the proletariat. The latest achievement in this line, in which ruler and ruled look equally comic, is the new German Empire of the Bismarkian Nation; here the capitalists and the workers are balanced against one another and both of them fleeced for the benefit of the decayed Prussian cabbage-junkers (p. 196).

Engels's assertion that the state is '*normally* the state of the most powerful economically ruling class' (my italics), but that in exceptional periods it acquires 'for the moment a certain independence in relation to both', is consistent with the position he and Marx took up throughout their long collaboration. In *The German Ideology* (1845–6) they had already arrived at the conclusion that

> the state is nothing more than the form of organization which the bourgeois by necessity adopts for both internal and external purposes as a mutual guarantee of their property and interests. The independence of the state is found today only in countries where estates have not fully developed into classes, where estates . . . still have a role to play, and where a mixture exists – countries where no one section of the population can attain control over the others. This is the case particularly in Germany.[1]

In 1852 in *The Eighteenth Brumaire of Louis Bonaparte* Marx argued that such a situation had developed in France where the bulk of the

1. Easton and Guddat, op. cit., p. 470.

bourgeoisie, led by 'the aristocracy of finance' and the industrial bourgeoisie, had lost all faith in bourgeois parliamentary democracy.

> If by its clamour for tranquillity the *parliamentary Party of Order*, as I
> have shown, committed itself to quiescence, if it declared the political
> rule of the bourgeoisie to be incompatible with the safety and stability
> of the bourgeoisie, by destroying with its own hands in the struggle
> against the other classes of society all the conditions for its own régime,
> the parliamentary régime, then the *extra-parliamentary* mass of the
> bourgeoisie, on the other hand, by its servility towards the President,
> by its vilification of parliament, by the brutal maltreatment of its own
> press, invited Bonaparte to suppress and annihilate its speaking and
> writing section, its politicians and its *literati*, its platform and its press,
> in order that it might then be able to pursue its own private affairs with
> full confidence in the protection of a strong and unrestricted govern-
> ment. It declared unequivocally that it longed to be rid of its own
> political role in order to get rid of the troubles and dangers of ruling.[1]

Marx sees Louis Napoleon as the representative of the great masses of
small peasants who, while objectively forming a distinct economic class
with their own mode of life and separate class interests, lack anything
other than local connection and consequently do not think or act as a class.

> They are consequently incapable of enforcing their class interest in
> their own name – They cannot represent themselves they must be
> represented. Their representative must at the same time appear as
> their master, as an authority over them, as an unlimited governmental
> power that protects them against the other classes and sends them the
> rain and sunshine from above. The political influence of the small
> peasants, therefore, finds its final expression in the executive power
> subordinating society to itself (p. 415).

The state appears here as an independent power with its own vast
artificial caste of bureaucrats whose proclaimed role is to protect the
nation from the political control of the bourgeoisie and to benefit all
classes. In 1852 Marx claimed that the attempts being made by
Napoleon to realize such objectives in class-ridden French society were
doomed to failure. Attempts by the state to protect and assist both
bourgeois and worker, peasant and landlord, meant the pursuance of
contradictory policies which would lead to economic confusion, social
chaos and the discrediting of the state.

Nineteen years later at the time of the fall of Louis Napoleon
(Napoleon III) Marx had somewhat modified his assessment of the
situation in France. He presented the Second Empire as 'the only form
of government possible at a time when the bourgeoisie had already lost,

1. *Karl Marx Selected Works*, Vol. II, pp. 397–8.

and the working class had not yet acquired, the faculty of ruling the nation', a state system under which 'bourgeois society, freed from political cares, attained a development unexpected even by itself'.[1] Five years earlier Engels had expressed the same sentiments in a generalized form in a letter to Marx:

> It is always becoming clearer to me that the bourgeoisie has not the stuff in it for ruling directly itself, and that therefore where there is no oligarchy, as there is here in England, to take over, in exchange for good pay, the management of state and society in the interests of the bourgeoisie, a Bonapartist semi-dictatorship is the normal form. The big material interests of the bourgeoisie carry this through, even against the opposition of the bourgeoisie, but allow the dictatorship no share in real power. The dictatorship in its turn, on the other hand, is forced against its will to further these material interests of the bourgeoisie.[2]

It appears, therefore, that Marx and Engels accept that the economic interests of the bourgeoisie may not require their wielding direct political power. The state may actually continue to assume its own semi-feudal or aristocratic form, as with the *junker* state in Germany, or some new form apparently independent of class, as long as it protects bourgeois property and removes restrictions on bourgeois economic progress. Though the bourgeois democratic republic is for Marx and Engels the natural form for the state to assume under the conditions of bourgeois society, it was apparent that this form was not in all countries destined to be realized. Partly this is because the material interests of the bourgeoisie do not require class rule where the old political order is willing to meet or adopt their economic demands, and partly because the bourgeoisie lacks the will and capacity for political power, in the face of the growing might of the proletariat. Engels wrote to Bernstein in 1884 'the logical form of bourgeois domination is precisely the democratic republic, which has only become too dangerous owing to the development already attained by the proletariat'.[3] Yet in *The Origin of the Family*, published in the same year he argues that the democratic republic 'is the form of state in which alone the last decisive battle between proletariat and bourgeoisie can be fought out'.[4] This does not

1. *The Civil War in France*, in *Karl Marx Selected Works*, Vol. II, p. 497.
2. Engels to Marx, 13 April 1866, in *Selected Correspondence*, pp. 205–6.
3. Engels to Bernstein, 24 March 1884, in *Selected Correspondence*, p. 435.
4. Engels, op. cit., p. 197. Engels reiterates this viewpoint in 1891: 'If one thing is certain it is that our Party and the working class can only come to power under the form of the democratic republic.' Engels to Kautsky, 29 June 1891: *Selected Correspondence*, op. cit., p. 486.

accord with Marx's earlier categorization of the Napoleonic Empire 'with the *coup d'état* for its certificate of birth, universal suffrage for its sanction, and the sword for its sceptre' as '*the ultimate form of the state power* [my italics] which nascent middle class society had commenced to elaborate as a means of its own emancipation from feudalism, and which full-grown bourgeois society had finally transformed into a means for the enslavement of labour by capital'.[1]

Four years later, however, Marx was to write of the democratic republic in his *Critique of the Gotha Programme* in exactly the same terms which Engels used in *The Origin of the Family*. 'It is,' wrote Marx, 'precisely in this last state form of bourgeois society that the class struggle has to be fought out to a conclusion.'[2] But while there seems some confusion on the point of what is to be the ultimate form the state is to take in bourgeois society both Marx and Engels are clear that the state can only survive in bourgeois society if it protects the economic interests of the bourgeoisie. Earlier, in the *Critique of the Gotha Programme*, Marx argued that while the form of present day states varied markedly from one country to another yet 'all have this in common that they are based on modern bourgeois society, only one more or less capitalistically developed' (p. 577). Consequently the political state was objectively always an instrument of class oppression. This was true even of the democratic republic with its popularly elected legislature. The machinery of the democratic republic might be used by the workers to gain parliamentary representation or even political power, but it could not be used for effecting the transformation of the social and economic foundations of society. In the words of *The Eighteenth Brumaire*: 'All the revolutions perfected the machine instead of smashing it.'[3]

If one examines why Marx insists that the existing state machine needs to be smashed, one sees that it is because that machine in the process of serving the changing needs of a class-dominated society has created a vast bureaucratic state apparatus. It is both the class purposes which the state serves in capitalist society and the form which it takes which Marx attacks. Marx lambasts the executive power of the French

1. Marx, *The Civil War in France*, op. cit., pp. 497 and 498.
2. K. Marx, *Critique of the Gotha Programme*, 1875: *Selected Works*, Vol. II, p. 579.
3. K. Marx, *Selected Works*, Vol. II, p. 413. But see p. 140 above for Engels' acceptance of the possibility of a peaceful social revolution in France, America and Britain.

Second Empire, 'with its enormous bureaucratic and military organization, with its artificial state machinery embracing wide strata, with its
host of officials numbering half a million, besides an army of another
half-million, this appalling parasitic growth, which enmeshes the body
of French society like a net and chokes all its pores' (p. 412). Every new
régime since the days of the absolute monarchy had strengthened this
machine – 'the division of labour within bourgeois society created new
groups of interests, and, therefore, new material for state administration.
Every *common* interest, was straightway severed from society, counterposed to it as a higher, *general* interest, snatched from the self-activity
of society's members and made an object of governmental activity'
(pp. 412–13).

It was precisely because the Paris Commune set out to smash the
class-orientated bureaucratic apparatus of the state that Marx set such
high value on the lessons of its brief existence. Provision was made for
the whole body of the community to serve as the militia and to elect all
state officials as well as Commune members, thus abolishing both the
standing army and the 'independent' bureaucracy. All public servants
were paid workmen's wages, were responsible to the Commune for their
activities and subject to recall by the electors. The Commune itself was
'to be a working, not a parliamentary body, executive and legislative at
the same time'.[1] The Commune for Marx was 'essentially a working
class government, the product of the struggle of the producing against
the appropriating class, the political form at last discovered under which
to work out the economical emancipation of labour' under which 'every
man becomes a working man, and productive labour ceases to be a
class attribute' (pp. 502–3). The Commune was 'a Revolution against
the *State* itself,[2] which aimed to restore 'to the social body all the forces
hitherto absorbed by the state parasite feeding upon, and clogging the
free movement of, society'.[3]

Although Marx, unlike Engels, did not categorize the Paris Commune
as the dictatorship of the proletariat there is no reason to believe that he
did not regard it as embodying the essential features of that transitonal
period. In 1875 he wrote, 'Between capitalist and communist society
lies the period of the revolutionary transformation of the one into the
other. There corresponds to this also a political transition period in

1. K. Marx, *The Civil War in France, Selected Works*, Vol. II, p. 498.
2. Notes written by Marx for *The Civil War in France*, quoted by Ralph Miliband in 'Marx and the State', *The Socialist Register, 1965*, p. 290.
3. *The Civil War in France: Selected Works*, Vol. II, pp. 501–2.

which the state can be nothing but *the revolutionary dictatorship of the proletariat.*'[1] Marx accepts that even in a communist society there will remain some social functions to perform analogous to the functions of the state in bourgeois society, but argues that it is impossible now to determine what these functions shall be. Marx is here almost certainly referring to the distinction which he saw the Paris Commune as making between the repressive features of the state as an instrument of class rule and the legitimate functions which in class society are carried out by an alien caste of officials. The former were to be abolished and the latter transformed – 'While the merely repressive organs of the old governmental power were to be amputated, its legitimate functions were to be wrested from an authority usurping pre-eminence over society itself, and restored to the responsible agents of society.'[2]

Marx himself not only gave no indication of what state social functions might be needed under communism but he also provided no clues, beyond his comments on the Paris Commune, as to what he regarded as the dictatorial element in proletarian rule. Engels dealt with both of these points in his own writings. On the former we have the famous passage on 'the withering-away of the state' in *Anti-Dühring* (1878) which Marx himself must have read. Engels wrote:

> As soon as there is no longer any class of society to be held in subjection; as soon as, along with class domination and the struggle for individual existence based on the former anarchy of production, the collisions and excesses arising from these have been also abolished, there is nothing more to be repressed which would make a special repressive force, a state, necessary. The first act in which the state really comes forward as the representative of society as a whole – the taking possession of the means of production in the name of society – is at the same time its last independent act as a state. The interference of the state power in social relations becomes superfluous in one sphere after another, and then ceases of itself. The government of persons is replaced by the administration of things, and the direction of the processes of production. The state is not 'abolished', *it withers away* (pp. 308–9).

It is doubtful however whether this passage really makes the matter any clearer. The 'state' as an instrument of class domination disappears, but the 'state' as the administrative and economic director remains.

On the dictatorship of the proletariat Engels is more revealing. In 1875 he tells Bebel that 'the "state" is only a transitional institution

---

1. *Critique of the Gotha Programme: Selected Works*, Vol. II, p. 577.
2. *The Civil War in France: Selected Works*, Vol. II, p. 500.

which is used in the struggle, in the revolution, in order to hold down one's adversaries by force, it is pure nonsense to talk of a "free people's state"; so long as the proletariat still *uses* the state, it does not use it in the interests of freedom but in order to hold down its adversaries'.[1] In 1886 he expanded on this theme.

> With the disappearance of an exclusively wealth-possessing minority there also disappears the necessity for the power of armed oppression, or state power. At the same time, however, it was always our view that in order to attain this end and the other far more important aims of the future social revolution, the working class must first take posses-sion of the organized political power of the state and by its aid crush the resistance of the capitalist class and organize society anew. . . . The anarchists put the thing upside down. They declare that the prole-tarian revolution must *begin* by doing away with the political organiza-tion of the state. But after its victory the sole organization which the proletariat finds already in existence is precisely the state. The state may require very considerable alterations before it can fulfil its new functions. But to destroy it at such a moment would be to destroy the only organism by means of which the victorious proletariat can assert its newly-conquered power, hold down its capitalist adversaries and carry out that economic revolution of society without which the whole victory must end in a new defeat and in a mass slaughter of the workers similar to those after the Paris Commune.[2]

While there is no reason to believe that Marx would have dissented from this analysis the fact remains that he did not expressly draw this con-clusion about the repressive role of the workers' state in the transition period. Neither Marx nor Engels could have envisaged that the concept of the dictatorship of the proletariat would be used by a Marxist party in Russia to justify the oppression of all other political parties, including working class and Marxist parties and the creation of a party-controlled authoritarian state complete with a vast bureaucracy, huge standing army and secret police machine.

READING

K. Marx, *Critique of Hegel's Philosophy of the State*, Easton and Guddat, op. cit.

K. Marx, *The Eighteenth Brumaire of Louis Bonaparte*. Excerpt in Feuer, op. cit.

K. Marx, *The Civil War in France*. Excerpt in Feuer, op. cit.

F. Engels, *The Origin of the Family, Private Property and the State*, Ch. 9.

Ralph Miliband, 'Marx and the State', *The Socialist Register, 1965*.

J. Plamenatz, *German Marxism and Russian Bolshevism*, Ch. 8, sections iii and iv.

1. Engels to Bebel, 18–28 March 1875, in *Selected Correspondence*, p. 337.
2. Engels to Van Patten, 18 April 1875, ibid., pp. 416–17.

Index